Achievement-Related Motives in Children

CHARLES P. SMITH, *Editor*

With contributions by VIRGINIA C. CRANDALL,
SHEILA C. FELD, JUDITH LEWIS,
CHARLES P. SMITH, *and* JOSEPH VEROFF,
and comments by JOHN W. ATKINSON,
HOWARD A. MOSS, *and* SEYMOUR B. SARASON

RUSSELL SAGE FOUNDATION, NEW YORK, 1969

PUBLICATIONS OF RUSSELL SAGE FOUNDATION

Russell Sage Foundation was established in 1907 by Mrs. Russell Sage for the improvement of social and living conditions in the United States. In carrying out its purpose the Foundation conducts research under the direction of members of the staff or in close collaboration with other institutions, and supports programs designed to improve the utilization of social science knowledge. As an integral part of its operations, the Foundation from time to time publishes books or pamphlets resulting from these activities. Publication under the imprint of the Foundation does not necessarily imply agreement by the Foundation, its Trustees, or its staff with the interpretations or conclusions of the authors.

Contributors

John W. Atkinson
Professor
Department of Psychology
University of Michigan

Virginia C. Crandall
Senior Investigator
Department of Psychology
The Fels Research Institute

Sheila C. Feld
Associate Professor
School of Social Work
University of Michigan

Judith Lewis
Psychologist, Infant Rearing Study
Department of Psychiatry
Children's Hospital of the District
    of Columbia

Howard A. Moss
Psychologist
Child Research Branch
National Institute of Mental Health

Seymour B. Sarason
Professor of Psychology and Director,
    Psycho-Educational Clinic
Yale University

Charles P. Smith
Associate Professor of Psychology
City University of New York

Joseph Veroff
Professor
Department of Psychology
University of Michigan

Preface

THE papers included in this volume were originally presented at a research conference on "The Development of Achievement-Related Motives and Self-Esteem in Children" at the Graduate Center of the City University of New York on October 19–21, 1967. The conference was made possible by a grant from the Russell Sage Foundation, and was held under the auspices of the Institute for Child Development and Experimental Education of the City University of New York. All of the original conference papers were revised for inclusion in this volume except that of Professor Stanley Coopersmith on "Self-Esteem: Formation and Change." His research is more fully reported in his recent book on *Antecedents of Self Esteem* (W. H. Freeman, 1967). The comments of the conference discussants, also included in this volume, are based on the original conference presentations. These comments initiated discussion of the papers by the panel of speakers and members of the audience, and some of the ideas expressed in those discussion sessions have been included in the concluding chapter of this volume. The conference provided a rare opportunity for the sustained presentation of related research reports and for the reactions of a knowledgeable audience.

One of the special emphases of the Russell Sage Foundation has been the use of knowledge from the social sciences in the interest of improving social and living conditions in the United States. This aim provided an impetus for the conference participants to present not only research on the socially relevant personality dispositions included under the rubric "achievement-related motives" but also to consider the relevance of their research for education and childrearing and to attempt to place these scholarly ideas on a level of social meaningfulness.

It is a pleasure to acknowledge the contribution of the Russell Sage Foundation and the active interest and support from the outset to the conclusion of the Foundation's President Dr. Orville G. Brim, Jr. Special thanks are also due to Professor Francis H. Palmer, Director of the Institute for Child Development and Experimental Education and to his administrative assistant,

Mrs. Charlene Jaffe, who ably handled many of the arrangements for the research conference. The urbane contributions of my colleagues Harry Beilin, William Ittelson, Harold Proshansky, and Ann Haeberle Rees who served as session chairmen at the research conference are appreciatively acknowledged. In her careful typing of the manuscript Mrs. Helen Feldman provided much-needed assistance. Numerous contributions to all phases of the preparation of this volume have been made by my wife, Carol Smith, to whom I am gratefully indebted.

CHARLES P. SMITH
City University of New York
October, 1968

Contents

CHAPTER ONE

Introduction

CHARLES P. SMITH

HOW a child develops a desire to do well in activities he undertakes, and how he becomes apprehensive about the possibility of doing poorly are problems of both theoretical and practical significance. This volume presents reports of four extensive research projects that deal with achievement-related motivation in children. New theories and methods of investigation concerning achievement motivation, anxiety about achievement, and expectancies of success and failure are described. Developmental trends dealing with both the stability and change of achievement-related motives over time are studied as well as the expression of these motivational dispositions at particular stages of development. That is, at any one age what situational and personality factors influence children's goal setting, persistence at tasks, performance in achievement situations, and reactions to success and failure?

"Achievement-related motivation" refers to the personality factors that come into play when a person undertakes a task at which he will be evaluated, enters into competition with other persons, or otherwise strives to attain some standard of excellence. Under such circumstances a variety of motivational dispositions and cognitive assessments of the situation are activated and influence a person's tendency to behave (e.g., his tendency to work more or less hard, to persist or to give up and turn to another activity, his thoughts of doing well or poorly, and his physical manifestations of stress). Specifically, the determinants of performance dealt with include approach and avoidance motives (the motive to achieve, and anxiety about failure or the motive to avoid failure), expectations (subjective estimates of the likelihood that one's efforts will lead to success or failure), and the incentive values of success and failure (e.g., the pleasure of winning, or making a good grade, or executing a difficult task flawlessly, or the pain and humiliation of criticism, of not being good at something, of doing less well than one's companions). How these personality determinants of motivation develop in children, how they can be measured, how they operate in specific settings, and their implications for education and childrearing are the concerns of this book.

There are a number of reasons for bringing together a set of papers on achievement-related motivation in children. Assertiveness, competition, and excellence are important aspects of behavior, particularly in our society, yet these kinds of behavior have been studied primarily in adults. The relatively small number of studies of achievement-related motivation in children have been seized upon eagerly even though they barely reveal the outlines of the problem. The early studies were provocative but by no means definitive, and as the material included in the present volume demonstrates, the topic is far more complex than had been recognized.

There have been three major traditions of research on these topics. Research on achievement motivation was begun by David McClelland, John W. Atkinson, and their colleagues at Wesleyan University[1] and has been continued at Harvard University by McClelland and his colleagues, and at the University of Michigan by Atkinson, Feather, Veroff, and their colleagues.[2] Another center for research on achievement behavior and achievement motivation has been the Fels Research Institute. This group of researchers, including Vaughn and Virginia Crandall, Howard Moss, Jerome Kagan, and their colleagues, has had a somewhat different theoretical orientation;[3] the work of several members of this group stems in part from the social learning theory of Julian Rotter. The third major center of research on achievement-related motivation has been at Yale University with the activities of Seymour Sarason and his colleagues and their research on test anxiety.[4] There have, of course, been other individual investigators such as Pauline Sears and Elizabeth French, who have carried out noteworthy research on achievement-related motivation over a period of years, but they have been less clearly identified with one of these three main traditions of research.

The papers included in this volume represent the influence of the Michigan approach (see chapters by Atkinson, Smith, and Veroff), the Fels ap-

---

[1] D. C. McClelland, J. W. Atkinson, R. A. Clark, and E. L. Lowell, *The Achievement Motive* (New York: Appleton-Century-Crofts, 1953).
[2] J. W. Atkinson and N. T. Feather (eds.), *A Theory of Achievement Motivation* (New York: John Wiley & Sons, 1966).
[3] Cf. V. J. Crandall, "Achievement," in H. W. Stevenson (ed.), *Child Psychology* (The 62nd Yearbook of the National Society for the Study of Education Part I [Chicago: University of Chicago Press, 1963]), 416–459; and H. A. Moss and J. Kagan, "The Stability of Achievement and Recognition Seeking Behavior from Childhood to Adulthood," *Journal of Abnormal and Social Psychology*, 62 (1961), 543–552.
[4] S. B. Sarason *et al.*, *Anxiety in Elementary School Children* (New York: John Wiley & Sons, 1960).

proach (see chapters by Crandall and Moss), and the Yale approach (see chapters by Feld and Lewis and by Sarason). Advocates of these approaches have not previously communicated as fully as might be desirable, and it is the intent of the present volume to bring about a confrontation of these viewpoints and to point up the common concerns and the differences among them so that future communication and integration will be improved. The concluding chapter is specifically addressed to this task.

The wide variety of themes covered in this volume should be of interest to students of personality, human motivation, and child development as well as to sociologists and persons interested in elementary school education. There are discussions of the components of children's achievement anxieties, childrearing practices that influence the development of motivation, the influence of reference groups on effective performance, male-female differences in motivation, Negro-white differences, the influence of motivation on academic performance, and the effect of desegregation on the achievement motivation of Negro children.

Generally speaking, there is a much greater body of published material on cognitive development than on motivational development. This is probably attributable to the greater ease with which cognitive variables can be manipulated and measured. One of the potential contributions of the present volume is the array of new or improved techniques for investigating and assessing achievement-related motivation described in the research reports. To maximize this contribution methodological considerations are dealt with in some detail and various assessment devices are included in appendixes.

The distinctive features of each of the chapters will be reviewed briefly to alert the reader to some of the noteworthy contents of the ensuing reports. Employing such questions as "What grade do you expect to make in this course?" and "What is the most difficult task in this series that you expect to be able to perform?" Virginia Crandall investigates motivation for academic and intellectual achievement. She deals with situations in which personal skill rather than external factors determines the outcome of events, that is, where reinforcement is contingent on performance; and she places special emphasis on *expectancy of reinforcement* as an important motivational variable. Her chapter summarizes a number of studies which bear on two major issues: the relationship of expectancies to performance, and sex differences in expectancies.

Crandall reports that sex differences in expectancy show up in the elementary school years and are still present in college-age men and women. The mystery is why girls should have lower expectancies of intellectual and academic accomplishment when their performances are typically as good as, or better than, those of boys; and the investigation of this problem reads like a detective story. Obviously sympathetic to the invidious situation in which her female subjects find themselves, the author pursues a variety of clues, checking out one inference after another. Are the girls' lower expectancies due to their giving what they consider to be socially desirable estimates? That is, are they concerned to have the approval of other persons and do they feel that girls are supposed to be modest and diffident while boys are expected to appear bold and prepossessing? Or is the sex difference due to differences in values for intellectual and academic attainment? Are the expectancy estimates of boys and girls affected in different ways by positive and negative reinforcement of their efforts at a task? These and other possibilities are explored.

At one point the trail leads to a consideration of a controversial educational issue—ability grouping. Crandall asks "What is the effect of ability grouping on a child's estimation of his own ability?" Does daily comparison of skills among classmates of similar aptitude help the low-ability child to maintain confidence in his ability? Crandall concludes her chapter with a discussion of the relevance of her findings for the psychological adjustment and future achievement of both boys and girls.

In the second paper Joseph Veroff elaborates on the importance of social comparison with respect to skills. Like Crandall, he deals with activities in which the child feels personal responsibility for the outcome. Veroff points out that responsiveness to the achievement standards of others (social comparison) and competition do not typically become important determinants of behavior until children enter school. He distinguishes between *autonomous* achievement motivation which involves internalized personal standards of excellence, and *social* achievement motivation which involves external standards of excellence. Although a particular individual normally develops both kinds of achievement motivation, some persons manifest more internally directed achievement striving whereas other individuals appear to be more responsive to external pressures for achievement.

In a three-stage theory of the development of achievement motivation Veroff describes an early period (approximately the first 6 years) which is critical to the development of autonomous achievement motivation. In this period exploration and coping lead to mastery and a sense of effectiveness. When the child comes to *evaluate his own efforts,* he may be said to have a sense of "achievement." If conditions prevent the development of autonomous achievement motivation during these years, or if emphasis on social comparison is introduced prematurely, then a mature form of achievement motivation can never develop.

In the second stage, during the elementary school years, the child learns

4

to respond to standards of accomplishment set by others. By comparing himself with other children, and by becoming aware of their standards, he is helped to define both the difficulty of tasks and his own level of ability. A certain amount of success in competition with these social standards is necessary for the child to acquire a disposition to strive for achievement in social settings.

In a third and final stage of development, which takes place during adolescence, autonomous achievement again becomes important. The child must regain a sense of independence and learn how to integrate the two kinds of achievement orientations. He must learn when to rely on internal standards and when to be responsive to external standards (e.g., knowing when to compete with others and when not to).

Satisfactory development in each stage, according to Veroff, depends on successful completion of the preceding stage. Different stages of completion define different motivational typologies; for example, persons can be high in both autonomous achievement motivation and social achievement motivation, or high in autonomous motivation but low in social motivation, or low in both. A study of the characteristics of these types of persons sheds light on some important but relatively neglected questions: Why do some persons turn every situation into a competitive one? What accounts for the apparent fear of success that some persons, especially women, display? Why are some people achievement-oriented in individual activities but unable to face competition with others?

In bringing evidence to bear on his three-stage theory, Veroff summarizes a number of studies carried out by himself and his students, and he describes in detail two new measures of autonomous and normative (social) achievement motivation. He provides data which indicate clearly that when presented with a range of alternatives, preschool children tend to select the easiest tasks in terms of socially defined difficulty (e.g., "Most children your age can do this task") while older children select more difficult tasks to work on. He suggests that willingness to compete does not play an important role in task selection until about the 2nd grade.

Veroff applies his theory to a wide range of socially relevant topics including sex differences (e.g., girls may remain more dependent on social comparison than boys), religion (e.g., Roman Catholics may have higher social achievement motivation and lower autonomous achievement motivation than Protestants), disadvantaged social groups (e.g., Negroes and females are perhaps less likely to complete the autonomy stage successfully), and education (e.g., the effect of school desegregation on the adjustment and achievement motivation of Negroes is considered; Negro boys tend to fare better than Negro girls).

5

Finally, Veroff illustrates the utility of his typology of achievement motivation by comparing groups of subjects with different combinations of autonomous and social achievement motivation. In a finding which complements the sex difference in expectation reported by Virginia Crandall, Veroff reports that boys select more difficult tasks than girls, but he finds that this is particularly true of boys with low autonomous achievement motivation. These boys (and his male Negro subjects frequently manifest this pattern of motivation and behavior) tend to overaspire impulsively. Low autonomy girls, on the other hand, tend to be more cautious in their goal setting. Veroff concludes with a provocative series of studies concerning children's reactions to experimentally induced success and failure, and shows which types of children profit most by success and failure and which motivational types profit least.

In addition to dealing with children's achievement motivation, the third paper by Charles Smith investigates another achievement-related personality disposition, test anxiety (conceived as a measure of motivation to avoid failure). Data obtained from 4th and 5th grade boys and their parents are brought to bear on McClelland's theory of how achievement motivation develops[5] and on Sarason's theory of how test anxiety develops.[6] The relationship between these two motives, the other personality variables to which they are related (e.g., self-esteem, defensiveness), and the ways in which they are manifested in goal setting and reading performance are also investigated.

Motives are viewed by Smith as learned dispositions to strive to attain positive incentives and to avoid negative incentives. Individual differences in the strength of motives are attributed to differences in childrearing and other learning experiences in the early life of the child. For example, the study examines the extent to which early independence training is associated with high achievement motivation and late independence training is associated with high test anxiety. With regard to another aspect of childrearing, parents were asked to describe the extent to which their children possessed certain personality characteristics and also the extent to which they would *like* them to possess these characteristics (childrearing values). These descriptions were examined to see if parents of boys with high achievement motivation and low test anxiety hold a more favorable view of their competence than parents of boys with low achievement motivation and high test anxiety. The results suggest that the parents of children with high test anxiety are dissatisfied with their children's dependence and lack

---

[5] D. C. McClelland, *Personality* (New York: Dryden Press, 1951) and *The Achieving Society* (Princeton: D. Van Nostrand Co., 1961). See also McClelland *et al., op. cit.*
[6] Sarason *et al., op. cit.*

of assertiveness, and that they put more pressure on their children to achieve than parents of boys with low test anxiety.

Smith's analysis of the childrearing values indicates that parental values for independence and achievement do not necessarily go together. That is, a parent can value independence highly and not achievement, or vice versa, which raises the possibility that these two aspects of childrearing may make different contributions to the development of achievement motivation. The results also indicate that parental values for achievement are not unitary. The achievement value items fall into two distinct groups labeled "assertive achievement" and "conscientious achievement," which suggests the distinction between competitive and individual achievement highlighted in Veroff's paper.

Paralleling the theoretical expectations regarding parental views of their children is the question of how the children view themselves. Is a positive self-concept associated with high achievement motivation and low self-esteem associated with high test anxiety? The results suggest that a negative view of his own competence is held by the child with high test anxiety, an attitude which probably makes him less responsive to education, and that the child with high achievement motivation holds a view of his "ideal self" that should make him more responsive to education.

The behavioral manifestation of these motives is studied in Smith's paper with respect to goal setting and reading performance. Atkinson's Motive $\times$ Expectancy $\times$ Incentive theory[7] is employed to investigate whether boys with high motivation to achieve and low motivation to avoid failure set more realistic goals for future performance than boys with low motivation to achieve and high motivation to avoid failure. Smith's study represents a related but somewhat different approach to goal setting than is presented in Crandall's study of expectancy and performance and Veroff's study of level of aspiration. The results show the importance of an additional variable, defensiveness, in accounting for unrealistic goal setting and suggest that it becomes more important as the child gets older.

Reading performance is selected by Smith as a way of investigating some of the task properties and situational factors involved in the influence of motivation on academic learning and performance. Two kinds of reading procedures are studied, the conventional reading curriculum and semi-programed reading materials which are intended to encourage self-directed learning. On the latter materials self-evaluation of performance is encouraged and social comparison among children with respect to reading

---

[7] J. W. Atkinson, "Motivational Determinants of Risk-Taking Behavior," *Psychological Review*, 64 (1957), 359–372.

proficiency is played down in order to reduce the pressure of competition and to enable each child to work at his own level and pace. An analysis of the properties of the programed reading materials led to the expectation that the deemphasizing of competition and external evaluation might make these materials more effective than the conventional reading curriculum for the highly anxious child. The results suggest that the self-directed materials have conflicting properties with respect to the role of anxiety—that they minimize the effect of anxiety in some respects and accentuate it in others.

In the fourth paper Sheila Feld and Judith Lewis deal exclusively with anxieties aroused in achievement situations and investigate three major issues: (1) Is an acquiescence response set a major determinant of answers to the Test Anxiety Scale for Children? (2) Does the Test Anxiety Scale for Children have a stable multidimensional structure, and if so, how does the content of the different dimensions affect the interpretation of the meaning of test anxiety scores? (3) What are the demographic correlates of the Test Anxiety Scale for Children, especially those pertaining to sex and race?

In approaching the response set problem the authors want to find out if a subject's position on the anxiety scale changes when the content is presented in a different form. In a methodological tour de force they devise a reversed item for each item of the original scale, determine the adequacy of the reversals, and then factor analyze the original and reversed items to see whether the resulting factors give evidence of a content or response set interpretation. Representing an unusually broad range of social and economic backgrounds, the subjects are all the 2nd grade boys and girls in an entire county public school system consisting of 111 schools and 8,875 pupils. The results indicate that while some minimal effect of response set cannot be discounted, the children's responses are primarily determined by the content of the items.

The factor analysis also reveals four dimensions for each sex within the original Test Anxiety Scale for Children: (1) anxiety about tests per se, (2) persistent thoughts about school when the child is away from school, (3) somatic symptoms of anxiety, and (4) negative self-evaluation in comparison with other persons. The latter factor again calls attention to social comparison with respect to a child's evaluation of his own competence. The high degree of similarity in the factor structures for boys and girls suggests that the sexes do not differ in the types of anxiety they experience.

As Feld and Lewis point out, the original Test Anxiety Scale for Children was intended to assess anxiety about academic evaluation, but it appears that the items deal with at least two different kinds of anxiety-arousing evaluation situations: taking tests, and performing in front of one's classmates. It may be important in understanding how anxiety influences school performance to distinguish between children who respond differently to these stimulus situations. We are again reminded of the distinction between individual achievement and competitive achievement. Some children may be anxious about both, some about neither, and some about one and not the other. For example, a child may not be apprehensive about written tests, but he may be terrified at the thought of being asked to work a problem on the blackboard in front of the entire class. Similarly it may be important to know the different ways in which different children experience anxiety. The authors note that a teacher may react differently to a child who shows somatic signs of anxiety than to an apprehensive child who suffers more covertly, or to a child who voices self-derogatory feelings.

Using the items with high obtained factor loadings, Feld and Lewis present subscales that can be used to assess the four different types of anxiety revealed by the factor analysis. Interesting sex and race differences emerge regarding these various dimensions of test anxiety. There is no difference between the test anxiety scores of Negro boys and girls, but for white children, girls have higher anxiety scores than boys—a fact which may help to account for the sex difference in expectancy reported by Crandall (or it may be that the lower expectancies found in girls produce their higher test anxiety).

Sizable differences attributable to race are found, with Negro children scoring significantly higher on all four test anxiety subscales than white children. These results provide some important information about the attitudes of Negroes toward education. Certainly there is no indication of indifference to school in these data, since Negro children not only report apprehensiveness about schoolroom evaluation, but also they report having a high degree of concern about school *even when they are away from school* (e.g., by dreaming at night of poor work on a test). The methodological contributions of this paper open the way for a more discriminating measurement of achievement anxieties, and the substantive findings provide a better understanding of the stimulus conditions which elicit anxiety and the range of anxiety responses to these situations which even a 2nd grade child can develop.

Following the research reports is an important set of commentaries which provide perspective on the investigations reported here. John W. Atkinson discusses the papers by Virginia Crandall and Joseph Veroff, Seymour Sarason comments on the chapters by Charles Smith and by Sheila Feld and Judith Lewis, and Howard Moss reacts to all four contributions. In an authoritative way these discussions propose theoretical refinements, suggest additional variables for consideration, and call attention to methodological issues of importance to all investigators interested in children's achievement-related motivation. The concluding chapter attempts to summarize and integrate the major findings, points up the methodological advances reported in this volume, calls attention to unresolved theoretical problems, and discusses the importance of the findings for education and childrearing.

CHAPTER TWO

Sex Differences in Expectancy of Intellectual and Academic Reinforcement[1]

VIRGINIA C. CRANDALL

MUCH research in achievement motivation or achievement behavior is carried out under theoretical systems which are basically expectancy $\times$ value formulations. While various investigators have found a number of additional constructs helpful in increasing prediction, expectancy and value remain central in their theoretical models. Because of this, it is imperative that we delineate the relationships of each of the two fundamental constructs to antecedent and response variables, not only to validate the utility of these intervening variables, but also to understand better how they develop and how they affect behavior. The series of studies to be described here deals with one of these major variables, expectancy of reinforcement, and specifically with sex differences in expectancy estimates. Obviously, a status variable like sex does not in itself explain the dynamic processes that determine the formation of expectancies. Nevertheless, if we can establish that a difference in expectancy is consistently associated with the subject's sex, perhaps this phenomenon will suggest hypotheses about

[1] The research reported in this paper was supported by National Institute of Mental Health Grant MH–02238 and by National Institute of Health Grant FR–00222. The author is grateful for the kind assistance of Esther Battle, Suzanne Good, and Laurel Paster in the preparation of this paper.

differences in the processes which determine expectancies that might come about because of the individual's history as a member of that sex. Our aims, then, in the studies to follow, are first, to demonstrate the consistency of differences in expectancy estimates between males and females, and second, to describe some beginning probes into the possible determinants of this difference.

THE DEFINITION OF EXPECTANCY

There are many disparate experimental paradigms and measures which have been used for the study of expectancy, and from these dissimilar operations it is apparent that the concept of expectancy has been defined in a variety of ways. In addition, several symbols and terms have been used to label what seem to be the same kind of expectancy. In order that the reader will better understand that form of expectancy with which we are concerned in the studies to follow, I will distinguish among three uses of the construct.

1. *Expectancy: the nature of the reinforcement available in a given situation.* This form of expectancy is synonymous with the individual's perception of the *kind* of reinforcement which he sees as likely to ensue from his behavior in a particular situation. For example, when one individual sits down at a bridge table, he may perceive that this situation provides an opportunity to demonstrate his card-playing *skill;* that is, the situation, as he sees it, provides reinforcements for achievement. Another individual, on the other hand, may structure the situation as primarily an affiliative one; he may be smiled at, spoken to, laughed with, and can exchange news and gossip. When the individual has generalized such an expectancy *across* situations, carries it with him, and "reads into" a variety of circumstances the expectation that they contain reinforcements relevant to a given need, Veroff[2] has labeled this a "disposition expectancy." As he says, "Such an expectancy about achievement would be the expectancy to see achievement possibilities in any ambiguous situation. The stronger the expectancy, the more likely the person is to see achievement in *any* setting." This form of expectancy, then, deals with the degree to which the individual perceives that reinforcements for a given need are available in a given situation. The reward or punishment value of that reinforcement is not the issue here. To use the first bridge player again as an example, this form of expectancy does not deal with whether he expects to win or lose; it deals with the strength of his certainty that card-playing skill is the issue.

---

[2] J. Veroff, "Assessment of Motives Through Fantasy" (Paper given at Midwestern Psychological Association, 1961); and "Theoretical Background for Studying the Origins of Human Motivational Dispositions," *Merrill-Palmer Quarterly,* 11 (1965), 3–18.

2. *Expectancy: the agent responsible for the occurrence of an outcome event.* This is the individual's expectation that his own behavior is or is not responsible for an outcome event. For example, in most probability learning studies, where the subject predicts whether a particular light will occur on the next trial or whether a card of a particular suit will turn up, expectancy estimates are being given for an event that he does not produce and whose occurrence he cannot control. This is in contradistinction to expectancy measures taken in situations where the outcome event is *contingent* upon the subject's instrumental behavior. This latter is the kind of event that the subject is predicting in most achievement tasks, for such tasks are usually presented in such a way that the outcome is perceived by the subject as dependent on his own skill. When the laboratory or life situation is somewhat ambiguous, however, then individuals may vary in the degree to which they feel that their own behavior causes the outcome to occur.

3. *Expectancy: the ability to obtain a specific reinforcement or class of reinforcements.* This form of expectancy is relative to the subject's perception of his own skill. It is the height of the probability held by the individual that his instrumental behavior will be adequate to obtain a single, specified reinforcement, or alternatively, the level of reinforcement on a single continuum which he predicts his behavior is able to elicit. That is, we can ask a subject what the odds are, or how certain he is that he is able to get 100 per cent (or any other given score) on a task, or we can ask him what score from 1 to 100 he expects to get. This is the form of expectancy which Atkinson and others[3] refer to as "subjective probability of success" (P_S) and it is this kind of expectancy with which we are dealing in the studies to follow. It will be noted that this kind of expectancy already assumes some positive value of the preceding two forms of expectancy. For example, in work in achievement the task characteristics, the instructions presented, or some other cues in the situation have already made it clear to the subject that *he* must perform some instrumental act in order to obtain the reinforcement and that the reinforcements which are available to him are those for achievement, that is, they are being given for the competence of his performance. The question remaining is "How good will that instrumental act be? How skilled am I in the behavior necessary to acquire that kind of reinforcement?" If I am unskilled, I will estimate that the odds are poor that I can get a score of 100 per cent, and/or I will predict that I can only get a particular score of $100 - x$.

---

[3] J. W. Atkinson, "Motivational Determinants of Risk-Taking Behavior," *Psychological Review*, 64 (1957), 359–372; J. W. Atkinson *et al.*, "The Achievement Motive, Goal Setting, and Probability Preferences," *Journal of Abnormal and Social Psychology*, 60 (1960), 27–36.

It is readily apparent that such expectations will depend on the kinds of skills involved. While it is possible to ask a subject "How good are you at doing *things?*" it is likely that he will find it hard to answer such a question, and will respond with something like, "Well, that all depends on what sort of 'things' you mean." In other words, he finds it difficult to generalize over varying skill areas. For example, one's expectancy of reinforcement might be high in activities requiring intellectual skill, but low in those dependent upon athletic prowess, or vice versa. And even within those areas, one might expect to do well in basketball but poorly at swimming, well at handling abstract ideas or logic but poorly in tasks requiring memory.

THE PREDICTION OF BEHAVIOR FROM EXPECTANCY

Although most investigators of achievement behavior use multidimensional theories, it is sometimes useful to examine the predictive utility of each single component variable. Since the work to be described below is based on a theoretical model which is primarily (though with modifications and additions) an expectancy $\times$ value formulation, it is necessary to hold value relatively constant in order to examine the relationship of expectancy to behavior. In order to do this an achievement area has been chosen where it might be said, at least broadly, that most subjects hold some positive value for that sort of achievement reinforcement. In today's culture, which puts so much emphasis on academic and intellectual achievement, perhaps it is safe to assume that being bright and getting good grades have a positive valence for most children. Given, then, that these constitute desirable goals, we would predict that the child who holds a strong expectancy that his effort is capable of producing good grades in school, or a good score on an intellectual task or a game requiring intellectual skill—this child should spend more time and effort in studying and in related intellectual and academic activities than should the child who does not expect to be able to attain the rewards. On the other hand, for the child who holds a low expectancy of reinforcement, it may seem useless to persist in attempts to reach the goal even though he may value it, because he does not feel that it is possible for him to obtain those reinforcements. The approach behaviors of the low expectancy child, then, should be more limited than those of the child with high expectancy.

This hypothesis has been tested. Forty children (20 males and 20 females, ages 7, 8, and 9) were given an expectancy measure in the laboratory.[4] Each child was shown a sequence of eight mazes which became in-

[4] V. J. Crandall, W. Katkovsky, and A. Preston, "Motivational and Ability Determinants of Young Children's Intellectual Achievement Behaviors," *Child Development*, 33 (1962), 643–661.

creasingly more complex. He was told that the maze at the one end was so easy that "Most children your age can easily do this one," and the last maze was described as so difficult that "Very few children your age are able to do this one." He was also told that he was about to be tested on this task and, starting from the easiest level, he was asked to indicate which mazes he would be able to do. A similar procedure was followed with a task that required that he remember and recall groups of toy objects after each group was uncovered for only three seconds. The number of toy objects in each group increased over the eight levels of the task. For both procedures, the stimuli at each end of the range were exposed, but all remaining stimuli were covered. This was done in order that the subject could not rehearse the solutions or give a specific expectancy for a particular maze or group of objects to remember. Thus, he was made to generalize his estimate of his skill on mazes and memory-for-objects from past reinforcements in tasks or situations that he perceived as requiring similar kinds of intellectual abilities. The highest level in the sequence at which the subject estimated he would be able to perform in each of the two tasks was averaged and considered an index of his generalized expectancy for intellectual reinforcement, for these tasks require intellectual skills, rather than artistic skill, or athletic skill, or some other.

The children were then put in an unstructured, free-play situation, and observers recorded the amount of time they chose to spend with intellectual puzzles, quiz games, reading materials, flash cards, checkers, chess, etc. They also observed and rated the intensity of concentration and effort the children displayed while they were engaging in those intellectual activities. The observers were specifically instructed to disregard the competence or quality of the child's products or performance so that the ratings would reflect only *goal-approach* behaviors. In accordance with the hypothesis, it was predicted that children who expected to be highly successful on those intellectual tasks should evidence more of these approach behaviors toward intellectual goals than should children who expected to be less successful.[5]

---

[5] Skills and abilities, per se, do not seem relevant to such behavioral measures as persistence, choice of task, intensity of striving, effort expended, etc., for these behaviors would seem to be determined by motivational factors. That is, for example, it seems most logical that it is not skill itself, but the child's *perception* of his skill, that will dictate whether or not he will choose the task, persist in his attempts to obtain reward, and work diligently toward that end. His perception of his ability may or may not be congruent with that ability. It is our conception that skill or ability itself does not constitute a dynamic, activating variable, but lies dormant or latent until and unless the subject is motivated to approach the goal. Even though measures of ability may *statistically* relate to goal-approach behaviors, they do not explain the dynamic processes through which that approach is made to occur. Thus, actual abilities, even if it were possible to obtain pure measures of them, would not seem to be theoretically appropriate predictors.

When, on the other hand, one is predicting *competence* of performance or excellence of product, then it would seem that both level of skill and motivational factors might be con-

The girls' expectancy estimates did not bear a significant relationship to the approach behaviors. For the boys, however, the expectancy estimates predicted both the intensity of their efforts in the intellectual activities as well as the amount of time they chose to spend in them ($r = .58$ and $.40$, $p < .01$ and $.05$, respectively).

In another study done in our laboratory, Battle[6] used 74 older children at the junior high school level, and found that *both* boys' and girls' expectations in mathematics predicted the amount of time they would persist in an attempt to solve a difficult math "magic square" problem. The correlation for boys was $.52$ and for girls $.38$ (both $p < .01$). For both sexes this time, height of expectancy had predicted the amount of goal-approach behavior that occurred.

Feather,[7] too, found that college-age subjects in general, who had high initial expectations of success on a difficult perceptual reasoning problem, persisted significantly longer in an attempt to solve it than did those subjects who had low initial expectancies.

A second motivational function of expectancy may lie in its more immediate effects in a present performance situation. For example, Tyler[8] has demonstrated that randomly selected subjects who were *given* a high expectancy of success (through "encouraging" remarks from the examiner during pretest trials) more frequently reached the correct solution of a novel pattern-learning problem than did those subjects who were given a low expectancy (through "discouraging" remarks). In addition, it was found that significantly more subjects in the low expectancy group than in the high expectancy group attempted to give the proper series of responses by rote memorization, rather than attempting to conceptualize the logical steps involved in the solution of the problem. Feather[9] also found that subjects in whom a high expectancy was induced with previous success trials

---

sidered to attain finer prediction. For example, correct solution of a Chinese puzzle would depend upon spatial relations skills, in addition to the factors motivating the child to attempt to solve it. In a study by E. Battle ("Motivational Determinants of Academic Competence," *Journal of Personality and Social Psychology*, 4 [1966], 634–642) in which report-card grades were used as a "product" measure, it was found, as would be expected, that children who were above the mean on both IQ and expectancy earned higher grades than those who were low on both measures. Nevertheless, those subjects who had low IQ but high expectancy had significantly higher grades than those who had high IQ but low expectancy. Thus, even with a competence measure, expectancy of reinforcement was a more powerful determinant of that performance than was ability when the two factors were in opposition.

[6] E. Battle, "Motivational Determinants of Academic Task Persistence," *Journal of Personality and Social Psychology*, 2 (1965), 209–218.

[7] N. T. Feather, "Persistence at a Difficult Task with Alternative Task of Intermediate Difficulty," *Journal of Abnormal and Social Psychology*, 66 (1963), 604–609.

[8] B. B. Tyler, "Expectancy for Eventual Success as a Factor in Problem Solving Behavior," *Journal of Educational Psychology*, 49 (1958), 166–172.

[9] N. T. Feather, "Effects of Prior Success and Failure on Expectations of Success and Subsequent Performance," *Journal of Personality and Social Psychology*, 3 (1966), 287–298.

were able to perform better on a subsequent anagrams task than those who were given a low expectancy with previous failure trials. It seems reasonable to assume that confidence in one's ability to perform well in the achievement task at hand may facilitate the maximum discrimination, abstraction, integration, recognition, and other cognitive processes that are necessary for correct problem solution, whether it is working on an experimental task, playing a competitive game, doing an assignment, writing a test, working a problem on the blackboard, reciting in class, or whatever. When, on the other hand, the child's expectancy is low, it may serve a debilitating function and prevent optimum cognitive performance, especially under test pressure or in situations where his intellectual product is open to public assessment. I am proposing, then, that low expectancy of reinforcement in a valued-goal area may underlie test anxiety, but this has yet to be established empirically.

Whether or not low expectancy actually calls forth the affective response of anxiety, however, we would expect it to function to depress performance. It may simply be that the low expectancy child decides, quite reasonably and without anxiety, that it is useless to try and he is wasting his time.

It then seemed reasonable to us that the greater approach behaviors of high expectancy children should result in the acquisition of more information and better problem-solving skills. These, in turn, should be reflected in higher grades and achievement test scores. Thus, expectancy measures should predict such measures of academic competence, but in a "derivative" fashion, that is, via the more extensive academic effort which is associated with a higher expectancy.

That expectancy is, in fact, related to final academic competence has been demonstrated by others as well as ourselves. The report on "Equality of Educational Opportunity"[10] is a good example. Embedded in a more extensive questionnaire were three questions asking the child how bright he thought he was in comparison with other students, whether he sometimes felt he was unable to learn, and whether the teachers presented the material too fast for him. While Coleman et al. apply the term "self-concept" to the responses from these three items, it is not difficult to infer also that this measure reflects the child's expectancy of reinforcement in intellectual-academic situations. In fact, these authors state, "If a child's self-concept is low, if he feels he cannot succeed, then this will affect the effort he puts into the task and thus, his chance of success."[11] Results from this nationwide study of approximately a million children in 6th, 9th, and 12th grades indi-

---

[10] J. S. Coleman et al., Equality of Educational Opportunity (Superintendent of Documents, Catalog No. FS 5: 238: 38001 [Washington, D.C.: Government Printing Office, 1966]).
[11] Ibid., 281.

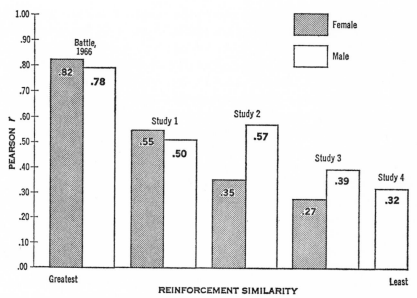

Figure 1. *Prediction of report-card grades from expectancy estimates as a function of degree of similarity between reinforcements on which expectancy estimates were based and grades.*

cate that this variable was more predictive of school achievement among white students than any of the thirty or so other attitudinal, demographic, and situational variables studied. Among nonwhite students it was the second most-predictive measure.

The prediction of academic competence from expectancy is demonstrated in Figures 1 and 2. These figures are based upon results from six different studies from our own project. Actually these several studies had been aimed primarily at the investigation of other issues. The original focus of each of the studies dictated the particular sample used and the exact nature of the task upon which the subjects made their expectancy estimates. Nevertheless, in each case, the subjects had given some sort of intellectual or academic expectancy and we obtained the students' academic grades and current achievement test scores (where they were available). The sample sizes range from 70 to 256 in these studies and all of the correlations are significant with p values (two-tailed) of at least .01 or better.

Figure 1 presents the correlations of various kinds of intellectual or academic expectancy estimates with *report-card grades*. The bars representing the correlations have been arranged along a dimension representing the degree of similarity of the reinforcements on which the expectancy estimate was based, to the reinforcements represented in report-card grades. That is, it would be expected that prediction of a given grade should be strongest if the subject has been asked to give a specific expectancy based on past feedback in that particular course, next most strong if he is basing his estimate on past academic work in other courses, next if he is asked about his intellectual capability, least if he is giving his expectancy relative to another skill area. Another way of saying it might be that when the task characteristics or the instructions for the expectancy measure cause the subject to focus on less relevant past reinforcements, prediction should be reduced to the degree that those past reinforcements are decreasingly relevant. In such a case the measured expectancies require increasingly greater generalization to the reinforcements represented in final course grades and may be presumed to be less commensurate with the specific academic expectancy which determines the individual's approach behavior toward that academic goal. A brief description of the expectancy measures used in these studies follows:

In the *Battle study*[12] junior high students gave separate estimates in early spring of the grades in math and English they thought they would receive at the end of the year. The bars represent the average (computed from z to r transformations) of the correlation of English expectancy to final English grade and of math expectancy to final math grade.

In *Study 1*, 12th grade high school students were asked for their estimates of their "true or native ability" in math, English, social science, and physical science. In this case we might assume that the subjects were giving us an estimate of what might be called their aptitude for each discipline, probably based primarily on grades received in past courses in that discipline, but also on reinforcements in other situations requiring the skills of that subject-matter area. Each of these estimates was correlated with the grade the student received in the course he was currently taking in that discipline. Again the average of the correlations (using z to r transformations) is represented in the bars.

In *Study 2*, the expectancy statements were made by college students at the beginning of an Introductory Psychology course. They were asked to estimate the final grade they anticipated receiving in the course, and these estimates were correlated with the grade they actually did receive. Since this was their first course in a new field, expectancies at the beginning of the course would have to be generalized from broader referents, perhaps primarily previous reinforcements of a general academic nature.

In *Study 3*, the estimates were given for a novel digit-symbol substitution

---

[12] "Motivational Determinants of Competence."

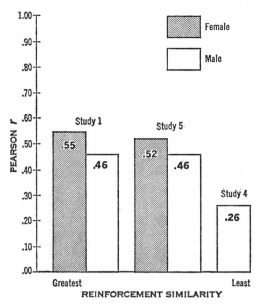

Figure 2. Prediction of achievement test scores from expectancy estimates as a function of degree of similarity between reinforcements on which expectancy estimates were based and achievement test scores.

task. These subjects were 8th graders and the examiner gave them an intellectual set for the task by telling them this was a type of task found in many intelligence tests. Here, in order for prediction to have occurred, we have broadened even further the demand for generality to those reinforcements that the subject conceives of as any indexes of his "brightness." These estimates were related to the average of grades received on the next report card.

In *Study 4*, 8th grade male subjects gave estimates for a novel angle-matching task. (There were no female subjects in this study.) Of course, it would not be expected that a very strong relationship would be found here, since this angle-matching task, with no intellectual set given for it, probably did not appear to be a matter of academic or intellectual skill, but of perceptual skill. In fact, the subjects were told "This is a test to see how well you can match up figures." It has been added to Figure 1 simply to demonstrate that there is still *some* generality of expectancies even from this remote skill area in order for any prediction to grades to have occurred at all.

Figure 2 presents correlations of the same expectancy estimates with *standardized achievement test scores* in those schools where current test scores were available to us (Studies 1 and 4 above).

Study 5 does not appear in Figure 1 because we had only achievement test scores for this sample. These were 9th grade students who were asked to make estimates on the same angle-matching task used in Study 4 above, with the exception that these subjects were helped to attain an intellectual set by explaining to them that this sort of task is often found on intelligence tests. We substantiated this assertion by showing them briefly the spatial relations section (Section 7) of the California Test of Mental Maturity.

As the reader can see, these correlations with achievement test scores do not run quite as high as those with grades.

If the correlations for Study 4 are omitted because the angle-matching task with no intellectual set appeared to have little connection with academic-intellectual reinforcements, the correlations from the remaining studies average .53 with grades and .50 with achievement test scores (z to r transformations). As the figures demonstrate, correlations are sometimes a bit higher for one sex, sometimes for the other, but height of expectancy on novel intellectual tasks or for future grades before they are earned, does predict those future grades at approximately equal levels for both sexes.

STUDIES DEMONSTRATING SEX DIFFERENCES IN EXPECTANCY

In view of the fact that expectancy does seem to facilitate approach behaviors,[13] it is important to note that girls' expectancy estimates are consistently lower than boys'. The following studies demonstrate these sex differences and are a beginning attempt to elucidate some of the reasons for such differences.

Study A

A group of the elementary school-age children (aged 7 years 2 months–12 years 2 months) in the Fels longitudinal sample, 17 boys and 24 girls, were given six different kinds of intellectual tasks from which expectancy estimates were obtained. It was thought that an average expectancy derived from six tasks should yield a reliable measure of the child's general intellectual expectancy. Stimuli for all tasks were especially constructed in our laboratory. Each of the six tasks was presented to the subject in eight levels of graduated difficulty as in the procedure used by Crandall *et al.*[14] As before, the child was told he would be tested subsequently on the tasks.

---

[13] Battle, "Motivational Determinants of Persistence"; Crandall *et al.*, "Motivational and Ability Determinants"; Feather, "Effects of Prior Success"; Tyler, "Expectancy for Eventual Success."
[14] Crandall *et al.*, "Motivational and Ability Determinants."

The most difficult level at which he predicted he would be able to perform constituted his expectancy estimate for that task. The tasks were:

1. *Estimating blocks.* Estimating the number of blocks in irregularly shaped constructions of greater and greater size and complexity, after each construction was uncovered for only ten seconds.

2. *Logical relations.* Solving easy to difficult "brain teasers."

3. *Spatial relations.* Constructing increasingly difficult jigsaw puzzles of *solid* colors.

4. *Numerical skill.* Solving easy to difficult addition problems without the aid of writing materials.

5. *Memory for objects.* Naming all toys in a group after seeing stimuli for ten seconds (from three objects, easiest, to twelve objects, hardest).

6. *Mazes.* Increasingly difficult.

Since all tasks were similarly presented in eight levels of difficulty, expectancy estimates were summed over all six tasks for each subject and the average of his six estimates was calculated. The mean of the males' average expectancies was 6.3 ($SD = 0.64$) and the females' mean was 5.6 ($SD = 0.76$). The t between these means is 3.04, $p < .01$, two-tailed. (In fact, girls' mean estimates were lower than boys' for each individual task.) The females, then, approached these new intellectual tasks with a significantly lower assessment of their intellectual skills than the males.

Was there any reason to believe that the males' estimates should realistically be higher? Perhaps the boys' past histories of intellectual reinforcement had been more positive in nature, resulting in a realistic expectancy that they would be able to perform very well on the new tasks presented to them here. Since these were *novel* intellectual tasks, it is obvious that the child could have had no reinforcement history on these particular tasks which he could use to form his current expectancy for his own performance. For this reason, it would have been necessary for him to use some generalization of the level of reinforcement he had received in other past intellectual situations.[15] Thus, intelligence test scores were used as an index of the adequacy of his performance in such past situations. If the child had received reinforcement at a level fairly commensurate with that adequacy, then it seemed logical that he would have derived an expectancy for success

---

[15] The expectancy tasks used here had been intentionally designed to be novel to the child, since a large proportion of the intellectual tasks and situations he ordinarily meets are, by virtue of his inexperience, new to him. When the individual is confronted with tasks that are unfamiliar to him he is compelled to use his previous successes and failures on tasks that he perceives as most nearly relevant to the particular task at hand in order to predict his probable success in the current task. It seemed important to attempt to investigate the origins of such current task expectancies because it has been empirically demonstrated at several age levels that such expectancies are consistently predictive of current approach behaviors and competence of performance.

in current intellectual task situations approximately equivalent to his IQ level.

Because male subjects had higher expectancy estimates we would anticipate that their IQ scores would also be higher. Analysis of the IQ scores, however, proved otherwise. The subjects' most recent Stanford-Binet scores from the Fels files yielded a mean for the males of 107 ($SD = 11.7$) while the females' mean was 114 ($SD = 15.7$). The t between these means was *not* significant. Thus, even though the girls' IQ's were slightly, though non-significantly, higher than the boys', their intellectual expectancies were significantly lower than the boys'. It seemed, then, that children of the two sexes had used their similar past feedback very differently in forming their expectancies.

To investigate this issue in a more precise manner, a single difference score was needed. Since expectancy scores and IQ scores could not be compared directly, it seemed most appropriate to make the comparison between the individual's relative position on the one dimension and his relative position on the other. Thus, the scores for all subjects were combined for each measure and transformed into standard z scores. The IQ z score was then subtracted from the expectancy z score to yield a discrepancy (D) score for each individual. If IQ level and level of expectancy had indeed been commensurate, then each subject's discrepancy score would have resulted in a value of zero. As can be seen in Figure 3, however, where males' and females' D scores are presented separately, most of the males have higher z scores on the expectancy distribution than on the IQ distribution ($+Ds$) while the reverse obtained for females ($-Ds$).

Of the 17 boys in the group, 13 had positive D scores, one had a D score of 0, and only 3 had negative D scores. The converse was true for the girls. Seventeen of the 24 girls had negative D scores and only 7 of them had positive Ds. The chi square for these data is significant (10.42, $p < .01$). Thus, the two sexes made estimates in opposite directions. The girls did not approach these new intellectual tasks with as confident expectancies of reinforcement as did the boys, even though their past intellectual performance had been similar. As indicated in Figure 3 the boys' mean discrepancy score was $+.80$ ($SD = 1.05$); the girls' mean was $-.56$ ($SD = 1.44$). Because of their opposite directions, those means were significantly different *from one another* ($t = 3.24$, $p < .005$). When the signs were removed from the D scores, however, the absolute amount of discrepancy from the zero value previously suggested was about equal for the two sexes ($t = 0.39$, *n.s.*).

As a beginning, the following three determinants were considered as possibilities which might account for these distortions in estimate:

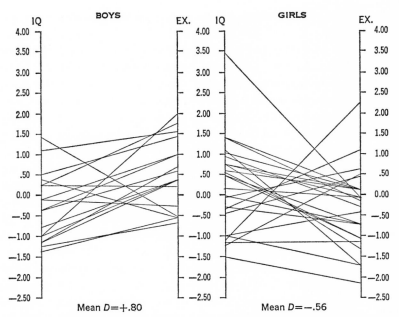

Figure 3. Discrepancies between Fels children's Stanford-Binet scores and their average expectancy estimates for six novel intellectual tasks.

1. Perhaps the child's *verbal report was a nonveridical statement* of his or her internally held expectancy. It might be that his verbal expectancy estimate had been distorted by some factor which, in this context, could be considered a response set since it influences the verbal estimates over and above the internally felt expectations that are assumed to determine approach behaviors.

(a) One such influence might be that the child was *responding to some sort of perceived cultural demand*. Perhaps the girls felt that the examiner would approve of them if they were modest about their intellectual skills, while the boys felt that they should appear confident and upward striving.

(b) Another influence upon estimates might be the *value the child holds for intellectual-academic reinforcements*. It may be that the more the child values intellectual reinforcements, that is, the more he *wants* to do well on intellectual and academic tasks, the more his verbal estimate might be wishfully pulled upward. Previous theory and empirical findings are contradictory on this issue. A negative relationship between value and expectancy has been proposed or found by some investigators[16] and a positive

[16] S. K. Escalona, "The Effect of Success and Failure upon the Level of Aspiration and Behavior in Manic-Depressive Psychoses," *University of Iowa Study of Child Welfare*, 16 (1940), 199–302; L. Worell, "The Effect of Goal Value upon Expectancy," *Journal of Abnormal and Social Psychology*, 53 (1956), 48–53.

24

relationship by others.[17] Some theories propose that the two variables are independent of one another,[18] while still other investigators have found the two variables related only under certain special circumstances.[19] Atkinson[20] proposes that expectancy and value are generally independent, but negatively related in achievement tasks. However, the studies testing these propositions have differed significantly from one another in design, the nature of the samples used, the form of expectancy measured, and/or the task characteristics. Thus, comparisons cannot be made and the present issue remains unresolved.

2. There is also the possibility that these expectations are not simply distorted verbal responses but that males and females actually form different internal expectations. It may be that these differences are the result of *different reinforcement histories* for the two sexes. While it does not seem likely, there is the possibility that males and females have actually received differential feedback from reinforcing agents even when their performances has been equivalent. Since Crandall,[21] Crandall, Good and Crandall,[22] Feather,[23] and others have shown that expectations are increased by positive reinforcement and decreased by negative reinforcement, it is possible that the reinforcement histories of males have been more positive and/or less negative than those of females. When responding to comparable intellectual performance, perhaps parents, teachers, and other

[17] F. W. Irwin, "Stated Expectations as Functions of Probability and Desirability of Outcomes," *Journal of Personality,* 21 (1953), 329–335; R. Jessor and J. Readio, "The Influence of the Value of an Event upon the Expectancy for Its Occurrence," *Journal of General Psychology,* 56 (1957), 219–228; K. MacCorquodale and P. Meehl, "Preliminary Suggestions as to a Formalization of Expectancy Theory," *Psychological Review,* 60 (1953), 55–63; R. W. Marks, "The Effect of Probability, Desirability, and 'Privilege' on the Stated Expectations of Children," *Journal of Personality,* 19 (1951), 332–351.

[18] J. B. Rotter, *Social Learning and Clinical Psychology* (New York: Prentice-Hall, 1954); E. C. Tolman, *Purposive Behavior in Animals and Men* (Berkeley: University of California Press, 1949).

[19] H. Burdick, "The Effect of Value of Success upon the Expectation of Success" (Technical Report #14, Contract Nonr 3591 [01] Office of Naval Research, NR 171–803 [Lewisburg, Pa.: Bucknell University, 1965]); Burdick and N. Stoddard, "The Relationship Between Incentive and Expectations of Success" (Technical Report #7, Contract Nonr 3591 [01] Office of Naval Research NR 171–803 [Lewisburg, Pa.: Bucknell University, 1964]); V. J. Crandall, D. Solomon, and R. Kellaway, "Expectancy Statements and Decision Times as Functions of Objective Probabilities and Reinforcement Values," *Journal of Personality,* 24 (1955), 192–203; Crandall, Solomon, and Kellaway, "The Value of Anticipated Events as a Determinant of Probability Learning and Extinction," *Journal of Genetic Psychology,* 58 (1958), 3–10; H. Hess and R. Jessor, "The Influence of Reinforcement Value on Rate of Learning and Asymptotic Level of Expectancies," *Journal of General Psychology,* 63 (1960), 89–102.

[20] Atkinson, "Motivational Determinants of Behavior"; J. W. Atkinson, *An Introduction to Motivation* (Princeton: D. Van Nostrand Co., 1964).

[21] V. C. Crandall, "Reinforcement Effects of Adult Reactions and Non-Reactions on Children's Achievement Expectations," *Child Development,* 34 (1963), 335–354.

[22] V. C. Crandall, S. Good, and V. J. Crandall, "Reinforcement Effects of Adult Reactions and Nonreactions on Children's Achievement Expectations: A Replication Study," *Child Development,* 35 (1964), 485–497.

[23] "Effects of Prior Success."

socializing agents give male children more praise and less criticism than females, and females more criticism and less praise than males. Thus, their different expectancies may be warranted simply because they have been given more of the one than the other.

3. Finally, internally held expectations may differ because the two sexes are *differentially sensitive to positive and negative reinforcements*. Even if boys and girls do actually receive objectively equal reinforcements, it may be that when those reinforcements are negative, the girls' expectancies are more sharply reduced by them than the boys'. And/or perhaps boys are more responsive to positive reinforcement and raise their expectancies more than do girls under such circumstances. If this were to turn out to be the case, the task would then be to find the antecedents of this differential assimilation of positive and negative feedback, but it would be necessary first to demonstrate whether sex differences in sensitivity to the reinforcements do, in fact, exist.

Or it may turn out to be some combination of differential reinforcement histories and sensitivity. While there has been much work done on cross-sex and same-sex examiner influence in social reinforcement and on the use of parent praise and criticism, there seems to be no empirical evidence bearing upon sex differences in reinforcement histories or reinforcement sensitivity in the intellectual area.

As mentioned in 1(a) above, it was thought that the discrepancy between a child's expectancy and his past performance might be a function of the child's attempt to state to the examiner an estimate which he thought he *should* hold, rather than that which he actually *did* hold. If this were true, the greater the child's need for the examiner's approval, the more his estimate might be distorted. Perhaps such need might have produced the too-modest estimates of the girls and the inflated estimates of the boys.

To measure the desire to present a socially acceptable façade to the examiner, our sample of Fels children were given our Children's Social Desirability scale.[24] This forty-seven-item scale has previously been demonstrated to have some validity as a measure of the individual's concern with others' approval-disapproval.[25] The scale was administered individually and orally. For this sample the girls' mean on the social desirability scale was 26.4, $SD = 11.7$; the boys' mean was 23.6, $SD = 10.8$. The t between these means was not significant.

---

[24] V. C. Crandall, V. J. Crandall, and W. Katkovsky, "A Children's Social Desirability Questionnaire," *Journal of Consulting Psychology*, 29 (1965), 27–36.

[25] V. C. Crandall, "Personality Characteristics, and Social and Achievement Behaviors Associated with Children's Social Desirability Response Tendencies," *Journal of Personality and Social Psychology*, 4 (1966), 477–486.

The IQ — expectancy D scores of the sample were arranged on a single dimension running from high positive, through consonant, down to high negative discrepancies. Correlations between the social desirability measure and the discrepancy scores, however, did not reveal any association for either of the sexes (boys' $r = .08$, girls' $r = .00$). Thus, the distortion represented in discrepancy scores could not be readily assigned to the desire to obtain social approval.

In 1(b) above, it was reasoned that the more the child valued intellectual reinforcements (i.e., the more he wanted to do well on these intellectual tasks), the more his verbal estimate might be wishfully driven upward. Therefore, we gave these children a measure of Intellectual-Academic Attainment Value, a measure of the importance they placed on doing well in intellectual and academic endeavors as opposed to getting reinforcements of other kinds. (See Appendix A.) This measure was especially constructed for the purposes of this study. It was made up of sixteen forced-choice items, each of which paired an intellectual or academic reinforcement with a reinforcement from the need areas of affiliation, dependency, dominance, physical comfort, and leadership. For example, "If you could have whatever you wanted, would you rather: (a) Be able to do well in your school work, or (b) Have lots of kids like you?"

This scale was also administered individually and orally. The girls' mean was 10.7, $SD = 2.6$; the boys' mean was 10.8, $SD = 3.5$.

Scores from this measure also did not correlate with the discrepancies of either sex (boys' $r = .18$, girls' $r = .13$). Thus, the value a child held for intellectual reinforcement did not cause his (or her) verbal estimate to be "pulled" upward. Again, distortions in estimate could not be assumed to be a function of a verbal response set.

Study B

The following findings bear upon the possibility that males and females may *assimilate* the same past reinforcements differently in forming their expectancies. That is, given past feedback *known* to be equivalent for the two sexes, will succeeding expectancy estimates still differ? The data to be presented were gathered from the entire class (except for foreign students) who enrolled at Antioch College in 1963 ($N = 380$). At entrance, and at each subsequent quarter's registration, expectancy estimates were obtained by asking the students to list the courses they were registering for and to circle on a 12-point scale the grade they expected to receive in each course at the end of the term. The scale was represented at each interval as follows: A, A—, B+, ... D—, F. At the end of each quarter the grades the

TABLE 1 *Tests of Difference Between College Males' and Females' Grade Point Averages and Expectancy Estimates*

Grade Point Average	Males			Females			t	p
	N	Mean	SD	N	Mean	SD		
End 1st Quarter	170	7.54	1.97	210	7.82	1.95	1.39	n.s.
End 2nd Quarter	166	7.75	2.00	205	8.14	1.72	1.83	n.s.
End 3rd Quarter	145	8.06	1.93	187	8.31	1.91	1.21	n.s.
Expectancy								
Beginning 1st Quarter	164	9.34	1.34	207	8.90	1.24	3.37	.01
Beginning 2nd Quarter	158	9.40	1.21	195	8.73	1.19	5.21	.01
Beginning 3rd Quarter	128	9.42	1.11	160	8.97	1.10	3.41	.01
Beginning 4th Quarter	115	9.50	1.21	152	9.05	1.14	3.11	.01

students actually had been given were obtained from the college registrar. It was considered that the grades the subject received for the preceding quarter were the most immediate referent available for him to use in estimating his grades for the coming quarter.

Table 1 contains the means and standard deviations of the grades received and the grades expected by each sex and the tests of difference between sexes on each measure. If the reader will refer to the first expectancy estimates he will note that even at the beginning of the first quarter in college, before any college courses were taken, the boys' *initial* estimates of their probable grades in their first courses were significantly higher than those of the girls. Significant differences between the expectancies of the two sexes continued for each of the remaining quarters of this analysis, and the males consistently gave the higher estimates. This was true even though there were no significant differences in the grades received by the two sexes. The males did not receive higher grades to warrant their higher expectancies; in fact, inspection of the boys' and the girls' mean grades reveals that the girls' grades were slightly, though nonsignificantly, higher than the boys' for each quarter.

In order to examine the accuracy or reality of the estimates, the grades of each sex for each preceding quarter can be compared with their estimates at the beginning of the next quarter. It will be noted that although these girls have lower mean expectancies than the boys, as was true of the younger Fels girls on their novel tasks, these college girls' estimates of their grades for each quarter were slightly higher than their own past grades. The males' estimates, however, like those of the young Fels boys, were again well above the past feedback they had received.

Table 2 presents between-sex comparisons of these discrepancies. Each

TABLE 2 *Discrepancies Between Last Grades Received and Estimate of Grades for Succeeding Quarter*

| | Males | | | Females | | | | |
	N	Mean	SD	N	Mean	SD	t	p
Gr. 1st Qtr. to Ex. 2nd Qtr.	157	+1.86	1.92	194	+.87	1.93	4.78	<.001
Gr. 2nd Qtr. to Ex. 3rd Qtr.	124	+1.60	2.08	157	+.71	1.65	3.89	<.001
Gr. 3rd Qtr. to Ex. 4th Qtr.	112	+1.29	1.90	150	+.57	1.70	3.17	<.01

of the three tests of difference demonstrates that the males overestimated significantly more than did the females each quarter. It will also be noted in the table that the absolute size of the discrepancy scores for each sex decreased as the subjects had more experience in college.

(Subsequent analyses of the discrepancy scores for the remainder of the five years of this study demonstrate that the sex differences in discrepancies noted in Table 2 continue, although these differences are slightly attenuated during the latter portion of the students' enrollment. An analysis of the difference between the overall average D scores for the full five-year period, however, was significant at the .001 level (males' $M = 1.00$, $SD = 1.07$; females' $M = 0.29$, $SD = 1.09$; $t = 4.34$). Although the females' mean D scores for the last several quarters were more often slightly positive than negative, the generally decreasing size of those scores led us to examine the *number* of students of each sex who had $+$ and $-D$ scores in their last academic year. Of the 129 students with sufficiently complete data to remain in the sample at that time, there were 57 females and 72 males. Thirty-three of the females had negative D scores, only 24 had positive ones; of the males, only 27 had negative D scores and 45 had positive ones. The chi square for these data is 5.32, $p < .05$. Thus, at the end of their academic careers more girls actually estimated lower than their past grades would warrant while more boys continued to estimate higher than their preceding grades. This is the same sex differentiated tendency initially noted in the younger Fels children with their novel task estimates.)

Study C

What would happen if a novel intellectual task were given to a sample of subjects of ages roughly comparable to those of the college students? If the reinforcements given the males and females *during* the task were exactly equal, would the two sexes assimilate this reinforcement differently? Would they change their estimates (pretest to posttest) in different amounts, even though they had been given the same feedback? As part of a larger longitudinal study of achievement, various achievement measures were given to the young adults (18–26 years old) in the Fels sample. At the time of this analysis 18 females and 23 males had been tested. One of the intellectual tasks required the storage, recall, and reproduction of different patterns of geometric figures which varied in color as well as form. The task was an adaptation of one developed by Glanzer, Huttenlocher, and Clark.[26] This modified form of the task involved twelve different storage loads and required that the subject recall a particular combination of ten of them on each trial. Six geometric forms (star, heart, square, triangle, diamond, and circle) in two colors (black and white) were used. Each stimulus consisted of some combination of five of the various black and white forms drawn on a rectangular card. The subject was given a complete set of cutouts of the six forms in black and a duplicate set in white. The stimulus card was shown the subject for ten seconds, then removed, and he was asked to reproduce the pattern of figures using his set of cutouts. After the task was explained to the subject, but before it was actually administered, his expectancy was obtained by asking him, "I am going to give you ten of these patterns now. How many do you think you will get right?" The task was sufficiently complex that the subjects were somewhat unsure of their responses until they were told "right" or "wrong" by the examiner. This allowed the examiner to manipulate the reinforcements to adhere to a designated schedule. All subjects were failed on trials 4 and 6 and succeeded on the remaining eight trials of the ten-trial series. Exactly the same verbal reinforcing statements were used for all subjects and the examiners were of the same sex as the subjects. After the series of ten trials, a second expectancy estimate was obtained in a similar fashion. It was expected, of course, that most individuals would raise their expectancies after this 80 per cent positive reinforcement schedule, but the point at issue was to determine whether the females would raise their estimates as much as the males. Perhaps this was why girls came to intellectual situations with lower expectancies—the positive feedback they receive in daily life does not have as great a reinforcing value for them as for males.

The first expectancy estimates of the females in this task, as in the preceding studies, were again lower than those of the males. The mean of the women's first estimate was 6.53, $SD = 1.74$; the men's mean was 7.57, $SD = 1.90$. The resulting t was 2.08, $p < .05$. After the series of trials, the mean of the females' posttest estimate was 7.50, $SD = 1.50$, and the males'

---

[26] M. Glanzer, J. Huttenlocher, and W. H. Clark, "Systematic Operations in Solving Concept Problems," *Psychological Monographs*, 77 (1963), 1, Whole No. 564.

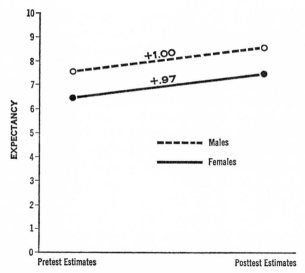

Figure 4. Mean changes in expectancy estimates after 80 per cent positive reinforcement on a novel intellectual task (Fels young adults).

mean was 8.57, $SD = 1.03$. The t of 2.64 between these means was again significant, this time at the .02 level. Again, the women's estimates were significantly lower than those of the men. Change scores were computed for each subject, constants added, and the t computed, in order to determine whether there were differences in the degree to which subjects of the two sexes were affected by the same reinforcements from the examiners. The females' mean change score was .97 while the males' mean was exactly 1.00. This difference between the sexes ($t = 0.06$) was obviously nonsignificant. These mean changes in expectancy are illustrated in Figure 4. Thus, although females started and ended the task with estimates significantly lower than the males, they did not seem to be any more or less sensitive to the same reinforcements than were the males, since the two sexes changed their expectancies equivalent amounts.

After all Ss had received the reinforcement schedule of eight successes and two failures in the task, it is obvious that the most realistic posttest estimate would be eight. It should be noted that the mean of the females' second estimate was 7.50 while that of the males' was 8.57. The difference between the posttest estimates and a theoretically expected estimate of 8.00 was computed for subjects of each sex. The t between these D scores for males and females was 0.04, clearly nonsignificant. Each sex, then, reflected past feedback with about equal amounts of accuracy, but the males again were somewhat optimistic and the females somewhat pessimistic relative to the reinforcements they had received for their own performance.

Certainly, however, the social reinforcement on the laboratory task given these young adults is far from comparable to the IQ scores used as an index of past performance for the little Fels children. Although both samples of females estimated low, and both samples of males estimated high relative to these different indexes of past performance, it will be necessary in future studies to control for, or *systematically* vary, each index across age when examining developmentally the manner in which the two sexes reflect past feedback in making their estimates. So far, however, it appears that the opposite direction of distortion in these estimates on new intellectual tasks may be predicted from sex regardless of age.

Even though the Fels young women started from lower levels of expectancy than the men, it should be noted that they were able to raise their estimates *during* the task just as much as the young men did. If this were the case in their daily experience, what then had made them and the Antioch College women and the young Fels girls give lower expectancies to begin with?

Study D

It occurred to us that the reinforcement given the Fels young women in the laboratory might be quite unlike their natural reinforcement histories in a very important respect. Perhaps the 80 per cent positive reinforcement schedule on a problem they had never tried before constituted such strong and clear-cut reinforcement that it created a "situational demand" to raise one's expectancy estimate for it. The laboratory reinforcement was more consistent and uniform than is normally the case in daily life. Depending on the idiosyncratic standards held by various reinforcing agents, the child's degree of competence on a particular task may exceed or fall short of that standard and he will receive praise, reproof, or fairly neutral feedback accordingly. It is well known that some teachers "grade hard," others are "easy graders." Mother may say that a score of 85 on a test is "great work," Dad may say it is "so-so," an older sibling may assess it as "pretty poor." When these sorts of inconsistent feedback occur, it may be that girls are more sensitive to the negative aspects of that inconsistency, while the positive ones are more strongly reinforcing for boys.

For the next study, then, feedback was controlled so that it contained different percentages of inconsistency or contradiction. The task was a novel digit-symbol substitution task and the 8th grade subjects were instructed that this was a test of intellectual competence. Expectancies were taken using a measure of social comparison. The task was explained to each subject and he was told that it was like part of an intelligence test. He was handed a legal-size sheet of paper with fifty small stick figures running down the length of the sheet. The top one was labeled "does the best on this test," the bottom was labeled "does the poorest on this test." He was asked to circle the child he would turn out to be when we finished testing everyone. Thus, expectancies could range from 1–50, and did. The subject was then assigned to a reinforcement condition so that 6 groups of boys and 6 groups of girls were matched across sex and across conditions on the basis of those initial expectations ($N = 204$, 17 per cell). To obtain matched groups on initial expectancy, data from an additional 24 male and 28 female subjects were discarded.

After each trial the subject was given the feedback on his performance via a display panel of ten lights. He was told that each light represented one of ten schools in which the test had previously been given. The sample was divided among 6 reinforcement schedules: 80 per cent positive, 80 per cent negative, 60 per cent positive, 60 per cent negative, 50 per cent positive, and 50 per cent negative. In the positive conditions the subject was informed that each of the lights which came on after each trial meant that he had "beaten the kids at that school." The negative conditions were produced by telling the subject that when any light came on it meant that "the kids at that school had beaten" him. The total task consisted of ten trials.

This form of feedback was adopted to provide the inconsistency with which a particular piece of performance (here a single trial) might be reinforced in daily life. In other words, the subjects were given quite-consistent-and-mostly-positive reinforcement, quite-consistent-and-mostly-negative, on down to highly inconsistent feedback which was half positive or half negative. The change score between pre- and posttest expectancies was considered the index of the manner in which the reinforcements had been assimilated. This change score, then, constituted the dependent variable on which a $2 \times 2 \times 3$ analysis of variance was computed. That is, there were the two sexes, by the two directions or signs of the reinforcement (positive and negative) by the percentage of reinforcement for each trial (80 per cent, 60 per cent, 50 per cent)—which indicated the amount of inconsistency. Because it was anticipated that girls might react more strongly to negative conditions but less strongly to positive conditions, while the converse mght be true for boys, it was expected that there would be no main effect for sex. Collapsing across conditions of opposite sign for each sex would probably preclude a significant F ratio for sex. The portion of the analysis relevant to the sex differences under investigation, then, would be a sex $\times$ sign interaction, indicating that the girls reacted more to negative reinforcements, boys more to positive, and perhaps a sex $\times$ sign $\times$ per cent

TABLE 3 *Analysis of Variance of Expectancy Change Scores*

Source of Variation	df	Mean Square	F	p
Sex	1	7.84	.16	n.s.
Sign (Pos. vs. Neg.)	1	1603.84	32.84	p < .01
Per cent Reinforcement	2	879.57	18.01	p < .01
Sex × Sign	1	34.60	.71	n.s.
Sex × Per cent Reinforcement	2	28.23	.58	n.s.
Sign × Per cent Reinforcement	2	22.97	.47	n.s.
Sex × Sign × Per cent Reinforcement	2	11.22	.23	n.s.
Within Group	192	48.84		

of reinforcement interaction indicating a greater difference between the sexes, each sex in its predicted direction, in the more inconsistent 50–50 conditions than in the more consistent 80–20 conditions.

The results are shown in Table 3. As predicted, there was no main effect for sex, but neither did the expected interactions occur. The main effect for per cent of reinforcement ($F = 18.01$) simply indicates that for all children (i.e., with sex and sign of reinforcement collapsed) the 80 per cent conditions caused more change than the 60 per cent conditions, which were more effective than the 50 per cent conditions. Secondly, the main effect for sign ($F = 32.84$) indicates that, for children of *both* sexes, the negative conditions as a group caused greater decreases in expectancy than the positive conditions caused increases, even though the positive and negative conditions were objectively equal mirror images of one another. Previous research,[27] however, had already demonstrated this latter phenomenon, and it did not contribute anything to the explanation of the sex differences in response to reinforcement for which the study had been designed. At least as it had been tested here, males and females did not respond differently from one another to either positive or negative reinforcement, nor to inconsistent mixtures of them.

The reader will remember that one of the hypotheses entertained earlier was that the children might be responding to cultural demands for different verbal behavior by the two sexes. These pressures may require that if a girl is to be *feminine* she must be modest in stating her intellectual capabilities; if a boy is to be *masculine* he should appear "upward striving" and confident. Perhaps, then, the more masculine a boy was, the more his expectancy estimate would exceed his past feedback, and the more feminine a girl, the more her estimate would fall below the level of her past reinforcement.

---

[27] Crandall, "Reinforcement Effects"; Crandall, Good, and Crandall, "Reinforcement Effects: A Replication Study."

To examine this possibility, the femininity subscale from the California Psychological Inventory[28] was given to the total sample of 256 children.

Again, the child's past grades were used as an index of the most specific and concrete feedback he had received about his intellectual capability. Boys' and girls' grades and their initial estimates on the novel task were each transformed into z scores so that a discrepancy between these z scores could be computed. It should be remembered that all subjects might have retained their same relative positions on both grade and expectancy z distributions, resulting in zero D scores, or that changes in either direction in those relative positions might be randomly distributed among males and females. Of the 126 boys in the sample, however, 90 had *positive* discrepancy scores; of the 130 girls, 92 had *negative* discrepancies. That is, about 70 per cent of the boys estimated high relative to their past feedback, and about 70 per cent of the girls estimated low relative to theirs ($\chi^2 = 37.18$, $p < .001$). In addition, the mean *amount* of the boys discrepancy was exactly equal to the mean *amount* of discrepancy of the girls (boys $= +.52$, girls $= -.52$), although the two sexes had again taken the opposite directions found in the previous studies.

We arranged the discrepancy scores into a single dimension running from high positive through consonant down to high negative discrepancies and found a correlation with femininity scores of $-.34$ ($p < .001$) for the total group of subjects. While the variance held in common was not large, it appeared that there was some tendency for the more feminine child to estimate relatively low compared to his past feedback, and the more masculine one to estimate relatively high.

However, masculinity and femininity are obviously associated with biological sex and it has already been shown that particular kinds of discrepancy scores were associated with sex. Thus, it seemed possible that the obtained correlation of $-.34$ between masculinity-femininity and discrepancy scores for the total group was caused by the common association of those variables with biological sex. Measures of relationship cannot in themselves ever establish cause, of course, but if, *within* each sex, greater and less femininity were to be associated with negative and positive D scores respectively, it would be much more persuasive. The correlations for the sexes separately, however, were essentially nothing for either sex (boys $= .03$, girls $= -.08$). If the reader will refer to Figure 5, it will be seen that the generally negative relationship for the total group is spurious. It is clear that masculinity-femininity as measured by the California Psychological In-

---

[28] H. C. Gough, *The California Psychological Inventory* (Palo Alto: Consulting Psychologists Press, 1957).

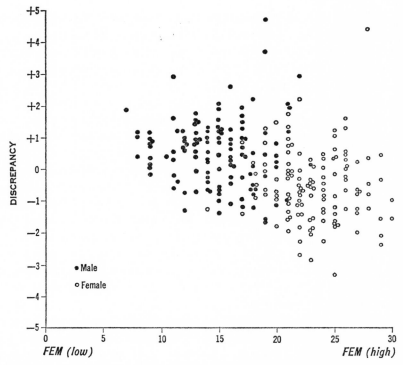

Figure 5. *Discrepancies between past grades and novel digit-symbol estimates as a function of femininity.*

ventory is strongly associated with biological sex; there is, in fact, practically no overlap for the boys' and the girls' distributions. Since the boys had more positive D scores and the girls more negative ones, it is these two facts which are accounting for the negative correlation with femininity for the total group. It will be seen that the distributions for each sex separately reveal no relationship at all between D scores and femininity for either sex. Thus, again, discrepancy between feedback and estimate could not be explained simply by cultural demands to make sex-appropriate verbal statements about one's ability, and it seemed necessary to continue to entertain the possibility that the internally held expectations of the two sexes were actually different.

In addition to the experimental data dealing with inconsistency and direction of reinforcement, and the femininity measure, there was still another source of data available to us for this subject sample which might provide some insight into the differential formation of expectancies. The particular school from which these subjects came used a rather extreme form of

36

homogeneous grouping in that it had divided these 8th grade children into nine ability levels. One of the rationales sometimes given for homogeneous ability grouping is that the child of poor ability is better able to maintain his confidence in his capability if he is in daily contact with others like himself and does not have to compare himself constantly with very capable children, as would be the case in a system where children of all abilities are put together. For this to be true, however, the child would have to ignore the assessment of the external world around him which sees him as one of the members of a group of low ability. In order to do this he must be oblivious to the larger world of parents, teachers, school administration, and peers outside his own classroom, and be cognizant of only the smaller group in his own room. If that were the case, then the child's assessment of his intellectual ability should be determined primarily by his relative standing within his own daily classroom and it should be influenced very little by the height of his ability group in the whole school. It seemed to us, however, that ability group level would constitute reinforcement of loaded value for most children.

For this reason analyses of variance for unequal Ns were computed for each of the sexes separately (126 boys, 130 girls) using ability group placement and standing within classroom as the independent variables and initial expectancy estimates on the novel digit-symbol task as the dependent variable. Subjects for this analysis were not used from the extreme groups 1 and 9.[29] The remaining seven groups were trichotomized into high (groups 2 and 3), medium (groups 4, 5, 6) and low (groups 7 and 8). The subjects from each of the several classrooms were also classified into thirds within their own rooms, using the range of grade point averages in a child's own classroom as the criterion on which to divide them.

Table 4 gives the means for each sex using this double classification. For the boys it will be seen that, in general, the means of their expectancies drop with decreases in both ability group level and standing within class. It will be noted, however, that the differences between ability groups (row means) are a good deal greater than those produced by differences in standing within one's own classroom (column means). The analysis of variance reflected this fact and yielded an $F = 9.88$, $p < .01$, for height of ability group, while standing within class did not significantly affect the boys' expectancies ($F = 0.65$). The interaction term was also nonsignificant

---

[29] Groups 1 and 9 were omitted partially to avoid possible ceiling effects on D scores and partially because these groups, by virtue of their special programs, were somewhat outside the main stream of the regular academic program of the school. Group 1 was an accelerated group with a very individualized, enriched program; group 9 was a slow learners' group made up of children of below 80 IQ. In addition, we felt that the latter children might be unable to give meaningful expectancy estimates.

TABLE 4

Means of Expectancy Estimates on a Novel Intellectual
Task (Digit-Symbol with Intellectual Set) Classified
by Standing within Classroom and Ability Group Level

		BOYS STANDING WITHIN CLASS						GIRLS STANDING WITHIN CLASS			
		High	Med	Low				High	Med.	Low	
ABILITY GROUP LEVEL	High	32.0	34.4	32.7	M 33.0	ABILITY GROUP LEVEL	High	31.5	26.9	24.9	M 28.4
	Med.	31.4	30.6	29.5	M 30.4		Med.	25.1	26.5	27.3	M 26.2
	Low	28.6	24.9	24.2	M 25.7		Low	18.7	19.8	27.7	M 20.3
		M 30.1	M 28.7	M 28.6				M 27 1	M 25.3	M 26.0	

($F = 0.67$). The boy's assessment of his intellectual capability, then, was significantly associated with the level of the ability group he had been put into, but was not associated with his standing among his peers in his own classroom.

For the girls, in general, the same thing is true. Ability group level was again significant ($F = 4.55$, $p < .025$) while standing within classroom was not ($F = 0.67$, *n.s.*). Inspection of individual cell means will reveal, however, that although the girls' expectancies in the top ability group (the top row) drop a little as standing within class goes down, those in the medium and low ability group levels actually *rise* as the standing within class decreases. This yielded a significant interaction term in the analysis of variance for the girls ($F = 2.84$, $p < .05$). Not only was ability grouping not maintaining the expectancy of intellectual success for the low ability group child *of either sex*, but girls who had lower classroom standing in the low and medium ability groups seemed to be resorting to some sort of inflated, unreal self-assessment.

To determine more definitely whether these girls' estimates were disproportionately high, the discrepancies between report-card grade and expectancy z scores were examined through this same double classification. These appear in Table 5. The reader will note that both boys and girls in the three cells around the upper left corners of each table give more conservative, cautious estimates than their past feedback might warrant. These are the children who are actually in pretty good positions as to both ability group level and standing within their own classrooms. Those in the

TABLE 5

Means of Discrepancies Between Past Grades and Current Expectancy Estimates on a Novel Intellectual Task (Digit-Symbol with Intellectual Set) Classified by Standing Within Classroom and Ability Group Level

		BOYS STANDING WITHIN CLASS					GIRLS STANDING WITHIN CLASS		
		High	Med.	Low			High	Med.	Low
ABILITY GROUP LEVEL	High	−.74	−.01	+.73	ABILITY GROUP LEVEL	High	−.87	−.94	−.76
	Med.	−.33	+.54	+1.34		Med.	−.93	−.06	+.92
	Low	+.19	+.62	+1.05		Low	−.83	+.02	+1.63

lower right cells are in poorer positions on both counts and it can now be seen that boys, as well as girls, in those poorer positions give inflated estimates. Although this was already apparent for the girls in Table 4, it could not be observed for the boys in that table because the expectancy estimates reported there had not yet been "anchored" to the grades the children had been receiving.

The most revealing part of Table 5, however, in relation to the sex difference phenomenon is in the cells that lie along the lower left to upper right diagonals. These cells represent the groups of children who have inconsistent or contradictory feedback about their performance. That is, the children in the lower left cells are in a low ability group but high in their own classrooms, while the children in the upper right cells are in a high ability group but are poorest in their own rooms. In the very center cell feedback is so neutral on both counts as to provide little to go on. It should be noted that under these conditions the boys' expectations are elevated, the girls' are depressed. In other words, when feedback is neutral or inconsistent and contradictory, the two sexes resolve the conflict in the opposite ways—the ways that have previously been found to be most characteristic of each sex.

A further analysis of variance was then computed to determine whether the sex differences under conditions of contradictory feedback were in fact significant. Subjects of both sexes were reclassified as to direction and consistency of feedback. Those who were either high-high or high-medium as to ability group and standing within classroom (upper left cells in

TABLE 6

*Means of Discrepancies Between Past Grades and Current
Expectancy Estimates on a Novel Intellectual Task
(Digit-Symbol with Intellectual Set) Classified by
Sex and Consistency and Direction of Reinforcement*

	Consistency and Direction of Reinforcement			
Sex	Consistent Positive	Contradictory & Neutral	Consistent Negative	
Males	−.35	+.51	+.96	M +.52
Females	−.91	−.52	+.62	M −.52
	M −.75	M +.03	M +.86	

Tables 4 and 5) were considered as having received quite consistently positive feedback; those who were low-low or low-medium (lower right cells in Tables 4 and 5) were considered to have had fairly consistent negative feedback. Those who were high-low or low-high on the two dimensions or medium on both (the diagonal cells) were classified as the "contradictory and neutral" group. Means for these groups are given in Table 6. The main effect for sex yielded an F ratio of 23.45 ($p < .001$), that for type of reinforcement was 38.32 ($p < .001$), and there was no significant interaction ($F = 0.98$). Tests of difference between cell means demonstrated that even though males and females both estimated low in the consistent positive condition, the females, true to their sex, estimated significantly lower than did males ($t = 3.01$, $p < .01$). Differences between the sexes in the consistent negative condition were also in the expected direction with the boys estimating even more positively than the girls, but here the difference in response was not significant ($t = 0.92$). It has been observed elsewhere[30] that on some occasions the effect of negative reinforcement can be so strong as to "wipe out" the effect of individual differences, and that may be what has happened here. The opposite response of the two sexes to "contradictory and neutral" feedback is, of course, very significantly different ($t = 5.62$, $p < .001$).

If the two sexes assimilated *this* contradictory feedback differently in forming their expectancies, why didn't they show differences with the inconsistent reinforcements given them on the digit-symbol task? One pos-

[30] Crandall, "Reinforcement Effects"; Crandall, Good, and Crandall, "Reinforcement Effects: A Replication Study."

sibility is that the method of communicating inconsistency, the use of lights displayed simultaneously for each trial to represent beating or losing to different schools, was not actually assimilated as inconsistency, and thus did not produce the conflict or dissonance which may be necessary to bring about the sex-differentiated distortion. It may be that the subjects simply interpreted the several lights as one single reinforcement of greater (80 per cent) or lesser (50 per cent) strength. To reexamine this hypothesis experimentally a different feedback procedure will have to be used.

The most probable reason for the significant results from the "real-life" school situation, however, is that the ability group and classroom factors are of much longer duration, involve many people's assessments of them, and touch upon a larger area of their lives, so to speak, than did our little laboratory task. The reinforcements that can be inferred from those school classifications probably have much greater value or impact.

SUMMARY OF STUDIES AND SUGGESTIONS FOR FUTURE RESEARCH

What conclusions can be drawn from these several studies? That girls give estimates of their own intellectual and academic capabilities lower than do boys seems quite well established and consistent over the various ages studied. Relative to their own past academic performance, the boys are overoptimistic, while the girls are at first slightly hopeful but become more pessimistic as their college careers progress. As to their capability in new intellectual situations, the girls' estimates are relatively *lower* than their past performance would indicate; the boys' estimates are equivalently higher.

Much additional research needs to be done before the two latter phenomena can be established conclusively across age levels. The measures of past feedback used as base lines to estimate the appropriateness of expectancies on new intellectual tasks have varied across age levels and they are extremely incomplete samples of the child's reinforcement history. And the use of intelligence test scores from which to infer reinforcement histories is a particularly crude measure. Much more accurate and complete reinforcement histories, at least in the intellectual skill area, are necessary, and comparable measures must be used at all age levels. In addition, the past grades to current academic grade estimates must be reexamined at other developmental periods. This latter, as opposed to the former problem, can be examined fairly readily.

The sex differences found do not seem amenable to prediction through indexes of cultural demand for sex-appropriate verbal responses. Of course, it may be that so far the proper tools have simply not been used to test this possibility adequately. It will be remembered that the verbal response hypothesis was based on the premise that males were trying *to appear* masculine and females feminine in giving their estimates. Thus, it would seem advisable to try a masculinity-femininity measure that did not disguise its purpose. Because the Femininity subscale of the California Psychological Inventory was empirically derived using biological sex as the criterion, many of the items do not have face validity as masculine or feminine. Thus, they do not allow the respondent to display an attempt *to appear* masculine or feminine. At any rate, since it is not yet possible to assign these sex differences to some sort of response set, it would seem advisable to continue to entertain the possibility that they are real.

The two sexes do not seem to assimilate laboratory task reinforcements differently, but there does seem to be a real difference in the way they derive their expectancies from contradictory life-school situations. When they have cues which tell them that on the one hand they are capable, on the other hand they are not, the girls seem to focus on the negative aspects of the situation, boys on the positive.

Do the sexes get different feedback from the culture? Girls, if anything, get more positive feedback, at least in the form of grades in the early school years. Nevertheless, from these grades as well as other behaviors, perhaps parents and other socializing agents give more praise to boys, more criticism to girls for their intellectual performance. Or perhaps they hold higher standards for girls, making it harder for a girl to produce a product that will meet their approval. These variables have been analyzed from some parent data in our files and no significant differences were found in the amount of praise or criticism for intellectual performance given by mothers or fathers to sons than to daughters. Nor do we find any differences in the standards held by parents of either sex for the intellectual performance of sons than of daughters. However, these parent data are mostly self-report data. It would seem advisable to obtain better measures through direct observation in the home and on structured tasks that are presented to the child in the parents' presence or on which parents and child work together—task situations similar to those used by Hess and Shipman,[31] Rosen and D'Andrade,[32] and Solomon and colleagues.[33]

[31] R. Hess and V. Shipman, "Early Experience and the Socialization of Cognitive Modes in Children," *Child Development*, 36 (1965), 869–886; and "Cognitive Elements in Maternal Behavior," in J. P. Hill (ed.), *Minnesota Symposia on Child Psychology*, Vol. 1 (Minneapolis–St. Paul: University of Minnesota Press, 1967).

[32] B. Rosen and R. D'Andrade, "The Psychosocial Origins of Achievement Motivation," *Sociometry*, 22 (1959), 185–218.

[33] D. Solomon, T. V. Busse, and R. J. Parelius, "Parental Behavior and Achievement of Lower-Class Negro Children" (Paper read at APA, Washington, D.C., September, 1967).

IMPLICATIONS FOR PSYCHOLOGICAL ADJUSTMENT
AND FUTURE ACHIEVEMENT

Probably more attention has been given here to the low estimation of girls than to the high estimation of boys. Perhaps such concern is unwarranted since girls' performance, at least at earlier ages, is as good as, or better than, boys'. In view of this fact, the motivational quality of expectancy may be called into question. However, the studies by Battle,[34] Crandall et al.,[35] Feather,[36] and Tyler[37] in which expectancy relates to clear measures of goal approach, and the several studies cited earlier in which novel task estimates relate to current or future grades earned would seem to argue for a motivational interpretation of expectancy. In addition, since higher expectancy is positively related to performance for girls *within their own sex* it might be said that girls who *are* able to hang on to a confident expectancy are the ones among their own sex who are able to perform best. The overall difference in performance *between* the sexes may prove to be attributable to other motivational factors in which girls have the advantage, such as, for example, intellectual attainment value[38] and perceptions of internal control.[39]

Nevertheless, Sontag, Baker, and Nelson[40] found significantly fewer girls than boys whose intelligence test scores had risen over the elementary school years, and significantly more girls than boys whose mental test scores had declined. It may possibly be that it is these lower expectations of girls that eventually, though not immediately, result in this poorer intellectual performance.

If these lower expectancies are, in fact, actually subjectively held, it is unfortunate that females must work under such a disadvantage. It has been suggested elsewhere[41] that girls frequently use achievement as a

---

[34] "Motivational Determinants of Persistence."

[35] "Motivational and Ability Determinants."

[36] "Persistence at a Difficult Task" and "Effects of Prior Success."

[37] "Expectancy for Eventual Success."

[38] Crandall, Katkovsky, and Preston, "Motivational and Ability Determinants."

[39] *Ibid.;* V. C. Crandall, W. Katkovsky, and V. J. Crandall, "Children's Beliefs in Their Own Control of Reinforcements in Intellectual-Academic Achievement Situations," *Child Development,* 36 (1965), 91–109; P. McGhee and V. C. Crandall, "Beliefs in Internal-External Control of Reinforcements and Academic Performance," *Child Development* 39 (1968), 91–102.

[40] L. W. Sontag, C. T. Baker, and V. L. Nelson, Mental Growth and Personality Development: A Longitudinal Study," *Monographs of the Society for Research in Child Development,* 23 (1958), Serial 68.

[41] V. C. Crandall, "Achievement Behavior in Young Children," *Young Children,* 20 (1964), 77–90; V. J. Crandall, "Achievement," in H. W. Stevenson (ed.), *Child Psychology* (The 62nd Yearbook of the National Society for the Study of Education Part I [Chicago: University of Chicago Press, 1963], 416–459; V. J. Crandall *et al.,* "Parents' Attitudes and Behaviors and Grade School Children's Academic Achievements," *Journal of Genetic Psychology,* 104 (1964), 53–66; F. B. Tyler, J. Rafferty, and B. Tyler, "Relationships Among Motivations of Parents and Their Children," *Journal of Genetic Psychology,* 101 (1962),

means of obtaining love, affection, approval from others—what Atkinson would call "extrinsic" rewards. But in order to obtain these valued goals girls must perform on tasks and in situations in which they feel less capable. If, in addition, the female "hunts for" and is unduly sensitive to reproof whenever the situation provides inconsistent feedback, it seems as though she has little chance of raising her expectancy.

On the other hand, if these are nonveridical verbal responses and females state low expectancies because the culture demands that they make such self-deprecatory statements in order for their behavior to be considered sex-appropriate, while at the same time the culture generally places a high value on intellectual competence, it would seem that females are put in another kind of psychological bind. They are supposed to *perform* competently in academic and intellectual situations, but are not supposed to *say* that they *are* competent. Whether internally held or erroneously stated, these low expectancies would not seem to bode well for their psychological integrity, comfort, self-esteem, or freedom from anxiety.

Although most attention has been given to the girls throughout this discussion because of their lower estimates, perhaps the boys' continued overestimation warrants as much attention. If the males truly *feel* highly confident, that should help them to continue to approach intellectual goals, which in turn should result in increased skill and insure future gratification. But if achievement pressures have forced them to defend by overstating, because it is too threatening to think of oneself as less capable intellectually, then there is cause for concern for them, too. It may be that their relatively poorer performance in this greatly valued intellectual area has forced them to be defensive about it.

The research findings presented here are meant to constitute only a very preliminary progress report. While the sex differences are consistent and stable through several age levels and with a variety of methods of measurement, little success has been achieved in the search for their antecedents. Any of the three possibilities presented here (differential reinforcement histories, differential sensitivity to positive and negative reinforcements, and culturally determined sex-appropriate verbal statements) or some combination of these antecedents may be found to underlie the observed differences, for the suggested antecedents are certainly not mutually exclusive. Or the origins of these sex differences may be found to lie in antecedents not yet probed here at all.

69–81; P. S. Sears, "Correlates of Need Achievement and Need Affiliation and Classroom Management, Self-Concept, and Creativity" (Unpublished manuscript, Laboratory of Human Development, Stanford University, 1962).

APPENDIX MATERIALS
A measure of Intellectual-Academic Attainment Value

If you could have whatever you wanted, would you rather:

1. (a) Be able to understand new ideas, or
   (b) Be the leader of your friends?
2. (a) Be able to do well in your school work, or
   (b) Have lots of kids like you?
3. (a) Have other people do what you want them to, or
   (b) Be able to understand new ideas?
4. (a) Have all your clothes, chairs, and beds be comfortable, or
   (b) Be able to do well in your school work?
5. (a) Always have your friends want you to play with them, or
   (b) Be able to understand new ideas?
6. (a) Be able to do well in your school work, or
   (b) Be the leader of your friends?
7. (a) Have someone you can talk over your troubles with, or
   (b) Be able to understand new ideas?
8. (a) Be able to do well in your school work, or
   (b) Have good things to eat?
9. (a) Have other people do what you want them to, or
   (b) Be able to do well in your school work?
10. (a) Have lots of kids like you, or
    (b) Be able to understand new ideas?
11. (a) Be able to do well in your school work, or
    (b) Always have your friends want you to play with them?
12. (a) Have all your clothes, chairs, and beds be comfortable, or
    (b) Be able to understand new ideas?
13. (a) Always have someone who can help you when you need help, or
    (b) Be able to do well in your school work?
14. (a) Be able to understand new ideas, or
    (b) Have good things to eat?
15. (a) Have someone you can talk over your troubles with, or
    (b) Be able to do well in your school work?
16. (a) Be able to understand new ideas, or
    (b) Always have someone who can help you when you need help?

CHAPTER THREE

Social Comparison and the Development of Achievement Motivation[1]

JOSEPH VEROFF

MY interest in the origins of achievement motivation began a number of years ago when a group of us attempted to reconcile a set of inconsistent findings contrasting the level of achievement motivation in Roman Catholics and Protestants. In a national study[2] our results did not support the previously reported advantage that Protestants have in strength of achievement motivation. In fact, our results indicated that under certain conditions Catholics have higher achievement motivation scores. To reconcile these results we talked of two different types of achievement motivation —one responsive to external pressures, and the other dependent on internalized standards. Presumably the externally based motivation was more typically Catholic, while the internalized one was more typically Protestant. If this interpretation is correct, it raises an interesting question. What is it about the Catholic or Protestant spirit in the socialization process that might orient children to become achievement-motivated in these different ways? The speculative answers to this question might furthermore be use-

[1] The research reported in this paper was sponsored by two grants from the USPHS (MH65423 and MH10554) and a subcontract grant from the Office of Education (Patricia Carrigan, principal investigator). Writing this report was facilitated during 1967–1968 by a USPHS Special Fellowship at the Institute for Human Development. The author wishes to acknowledge the helpful critical readings M. Brewster Smith, Charles Smith, and Joanne Veroff made of an earlier manuscript.
[2] J. Veroff, Sheila Feld, and G. Gurin, "Achievement Motivation and Religious Background," *American Sociological Review*, 27 (1962), 205–217.

ful as a basis for a general theory of the development of achievement motivation.

With such a question in mind, I became involved in trying to construct valid measures of assessing different kinds of achievement motivation in young children, with the ultimate goal of setting up short-term longitudinal studies investigating the effects of parental and family influences, social group, and school settings on the development of achievement motivation. Although in this paper I will be describing research originally undertaken as validity studies, I would like to focus primarily on these researches as they help us explore the development of achievement-related motivations.

In the beginning let me distinguish two types of achievement motivations suggested by our investigation of Catholic and Protestant differences, and by formulations developed by Vaughn Crandall and his co-workers:[3] *autonomous* achievement motivation, contrasted to *social* achievement motivation. I will define achievement motivation as the overall tendency to behave with respect to achievement goals (defined in terms of competing with standards of excellence). *Autonomous* achievement motivation brings *internalized* personal standards into play. *Social* achievement motivation brings standards of excellence based on *social comparison* into play. I am making a distinction between competition with the norms set by others (social comparison) and competition with one's own norms (autonomous achievement). Usually social comparison entails relative standards of performance—the most excellent is the "best" of the group. Social comparison does not necessarily mean aggressive competition, but it often does. Furthermore, successful social comparison does not have to mean social approval, but it often does. Turning to the meaning of autonomous achievement, we will find that it can entail some absolute criterion of performance, but not necessarily. Competition with one's self can also reflect one's relative capacity—how well one feels he is doing compared to some previous point of accomplishment. Social approval can also be a consequence of successful autonomous achievement.

Both motivations for social comparison and for autonomous achievement may be operating in the same situation, but their strength can vary. With each motivation one can discern a specific motivational disposition— a social achievement motive or an autonomous achievement motive. Although each motive may be strong in a given individual, each may be weak, and, more often than not, one may be strong while the other is weak. I will not elaborate that point now, because these assertions lead directly

---

[3] V. J. Crandall, W. Katkovsky, and Anne Preston, "A Conceptual Formulation for Some Research on Children's Achievement Development," *Child Development*, 31 (1960), 787–797.

into some of the developmental theory that I will soon outline. All that I want to make clear now is the hypothesis that some social groups, some parents, some social situations foster one type of achievement motivation and some another, and some may foster the mongrel types. We can classify children into different groups based on different types and then can see whether different groups are affected differently by the same life situation. These hypotheses imply that it is no longer proper to talk only about high or low resultant achievement motivation. Rather it is important to specify what kind of resultant achievement motivation, and in what combination, a researcher is talking about. I will use developmental speculations, backed up with data where available, as a basis for classifying these types and for demonstrating their usefulness in understanding different kinds of children in different kinds of achievement situations.

DEVELOPMENTAL SPECULATIONS

Achievement gratification as pride of accomplishment is not a primordial experience. Rather it evolves from the child's more primitive feelings of effectiveness in attempted autonomy. Mastery emerges out of exploring and coping with the environment as an individual organism. White[4] and Hunt[5] have been particularly effective in calling attention to these intrinsic experiences in very young children. They are fundamental in the development of achievement goals. They are not themselves achievement goals, but it is out of these experiences that autonomous achievement goals develop. Wenar[6] has begun to classify various types of behaviors in the infant (under one year) that can be labeled as "competent." Behaviors that he has attempted to code systematically as indications of competence are a high "intensity" of behavior, a "self-sufficiency" (independence from social elicitation), an orientation to complexity, and "objective" observing (especially in social curiosity). At no point does Wenar make any assumption about the child's *awareness about himself and what he is doing.* In particular there is no assumption about the child's evaluation of his competence. Although the child is obviously not passive in any of the above dealings with the world, nevertheless, he is not necessarily evaluative. And it is the *evaluation of competence* that makes the experience an "achievement"—that would underlie what I have singled out as autonomous achievement motivation. A child has to be aware of what he has done and act evaluatively toward it. In order to be evaluative toward his behavior the child must have a

---

[4] R. W. White, "Competence and the Psychosexual Stages of Development," in M. Jones (ed.), *Nebraska Symposium on Motivation* (Lincoln: University of Nebraska Press, 1960).
[5] J. McV. Hunt, *Intelligence and Experience* (New York: Ronald Press, 1961).
[6] C. Wenar, "Competence at One," *Merrill Palmer Quarterly*, 10 (1964), 329–342.

sense of personal agency in accomplishment, some notion that *he* did it. The joy an infant may experience from the exercise of muscles or vision even when oriented to complex stimuli is, no doubt, inspired by competence, but it is *not* the result of autonomous achievement. No evaluation, however primitive, has presumably taken place. Piaget[7] talks of the period of 4–8 months as a time of the development of crude intentionality in the child. During this period the infant will try to make an object that has disappeared reappear. Such behavior shows that the child can operate *without* the immediate stimulus. When a child can act in this manner with respect to competence goals, then one might say that he has a primitive evaluative system for his own competence, a primitive autonomous achievement motivation. He behaves in order to bring about a condition of *greater* competence *on his own*. Thus, he *evaluates* on his own. Stunning progress of such autonomous achievements in very young children emerges at the onset of language which can be seen as both a condition for and a result of an adequate conception of "self." And so, although I would trace autonomous achievement motivation to the differentiation of competence in early infancy, I would contend that well-organized autonomous achievement orientation cannot blossom until 1½–2½ years when the child's burgeoning capacity for language enables him to reflect better on what he has done and whether he accomplished his intended achievement or not. The child's autonomous achievement motivation can become more and more intense as his capacities and skills become clearer and clearer, especially in conjunction with the rapid growth of early childhood. A child learning to walk, discovering the possibilities of language, climbing stairs, running, dressing himself, or merely effectively manipulating objects experiences autonomous achievement pleasures constantly. Autonomous achievement goals generate from these repeated experiences of pleasure in the child's new found capacity to do what he was previously unable to do.

But what of social comparison? How early does it begin? From the developmental standpoint it is apparent that social comparison and evaluation are only secondary and later processes imposed on an already formed orientation to one's own intrinsic goals. The early feeling of competence in autonomous achievement does not involve social comparison. Of course, much of human cognitive capacities develops within the medium of social interaction. I would contend, however, that Festinger's hypothesis[8] about the automatic generation of social comparison tendencies when a person's

---

[7] J. Piaget, *The Origins of Intelligence in Children* (New York: International University Press, 1952).
[8] L. Festinger, "A Theory of Social Comparison Processes," *Human Relations,* 7 (1954), 117–140.

ability is being evaluated under conditions of ambiguity, does not apply to *very young* children, especially those younger than 5 or 6. The child is too egocentric at this age. Of course, there are often standards about what or how well a 4-year-old should perform, and the 4-year-old often can learn these standards, *even if* these standards represent social comparison. A 4-year-old can compare himself to another if asked to, or if oriented that way, for example, by competitive siblings. I am only saying that he does not automatically do it. He does not automatically think of his performance in contrast to other people's performances. Only considerable reinforcement, usually from siblings or parents, can cause such a disposition to develop as a general motivation in a very young child.

Only in slightly older children in our culture, those in the early school years, does there exist both a pressure for social evaluation and a desire for it. At this age the larger socialization by the community through the school occurs. Social comparison then becomes an automatic response generated by evaluations of performance. This then would be the second stage of the development of achievement motivation. The autonomous orientation to achievement is the first stage.

During this second stage social comparison is functional; it allows a child to accommodate to his own failures, to note how his aspirations may be realistic or unrealistic vis-à-vis other children's performance. Social comparison allows a child to learn about himself in relationship to the world. It has an *informative* function. But more than that, social comparison, if favorable, often means social approval not only from a significant other, but also from the world at large. It has a *normative* function. When a child is placed in the school setting it is therefore not surprising for him to orient himself quickly to social comparison even if his family does not expressly encourage it. It would not be surprising to find a more precocious interest in social comparison developing in children who have been to nursery school. It also would not be surprising to find precocious social comparison developing in younger siblings, particularly those in large family settings. In either case the social world, being more diffuse psychologically, compels the child to compare his performance with others.

If social comparison goes right—if the child can see himself as not being discrepantly incompetent—a child can learn to be reassured about his own standards, about his own autonomy. He can perhaps learn to differentiate situations in which his performance relative to others is different from the situations in which it is the same. Social comparison conveys both norms for proper performance and information. An integration of autonomous achievement and social comparison can occur when social comparison does not get imbued with other values, when the normative function of social comparison does not completely dominate a child's thinking about achievement. If the normative function supersedes the informational function, then social comparison motivation will overrule any autonomous achievement motivation. If the information function supersedes the normative function, then an integration of these two motivations can occur. By an "integration," I do not mean that the two motivations are fused but rather that they are held separate and used in the appropriate situation. This type of accommodation of one's own achievement standards to the standards of the world describes the final "mature" orientation to achievement. Thus, three stages of development of achievement motivation are posited: (1) autonomous competence; (2) social comparison about achievement; and (3) autonomous achievement motivation integrated with social comparison strivings.

Following other theories of stages of personality development, I will assert that successful mastery of each previous stage of achievement is necessary for successful mastery of the next stage. Some degree of autonomous competence is a prerequisite for attention to social comparison, and both social comparison and some degree of mastery competence are necessary for a mature competence orientation that combines with the social orientation. Therefore, the quality of a child's early sense of effectiveness is critical. If he does not learn to cope effectively in infancy and early childhood, no amount of social demands for achievement will be useful in promoting later achievement interests.[9] If he *does* learn to cope effectively, later social demands can have a strong impact. Successful social comparison depends on an adequate sense of effectiveness or autonomy. Furthermore, in order for a child to be able to integrate both autonomy and social comparison motivation, a child must be successful in social comparison, especially in his middle childhood. Similar to Harvey, Hunt, and Schroder's formulation of development[10] I would conceive of achievement motivation as following consecutive steps of differentiation and integration. From a successful phase of autonomy orientation (Can I or can I not do it myself?) there can develop autonomy motivation[11] from which in turn can develop a social comparison orientation (How do I compare with others?) with its social comparison motivation. With both orientations mastered

---

[9] In this assertion there is an implicit assumption about the validity of the "sensitive stage" idea proposed by various theorists including the present author with regard to achievement motivation (J. Veroff, "Theoretical Background for Studying the Origins of Human Motivational Disposition," *Merrill Palmer Quarterly*, 11 [1965], 3–18).
[10] O. Harvey, D. Hunt, and H. Schroder, *Conceptual Systems and Personality Organization* (New York: John Wiley & Sons, 1961).
[11] I am using a distinction between "orientation" and "motivation." By "orientation" I mean the cognitive or motoric readiness to react to a given situation. By "motivation" I mean the tendency to act with respect to certain goals. All motivations are orientations but not all orientations are motivations.

TABLE 1 *Types of Achievement Orientations Based on Stages of Development*

Types	Stage of Autonomy	Stage of Social Comparison	Stage of Integration
1. Integrated Achievement Orientation	+	+	+
2. Competitive Orientation	+	±	−
3. Fear of Failure Orientation (a)	+	−	−
Fear of Failure Orientation (b)	±	±	−
4. Fear of Success Orientation	±	+	−
5. Low Achievement Orientation (a)	±	−	−
Low Achievement Orientation (b)	−	−	−

Note: Symbols used are
+ Mastery of Stage
± Partial Mastery of Stage
− Lack of Mastery of Stage

and motivation developed, there can develop an integrated stage of both autonomy and social comparison orientation (Can I do it well on my own and measure up to other people's standards of excellence?) out of which both motivations can operate freely.

With such an underlying conception of the order in which the two types of achievement orientations and motivations have to be learned for subsequent development of "mature" achievement motivation, we can ask what happens when a child does not consecutively and successfully go through each of the stages. Since we are considering various combinations of presence and absence of motivation, it was convenient for me to answer this question in terms of achievement types. I have schematically outlined these types in Table 1.

In Type 1, a child has for the most part mastered successive stages of achievement orientation; he has mastered autonomous achievement motivation, social comparison motivation, and integration. In Type 2, only autonomy has been mastered, social comparison has been partially mastered but the further integration has not been mastered. In Type 3a, autonomy is mastered, but social comparison and the integration are not mastered. In Type 3b, the stages of both autonomy and social comparison are only partially mastered, and, hence, integration is impossible. In Type 4, autonomy is partially mastered, social comparison is mastered, but the integration is impossible. In Types 5a and 5b, autonomy is not mastered or is only partially mastered, and neither social comparison nor integration is mastered.

Before I describe these types in more detail, let me ask what is meant by successful mastery of any of these stages. How do we know that there is some degree of successful achievement of one of these stages of development? These are complicated questions to answer; they lie at the heart of general developmental issues. Let me take a quick stab at some answers here.

Elsewhere I have described a sensitive stage hypothesis with regard to the development of motivational dispositions.[12] What I suggested and presented some evidence for is that there is an optimal timing of demands for particular behaviors in the child which leads to the development of strong motives and expectancies. One can use this general idea to help identify when successful mastery or partial mastery of an achievement demand occurs.

For *successful mastery of autonomy* in the very early stage, demands and opportunities for autonomy have to be appropriately timed. They must be neither too early nor too late. The parents must allow free exploration of the environment. They must allow the child to learn to acquire a range of verbal and manipulative skills at an appropriate time. Between the ages of one and four a parent must appropriately gauge the capacity of his child and allow him to master challenges on his own, to gain what may be called a sense of effectiveness. With successful mastery, high autonomous achievement motivation develops. Ineffective pacing can lead to partial mastery of the autonomous stage and hence to low autonomous achievement motivation. Often such partial mastery can induce anxiety about autonomous achievement and only moderate positive autonomous achievement motivation. Lack of pacing can lead to total lack of mastery of autonomous achievement. Very early in his career a child can learn that he can master his fate and in his own way control his environment. Any arrangement of the child's experiences with the world that encourages such a generalized expectancy will promote the successful mastery of this first stage of achievement development and the development of strong autonomous achievement motivation. One such arrangement might merely be the free motoric access to a large territory. McClelland[13] reported a greater use of playpens by mothers in predominantly Catholic cities than in predominantly Protestant ones. This may only reflect the response of mothers to larger family size. Nevertheless the fact that German-Catholic adolescents have lower achievement motivation scores than do Protestants is very provocative, juxtaposed with the playpen finding. Perhaps it was this very early limitation of motoric exploration that hampered initial feelings of

---

[12] Veroff, "Studying Human Motivational Disposition."
[13] D. C. McClelland, *The Achieving Society* (Princeton: D. Van Nostrand Co., 1961).

53

competence among Catholics. The results are only suggestive, since many things can account for this correlation, but within the present discussion these results may have special significance.

What relationship exists between social rewards or punishments and early learning of autonomous achievement motivation? Social approval in and of itself is not critical in gaining confidence in competence. A child can learn about this mastery without social rewards. White has been particularly eloquent on this topic.[14] Social rewards for competence probably extend the affective associations to autonomous achievement, perhaps thereby building *very* strong autonomous achievement motivation, but they are not required for the development of this orientation.

On the other hand, social punishments in the form of belittling or other criticisms of a child's adequacy at this age can be strong deterrents to the development of autonomous achievement motivation. Sarason *et al.*[15] have suggested that early social criticism of a child's performance may underlie the dependency syndrome which, in turn, may be the major determinant of test anxiety. Parental criticism often implies inadequate autonomy; the child turns to others for guidance partially out of fear of his own provoked aggression but also because he feels himself to be inept.

In summary, what does seem critical for the successful mastery of autonomy are the following: the freedom of access to environment, sufficient exposure to stimulation requiring autonomous mastery, and sufficient support for autonomous action. I have previously noted that optimal timing of parental achievement induction is a good predictor of children's autonomous achievement disposition. Perhaps the reason for this is that with such optimal timing the parent allows, encourages, and supports a child's freedom and at the *same time* challenges a child's autonomy. The child is encouraged to explore his environment at a time when he is able to meet new challenges and cope with them. The optimal time may be that time when the child cannot accomplish without effort, but can accomplish with persistent striving.

For *successful mastery of social comparison,* a child has to compare favorably with a reasonably large majority of others of the same age and sex with respect to the valued attributes of the social group to which he refers himself. It is difficult to specify what favorable comparison is. Is it being relatively competent on a number of characteristics? Is it being very competent on a few characteristics? Or is it being not incompetent on any or few? I cannot answer these questions and they are excellent ones to pur-

---

[14] White, *op. cit.*

[15] S. B. Sarason *et al., Anxiety in Elementary School Children: A Report of Research* (New York: John Wiley & Sons, 1960).

sue. The only thing that is clear is that the child must feel like an adequate person in comparison to others who are significant for him. Early in the game positive social comparison means positive social approval for meeting group standards. It may be that certain reference groups stress competence at a number of different skills while others limit themselves to only certain skills. In our society, boys are notoriously singleminded about valuing athletic skills. It may be that for many boys adequate social comparison in athletics is the major basis for adequate social comparison in general.

Earlier I noted that adequate social comparison meant the capacity to treat social comparison as information rather than as norms for social approval. The latter basis for social comparison becomes figural when a child's reference group values competition so strongly that no other basis for evaluation can come to the fore. This can occur among the single-minded athletically oriented boys mentioned above or it could occur in a highly competitive school system or neighborhood. In these settings competition can so dominate a person's basis for esteem that even with successful social comparison a child may be locked into a framework of normative social comparison. But, generally speaking, one might say that with adequate social comparison about valued characteristics a person can relax about social comparison, treat social comparison as information about how well he could be doing or how well he actually is doing, and then move back into considering his own autonomous capacities for mastery.

However "favorable comparison" is defined, I contend that appropriate timing of social comparison is important. At around eight or nine a child has sufficient awareness of steps of difficulty in performance variations that he can become aware of *relative improvement* if he attempts to achieve in contrast to others. Too early demands for social comparison may blind him to relative improvement or make him very anxious about his own performance vis-à-vis others. *A very young* child can overdramatize his incompetence compared to others. Demands for social comparison *after* a critical time have little challenge to the child. The child cannot easily generalize these demands when they are applied only to situations in his later years of elementary school. My best guess is that for favorable comparison a child must be in a group where he can excel in *something* and yet be challenged. There are social settings that can promote such experience and social settings that can not. For some children homogeneous ability grouping in school can be very effective in successful mastery of social comparison of those abilities relevant to the grouping. Heterogeneous groupings in school can be disastrous to those lacking in autonomous motivation and very unchallenging to those with very strong autonomous motivation.

Thus, proper pacing of challenge is again what is critical in these phases of the life cycle within each of the major social settings in which the child finds himself.

For *successful mastery of the integration of autonomous and social comparison motivation,* a child must regain a strong sense of his own independence—some sense of his own effectiveness apart from the social groups to which he belongs. It is a speculation of mine that this can come about most dramatically when a child learns to commit himself to some area of very personalized and autonomous skill, the kind of skill that emerges only when a child *overcomes* considerable obstacles to this skill. A sense of independence and effectiveness, however, should certainly be facilitated in grade school by the simultaneous occurrence of sufficient encouragement of autonomy along with comfortable reference groups for social comparison. Indeed, one would think that intense social comparison might drop out in the later years of elementary school. In any case, appropriate interest in autonomy becomes even more figural in early adolescence. What with the dramatic physical changes and the awareness of encroaching adulthood, a child feels a strong push for differentiation from his parents as well as his peers. An adolescent needs the freedom to belong as he chooses, to act on his values as he sees them, to try to integrate inconsistencies in his perspective. Such freedom, however, must be appropriately timed. If it occurs too early, the child may be cast adrift in a sea of confusion. If it occurs too late, it would be a little like unlocking the barn door after the horse has come home or become too unsure of himself to leave in the first place. Appropriate "letting go" can help a child integrate social comparison and autonomous achievement motivation. Without it, a child's achievement interests can be overwhelmed by a domineering parent.[16] Obstacles to appropriate sexual identities, in particular, might stand in the way of successful integrations of these apparently conflicting motivations of autonomy and social comparison. An adolescent boy, unsure of his masculinity, can easily become compulsively blinded to social comparison. He reads any comformity to norms as a degradation of his autonomy. Or he may be so frightened of assertion that he remains inextricably tied to social comparison only. With an inadequate sense of being masculine or feminine, a child is often unsure about his own evaluation as a person and about what kind of competences he should be concerned about. He thus may not know how to differentiate those situations that may ap-

---

[16] Cf. F. L. Strodtbeck, "Family Interaction, Values, and Achievement," in D. C. McClelland *et al.* (ed.), *Talent and Society* (Princeton: D. Van Nostrand Co., 1958), 135–194; B. C. Rosen and R. D'Andrade, "The Psychosocial Origins of Achievement Motivation," *Sociometry,* 22 (1959), 185–218.

propriately arouse autonomous achievement motivation from situations that appropriately arouse social achievement motivation.

Having briefly discussed the problem of what successful mastery of any of these stages of achievement might be, let me now describe the typology outlined in Table 1 in more detail.

The first type I will call the *integrated achievement motivation*. This type of person can become motivationally engaged not only when the means of evaluating his performance are clear from his own bearings, but also when his *own* goals and means of evaluation are ambiguous. In the second case he uses social comparison informationally. I would contend that many of the highly motivated achievers in college samples are likely to be of this type. Furthermore, returning to my initial discussion of Catholic-Protestant differences in achievement motivation, I would contend that this type and the subsequent one are more prevalent among Protestant groups than among Catholic groups.

The second type I will call the *competitive orientation*. People of this type are those who are not able to master what it means to integrate competition with others with achieving on one's own, probably because they had not fully mastered their problems in social comparison. This type includes people who overly evaluate the competitive situation. Even when a situation in fact demands their own autonomous strivings and standards of excellence are clear without social comparison, such people tend to interpret the situation as one where competition is required.

The third type, where social comparison itself is not mastered, is very likely to be a group that many researchers have called *"high in fear of failure orientation."* Atkinson has used measures of test anxiety to help him and his collaborators isolate students who are high in fear of failure. He uses it as a way to assess those people who are characteristically upset by anticipated failure in competing with standards of excellence. Atkinson does not distinguish a subject who is fearful of failure in competition with himself as opposed to competition with others. I would contend that fear of failure should be limited primarily to the latter kind of person. Test anxiety may be a good gauge of such fear because tests usually are reflections of competition with others. But I limit discussion of fear of failure orientation to a fear of competing with others, because I think people with this orientation must have experienced some success in autonomy but they experience difficulty in comparing themselves favorably with others. They must have met with enough success to keep them striving for it. It may have been inconsistent success; they may be those who have experienced social criticism for failure in autonomy as well as inadequate social comparison. Nevertheless they experienced some early success with autonomy.

These people then characteristically experience failure and success intermittently at both the stage of autonomy and the stage of social comparison (as shown by the ± ± types) or they experience considerable success in autonomous strivings but do not experience such success in social comparison. In either case these people anticipate considerable social disapproval. The major concern of a person with fear of failure is to avoid standing out in social evaluation—to avoid disapproval. Lacking adequate sense of his own control of the social evaluation process, he finds the world hostile and somewhat unmanageable.[17] The kind of person, described by Marlowe and Crowne as high in social approval,[18] and the kind of person Crandall, Crandall, and Katkovsky[19] see as oriented to doing what is socially desirable are both likely to be high in fear of failure. Such a "hang-up" about avoiding disapproval in social comparison often precipitates another related characteristic—cautiousness in both setting expectations for oneself and in asserting oneself. Such cautiousness often leads to failure and a vicious circle is activated. Returning again to Catholic-Protestant differences in achievement styles, I would contend that this type is more prevalent among Catholics than among Protestants.

The fourth type I have called a *fear of success orientation*. Unlike the person with fear of failure, the type of person who is high in fear of success is someone who goes on to master social comparison in spite of earlier inconsistent experiences with successful autonomy strivings. This type of person is successful in competition with others and is fearful of what that success means. Why should such a person be fearful of success? We can only speculate, but it seems clear that there must have been some painful associations to earlier successes. Perhaps there was both acceptance and rejection of the child's earlier manifestations of successful autonomy. A mother might see her son as successful at sports, while his father may belittle his skill. A father might be thrilled by his daughter's verbal skill, but simultaneously reprimand her for being too intrusive with adults. Very personal family dynamics can account for these peculiar inconsistencies. Neurotic oedipal triangles are often assumed to engender such ambivalence.

Fear of success is apparently more common in women than in men.[20]

---

[17] R. C. Birney, H. Burdick, and R. Teevan, *Fear of Failure* (Princeton: D. Van Nostrand Co., in press).

[18] D. P. Crowne and D. Marlowe, *The Approval Motive* (New York: John Wiley & Sons, 1964).

[19] V. C. Crandall, V. J. Crandall, and W. Katkovsky, "A Children's Social Desirability Questionnaire," *Journal of Consulting Psychology*, 29 (1965), 27–36.

[20] Tina Horner, "The Motive to Avoid Success: A Thesis Proposal" (Unpublished, University of Michigan, 1965).

I am not talking about the deliberate avoidance of appearing competitive with a man which the woman may see as jeopardizing her attractiveness. Rather I am addressing myself more to the early experiences of conflict about autonomy that more girls than boys probably experience in the first stage of achievement motivation. Although it is hard to document, most developmental psychologists assume that there is greater ambivalence about autonomy in girls than in boys. These social role expectations can be subtly transmitted even in early social learning. It may be important, too, that women are the major caretakers of both boys and girls. Perhaps because women feel more similar to girls than to boys they can treat their sons with greater respect for autonomy than they can their daughters. Girls are more likely to be extensions of a mother's self than are boys. Thus, girls may emerge from the autonomous achievement stage with greater ambivalence. If you couple this supposition with the fact that girls are likely to do well in school via compliance in comparison with boys, it may be no wonder that many of them emerge from their school experiences with a fear of success.

The fifth type is called *low achievement motivation.* For this group there has been not only little emphasis or possibility for satisfaction from mastery of autonomy, but also there has been a lack of mastery of compliant social comparison. This type is likely to have unrealistic appraisals of aspirations and abilities, not only for himself but for others. In this group might be those who are impulsively overaspiring. Because they have so little experience with a sequence of partial goals leading to ultimate goals, they may always assume "the higher, the better" even when it is unrealistic.

Although there are obvious variants and combinations of any of the above types, these basic types can serve as the structure for the rest of this paper. I have contended that such differentiations will further our understanding of developmental processes underlying achievement orientations as well as promote explanatory distinctions between people as they behave in an ongoing situation that hitherto have not been made.

Is there any evidence for this contention? I have made a number of highly speculative assertions about the nature of achievement motivations in young children and their development. I would like to back up some of these assertions with whatever limited amount of data I have available for them. In order to do this, I will be reporting information from studies that I and some of my students have been working on for a number of years. To describe the evidence that I would like to offer in support of these assertions, I would like to present briefly the rationale for the assessment techniques used, especially because some of them are novel procedures. Then I will describe studies that have been done using these techniques.

MEASUREMENT OF ACHIEVEMENT MOTIVATIONS IN CHILDREN

Assessment of Autonomous Achievement Motivation

Let me first describe a promising new technique for measuring autonomous achievement motivation in nursery school and 2nd grade children. The measure is responsive to achievement arousal;[21] it has been negatively related to test anxiety under achievement arousal; it is positively related to underachievement,[22] it is associated with moderate maternal expectations for children's achievement. Sex and developmental differences occur that fit into an interpretation of the measure as one reflecting autonomous achievement motivation.[23] Older children are more likely to be high in this measure than younger children; and older boys are more likely than older girls to increase their motivation scores after achievement arousal. All of these data suggest that there is considerable validity to the technique. I will go into detail about some of these specific results later on, but at this point let me just describe it and its rationale.

The theoretical work of Atkinson on the delineation of achievement motivation in the past decade pointed to a potential measure of the achievement motive in the overt aspiration choices of children. Atkinson and Feather[24] have noted that risk-taking behavior can be a joint function of the motives to approach success and to avoid failure. In a level of aspiration setting, the selection of calculated risks as opposed to "sure things" or "outside chances" is characteristic of persons high in approach achievement motivation. Conversely, those who select "outside chances" or "sure things" in a series of aspirations are characteristically low in approach achievement motivation relative to their avoidant achievement motivation. A number of studies have been offered in support of this position.[25] This theory thus suggests one ought to measure a child's characteristic response to achievement challenge.

Two studies stand out as ones that offer some clues as to how one might

---

[21] The results of the study demonstrating this are reported later in this chapter under Assertion 4 and in Table 11.

[22] Second-grade children high in test anxiety and low in autonomous achievement motivation can be singled out as those most likely to be reading at a level much lower than their measured ability.

[23] These results are reported under Assertion 2 and in Table 8.

[24] J. W. Atkinson, "Motivational Determinants of Risk-Taking Behavior," *Psychological Review*, 64 (1957), 359–372; and *An Introduction to Motivation* (Princeton: D. Van Nostrand Co., 1964); J. W. Atkinson and N. T. Feather, *A Theory of Achievement Motivation* (New York: John Wiley & Sons, 1966).

[25] See Atkinson, *An Introduction to Motivation*.

go about measuring a child's characteristic response to achievement challenge. Crandall and Rabson[26] examined a child's interest in repeating tasks at which he either failed or succeeded. These researchers found that a child's willingness to repeat a failed task increased with age, a result corroborating Rosenzweig's earlier findings.[27] They also found that girls are less likely to repeat failed tasks than boys. Coopersmith[28] obtained a similar measurement from older children and related it to assessments of self-esteem. He found that children willing to repeat a failed task were the most likely to show discrepancies between their own judgment of their self-esteem and their teachers' judgment. Furthermore, a fantasy measure of achievement motivation was significantly related to repeating failed tasks. The authors of these two studies did not conclude that measures of repetition of challenging tasks reflected dispositions to achieve, but I would like to offer such an interpretation.

Let us follow the leads of Coopersmith and Crandall and Rabson and examine the significance of a child's repetition behavior in the risk-taking situation. From Atkinson's theory of achievement motivation, I will assert that those who are interested in repeating tasks that are moderately difficult for them, rather than tasks that are relatively easy or very difficult, are people who have a high positive motive to succeed relative to their negative motive to avoid failure. This is the general rationale for the technique for assessing autonomous achievement motivation that I am about to describe. A complete description of the procedures appears in the Appendix to this chapter.

The measures used ask the child to perform a series of tasks reflecting different skills. The child is presented with an easy version of each skill and then steps of that skill in increasing difficulty until he fails two in a row. At that point the administrator turns to the child and says, "Let's do just one more. Which one of these would you like to do again? This one here [pointing to the first one] which was easy for you; this one here [pointing to the task that the child was able to do right before the first failure] that was not so easy for you, but you did OK; this one here, that was hard for you [pointing to the first failure]; or this one here that was very hard for you [pointing to the second failure]?" The tasks were so arranged that all children could pass the first two items. The subject then

---

[26] V. J. Crandall and Alice Rabson, "Children's Repetition Choices in an Intellectual Achievement Situation Following Success and Failure," *Journal of Genetic Psychology*, 97 (1960), 161–168.

[27] S. Rosenzweig, "An Experimental Study of 'Repression' with Special Preference to Need-Persistive and Ego-Defensive Reactions to Frustration," *Journal of Experimental Psychology*, 32 (1943), 64–74.

[28] S. Coopersmith, "Self-Esteem and Need for Achievement as Determinants of Selective Recall and Repetition," *Journal of Abnormal Social Psychology*, 40 (1960), 310–317.

said which one he preferred to repeat and then repeated his particular choice. The choice of either of the two *middle* tasks was assumed to be a choice of challenge, because each of these represented ones that the child had just been able to succeed at or had just missed. It is important to note that "middle tasks" are relative to the child's ability. In this way, the child is asked to respond to a challenge defined by his own capacities, and we assumed that the choice would reflect *autonomous achievement* striving. The number of such choices across the four series was assumed to be a measure of resultant autonomous achievement motivation. The four types of scaled tasks were presented in the order listed below:

(a) reproducing different strings of "snap-it" beads from memory;
(b) a ball-throwing task—throwing a rubber ball in a basket from behind lines set at different distances;
(c) an object-memory task—recalling the objects pictured on sheets of paper;
(d) a drawing task—copying designs of varying complexities.

It should be noted that each of these tasks samples somewhat different types of skills: motor coordination, visual memory, memory span, copying ability. It is hoped that sampling skills from somewhat different domains would be an advantage in trying to develop a measure of general achievement orientation. Crandall, Katkovsky, and Preston[29] have argued that different measures of achievement reflect different behavior potentials in a given child and that to conceive of a generalized potential might sometimes be in error. I recognize this, but these same authors also find results that suggest that generalized expectations about achievement can exist across domains. These generalized orientations to achievement are what I am trying to get at. The assumption used in this measure is that to the extent that the person has a strong autonomous achievement motive, he would generalize across domains of achievement. Hence, the measure of achievement motivation is equal to the sum of "challenging" choices across the four domains of skill.

Assessment of Social Achievement Motivation

1. *Normative level of aspiration.* In this measure a child is asked whether he would like to try a task that "most boys [or girls] your age can do," or a task that "some boys [girls] your age can do, and some boys [girls] cannot," or a task that "most boys [girls] your age cannot do." In

---

[29] V. J. Crandall, W. Katkovsky, and Anne Preston, "Motivational and Ability Determinants of Young Children's Intellectual Achievement Behaviors," *Child Development*, 33 (1962), 643–661.

this measure, the child does not know what the specific nature of the task is, nor does he know with any certainty how he himself might be expected to perform on this particular task. The tasks are located in $3'' \times 5'' \times 2''$ boxes for some administrations or in $5'' \times 7''$ envelopes for others. In either case the containers are very similar visually. What we measure is the child's preference for taking a task that is a moderate challenge in contrast to a high or a low challenge in general social comparison to others. Selecting the container where "some boys can do and some boys cannot" is coded as high social comparison motivation. In making his preference we assume that the child is using social comparison as the basis for his achievement interest. An obvious contaminating factor in this measure is the child's actual capacity in most achievement settings. A child who generally succeeds may have a different reference group for social comparison than one who does not generally succeed. The present measure may be especially useful for those of moderate ability. Using the "general other" as a basis of social comparison may be misleading in assessing achievement strivings for those who are either very high or very low in general ability.

2. *Embedded figures test.* This is a measure of field dependence in perception. The child's ability to see an embedded figure is taken to mean that his capacity to differentiate his own perceptions or his own body is highly developed. When such orientations are not strong, there may be difficulties in perceiving a figure embedded in its context. This is presumably because such a child attends too much to external cues so that he cannot sort out relevant information; he is field dependent. For the purposes of the present discussion, I would also like to assume that such a child is more likely to have a high social achievement motivation than not. Such an assumption is not a totally defensible one, since high scores on field dependence can also mean lack of capacity to follow instructions or sort out any information. Low scores on field dependence can mean either that a person has *mastered* the social orientation or has never confronted it. Here I am stretching the meaning of the measure, but some of our results using this measure turn out to be most interesting if interpreted in this way.

3. *Test and general anxiety.* Although scores derived from questionnaire measures of General Anxiety or Test Anxiety have been factor analyzed into a number of important components (e.g., in Chapter 5 Feld and Lewis report four factors in Test Anxiety), the measures still seem to be oriented toward admission to inadequacy of some sort or another. I suspect such inadequacy is very strongly felt in the social comparison setting. Taking tests usually involves social comparison; other anxiety situations also involve social comparison. Therefore, we will use anxiety measures as

an indirect indication of a child's social orientation to achievement motivation. Comparing this measure with the normative level of aspiration, one sees in this measure the obvious avoidant component of anxiety assessment. Perhaps the two measures *in combination* would give us a very powerful assessment of social achievement motivation.

Assessment of Integrated Achievement Motivation (Fantasy Achievement Motivation)

Although for some people one could use high scores on the Embedded Figures Test to indicate successful experiences with social comparison, it cannot be unambiguously interpreted in this way, especially for very young children. Is there another measure of integration of autonomous and social orientation to achievement? I propose that a fantasy-based measure might come close to it. What does a fantasy achievement motivation score mean? I assume that it represents an integrated orientation to achievement. In order to score high in fantasy measures of motivation, a child or an adult not only has to be somewhat sensitized to his own push for achievement (autonomous strivings), but also must be sensitive to the potential achievement orientation in characters in the story (social comparison). The apperceptive process is a difficult one to pin down. Taking the role of another's thoughts and feelings in a story requires a modicum of sensitivity about social comparison. To develop the thought sequence with regard to the achievement syndrome requires a modicum of autonomy concerns. This sort of primitive analogous reasoning leads me to conclude that the measure of fantasy achievement motivation seems to come close to tapping what I have called the integrated type. Obviously it will not be a measure of a mature achievement motivation. There would be many fallacies in that assumption. Fantasy can be defensive. Indeed, Raphelson[30] has noted that high fantasy scores due to achievement motivation do not necessarily counterindicate fear of failure. Therefore, most investigators have used another measure (test anxiety) along with a fantasy measure to get at the achievement motivation type that defines a positive achievement orientation (hope of success) and a negative achievement orientation (fear of failure). But I think Atkinson, Raphelson, and others, in dealing mostly with college populations, are assessing groups who, compared to the population at large, tend to have integrated achievement motivations. Of course, when fantasy achievement motivation scores are paired with test anxiety scores, greater precision in predicting more

[30] A. Raphelson, "The Relationships Among Imaginative, Direct Verbal and Physiological Measures of Anxiety in an Achievement Situation," *Journal of Abnormal and Social Psychology*, 54 (1957), 13–18.

specific behavioral sequences occur. A college population compared to other populations, should, by and large, reflect an integrated achievement orientation in its behavior. Atkinson and others are getting at refinements within this general type.

There is a wealth of information on fantasy measures of achievement motivation.[31] Because of this I was especially interested in using such a measure for young children. It was difficult to know where to begin. Kagan,[32] in summarizing the work done on projective assessment of personality with children, was very pessimistic about the usefulness of thematic devices. It is difficult to base any new technique on what has gone on previously. Systematic standardized work on children's fantasy gives few direct leads. Having an opportunity to try a short fantasy assessment on approximately 3,000 children, I arbitrarily put together two pictures we had used in other settings—a man in white shirt and tie at a desk and two men at a machine, for both girls and boys. These two pictures[33] were found useful in distinguishing men from different social backgrounds. Therefore, it seemed like a good thing to try them with children, if we were especially interested in their social backgrounds, as we were in this case. This is a set of pictures about adults. This may make it particularly good for assessing achievement motivation in children. Children who see adults in achievement settings, perhaps, have a well-developed future orientation. Since it is believed that a future orientation is necessary for well-developed achievement motivation,[34] then using a projective measure about adults may give us a reasonably valid measure of achievement motivation in children. Furthermore, stories about adults can be projective assimilations of their own perceptions of men at work or their conceptions of what fathers do at work. Both these assimilations may be important ingredients for those who have high achievement motivation.

We standardized the assessment procedure pretty much as outlined in previous work on a national survey.[35] We asked the children the following questions about each picture: (1) What is (are) the man (men) doing? (2) What is (are) the man (men) thinking? What does (do) he (they)

[31] Cf. J. W. Atkinson, *Motives in Fantasy, Action and Society* (Princeton: D. Van Nostrand Co., 1958); Atkinson and Feather, *op. cit.*
[32] J. Kagan, "Thematic Apperceptive Techniques with Children," in *Projective Techniques with Children* (New York and London: Grune and Stratton, 1960).
[33] J. Veroff, Sheila Feld, and H. Crockett, "Explorations into the Effects of Picture Cues on Thematic Apperceptive Expression of Achievement Motivation," *Journal of Personality and Social Psychology,* 3 (1966), 171–181.
[34] W. Mischel, "Delay of Gratification, Need for Achievement and Acquiescence in Another Culture," *Journal of Abnormal and Social Psychology,* 62 (1961), 1–17; Strodtbeck, "Family Interaction."
[35] J. Veroff *et al.*, "The Use of Thematic Apperception to Assess Motivation in a Nationwide Interview Study," *Psychological Monographs,* 74 (1960), 12, Whole No. 499.

TABLE 2 *Description of Achievement Imagery for Coding Young Children's Responses to Pictures*

A. Achievement Imagery

1. Explicit Standard of Excellence
   Concern by a character with making something right, correct, or perfect; or with not making something wrong or incorrect (if comments are by author—"it will turn out all right" or "he will do it right"—don't score here).
   Note: Positive or negative affect about accomplishment or failure, respectively, is to be taken as an indication of implicit standards of excellence and therefore will be coded under 1. (E.g., "He is trying his best to find the answer.")

2. Career Orientation
   Character becomes famous or is concerned about it; becoming an artist; setting up business (wanting money, however, should not be coded here). (E.g., "The man wants to be a writer.")

3. Making Something
   Writing stories, blueprints, paintings, drawings, buildings from plans unless making something is clearly seen as a daily job, part of routine; this category is coded when there is any emphasis on making a special creative product. (If character is only concerned about being "finished" or if there is no further elaboration or process beyond "making something" code in 5.) (E.g., "They are making a new machine—a rocket.")

B. Task Imagery

4. Executing Tasks
   Any emphasis on merely executing a task—character in the story is concerned with steps in the process of overcoming obstacles, working hard. If it is explicit concern about being finished, code in 5. If there is elaboration of thinking, doing, such as pointing out steps toward goals, code in 3. (E.g., "The men are working hard at their job; they want it to work.")

5. Doing Something
   Doing something, fixing something, working at something with no emphasis either on creativity or on the process of executing work; "working," "doing something," "writing" without ideas about the goal or goal attainment, code in 5. Explicit concerns with being finished or having an object being worked on should be coded here. (E.g., "They are trying to finish their job.")

C. Unrelated Imagery

6. Passive Activity
   Reading a story, code in 5; looking at something.

7. Affiliative Goals
   Reference to being with, needing and enjoying people.

8. Other Goals
   Specific or nonspecific or not coded elsewhere.

want? (3) What will happen? These questions were not probed, in order to guarantee standardization of responses. Interviewers attempted to write verbatim transcripts. Coding these stories was a problem. Although the intercoder reliability averaged in the .80s, arbitrary rules had to be devised in order to guarantee reliability. Often there were only fragments of fantasy, especially in the case of very young children's responses. Nevertheless, we viewed the coding procedures as being provocative enough to warrant discussion for future use. The categories appearing in Table 2 were adopted. The first three categories were equated with achievement imagery (2 points), the next two categories were equated with task imagery (1 point), and the last categories were equated with unrelated imagery (0 points). Subcategories were not scored. Thus, a child received

TABLE 3 *Intercorrelations of Various Measures of Achievement Orientations in Children (Boys and Girls Combined)*

Measure of Achievement Orientation	1. AAO r (N)	2. NLA r (N)	3. EFT r (N)	4. TA r (N)	5. GA r (N)
1. Autonomous Achievement Orientation					
2. Normative Level of Aspiration	.16* (2069)				
3. Embedded Figures Test	.04 (100)ᵃ	—ᵇ			
4. Test Anxiety	.04 (160)	—.01 (160)	—ᵇ		
5. General Anxiety	.02 (1340)	—.03 (1332)	—ᵇ	—ᵇ	
6. Fantasy Achievement Motivation	.02 (2085)	.07* (2076)	—ᵇ	—ᵇ	—.08* (1335)

* p < .05

ᵃ Males only
ᵇ Not available

a score of 2, 1, or 0 on each story and a total score on two pictures ranging from 0 to 4. We will be looking only at total scores across two pictures. The correlation between number of words used to tell the stories and the achievement motivation score was .11 ($N = 2085$, $p < .05$). It is significant but not high enough to warrant a major correction.

For general interest I present the intercorrelations of all of these measures of achievement motivations in Table 3. Controlling on the age and sex variable at times does make a difference. I will go into some of these differences in presenting results, but for now what is of general interest is the overall intercorrelation trends in these measures. Generally they are low, but they are at times significantly high as age and sex differences are explored.

Let us now turn to results that seem to support some of my speculative assertions about the development of achievement motivation. I will present results from different studies as a help in understanding a series of these assertions. The first half of the results section of this paper will present information about developmental assertions. I then have organized the results into a second section, where I consider the value of considering this typological analysis in understanding children's behavior, first with respect to sex differences and then with respect to reactions to success and failure. Therefore, the results will be presented in two major bodies, the first testing some assertions about developmental ideas of achievement motivation, and the second testing some assertions about the relationship of types to various aspects of children's achievement behavior.

Results About Developmental Assertions

ASSERTION 1: *Social comparison is not necessarily an aspect of achievement incentives for preschool children; it is only in the larger social setting of a grade school that social comparison is inevitably used in evaluating performance and hence in setting standards for the bases of achievement satisfaction.* In a study of nursery school children Callard,[36] while controlling for sex of child and social class background of the child, found very few children (male or female, high or low socioeconomic status) preferred to try a task that is even moderately difficult when *other children* are used as a standard of comparison. The sample in her study consisted of 80 four-year-old children and their mothers residing in or near a large urban area in southeastern Michigan. The sample was homogeneous in two respects: The mother in each case was the person who took the major responsibility for the care of the child; and each child was enrolled in nursery school at the time of the investigation. The 80 children were broken down into four subsamples: 20 middle-class boys, 20 working-class boys, 20 middle-class girls, 20 working-class girls. At the outset class distinctions were made according to how parents answered the classifications on the basis of area residence and of occupation. Middle-class included classes one, two, and three (according to Hollingshead's scheme), and working-class included classes four and five. Children were included in the middle-class group only if their mothers had at least one year of college; children were excluded from the working-class sample only if either parent attended college. It was a characteristic in the working-class group for mothers to receive social assistance. At the time of administration of measures of achievement motivation, each child was no less than 48 months old, not more than 60 months of age. The subjects were tested individually by female experimenters. Subjects were given the measure of autonomous achievement motivation (task repetition), a normative level of aspiration, and a measure of persistence. Subsequently, the subjects were also tested for IQ by the Columbia Mental Maturity scale and the Stanford-Binet.

The major result of this study relevant to this discussion is that, in the normative level of aspiration, only 6 per cent selected the challenging task; 81 per cent selected the easy task. This was true for both sexes and in the two social classes (cf. Table 4). It seems clear that children at nursery school age do not become "concerned" about normative evaluation of

---

[36] E. Callard, "Achievement Motive in the Four Year Old and Its Relationship to Achievement Expectancies of the Mother" (Unpublished doctoral dissertation, University of Michigan, 1964).

TABLE 4 *Nursery School Children's Distribution of Social Comparison Choices in the Normative Level of Aspiration (by Sex and Social Class)*[a]

| | N | Choice of box | | |
		Easy	Challenging	Hard
Middle-Class Girls	(20)	95%	5%	0%
Working-Class Girls	(20)	85%	5%	10%
Middle-Class Boys	(20)	85%	5%	10%
Working-Class Boys	(20)	80%	10%	10%
Total	(80)	86%	6%	8%

[a] After Callard, op. cit.

their performance. They prefer the "easy" choice; they avoid the "challenging" or "difficult" choice in task selection when other children's norms are used.

Some parallel results were available in a sample of nursery school children who were predominantly from middle-class backgrounds. Nursery school children in two separate studies were tested on a normative level of aspiration along with the measure of autonomous achievement motivation. In those studies, only 15 per cent out of 147 selected moderately difficult tasks, whereas 72 per cent selected the easiest task. These results suggest that social comparison as a quality of the achievement goal is not a critical aspect of the achievement strivings for 4-year-olds. In selecting his task preference in this measure, a child is confronted with choosing among three tasks that are unknown to him. In such a circumstance, choosing the easiest task perhaps is still of sufficient challenge to most 4-year-olds. Could it be that conquering the unknown is itself momentous enough to incite mastery strivings, and that the addition of a social comparison incentive may make it too threatening to most 4-year-olds?

Social comparison interests gradually become more positive in children as they get older. In Table 5, I present data from a large-scale sampling of school children's response to the normative level of aspiration tasks. It was part of what I will call the Normative Study. It was designed to test the effects of desegregation in a school system in a Midwestern town on the achievement orientations in youngsters. In working out this naturalistic experiment, we collected data on a large population of boys and girls in kindergarten through 5th grade and then retested them and other children a year later. The critical group in this study is a desegregated group—a group of Negro youngsters who had attended a predominantly Negro elementary school and who were now being bused to predominantly

TABLE 5 *Percentage of Pupils at Various Ages Selecting "Easy," "Challenging," and "Hard" Unknown Tasks in Normative Level of Aspiration (by Sex and Type of Presentation of Task)*

| | | Type of Task | | | | | | | |
| | | Box | | | | Envelope | | | |
Grade	Sex	N	Easy	Challenging	Hard	N	Easy	Challenging	Hard
K	Boys	113	77%*	11%	12%				
	Girls	128	89%	4%	7%				
1	Boys	120	60%	23%	17%	163	71%	16%	13%
	Girls	108	69%	23%	7%	175	83%	7%	10%
2	Boys	104	43%	31%	26%	131	41%	31%	28%
	Girls	111	59%	24%	17%	134	51%	36%	13%
3	Boys	94	22%	39%	38%	165	23%	48%	29%
	Girls	98	38%	36%	27%	157	34%	47%	19%
4	Boys	108	16%	50%	34%	116	16%	50%	34%
	Girls	92	23%	59%	18%	122	25%	54%	20%
5	Boys	91	14%	45%	41%	90	17%	51%	32%
	Girls	91	27%	48%	24%	109	17%	59%	24%
6	Boys					129	10%	53%	37%
	Girls					134	15%	54%	31%

* Percentages have been rounded here and in Table 6.

white receiver schools. In our study we included measures of autonomous motivation, normative level of aspiration, general anxiety[37] (the latter only for the 2nd grade and above), and the fantasy measure of achievement motivation. Aside from the anxiety measure, the tests were administered individually by female graduate students or mature women from the community. All the testing was done in one session. The anxiety scale was administered to homeroom classes of children by male and female administrators.

A striking age trend can be noted in Table 5. Analyses of variance yield highly significant F ratios due to age (for example, for the envelope choice $F_{(age)} = 73.32$; $df = 5/2061$; $p < .001$), and sex (for the envelope choice $F_{(sex)} = 33.32$; $df = 5/2061$; $p < .001$). Boys more than girls consistently select the more difficult choice. Boys and girls emerge with similar scores on social achievement motivation because approximately the same percentage of boys and girls select the moderate choice. However, more boys select the most difficult choice and more girls select the easiest. But it is the age result that concerns us. Similar to our findings in nursery school studies, we find a preponderant choice of the easy alternative in kindergarten and 1st grade. However, only 10–20 per cent of the 5th and 6th graders select the easy choice in the normative level of aspiration. One might say that the older children have learned that the easy choice is socially disapproved, but I would further argue that as children get older they become more receptive to social comparison. Taking the easy route in a choice of alternatives does not give them any new information in their concerns about social comparison. And as children grow older, they seek out new information about their standing vis-à-vis others.

It is also apparent that the frequency of choices of the most difficult alternative increases with age. Again, one may argue that social approval for taking the most difficult task is more apparent for older children, but two other possibilities also exist. First, taking the most difficult choice could be a defensive reaction to lack of adequate social comparison in grade school experience. Or taking the most difficult choice can be an indication of high achievement motivation among those who in fact do successfully master social comparison. It is for this reason that we looked at the same data for three groups of children: low IQ (defined by their standing on the Lorge Thorndike IQ Test), moderate IQ, and high IQ, this time lumping boys and girls together. We looked for the same age

---

[37] Thirty-Item General Anxiety Scale, in S. B. Sarason *et al.*, *Anxiety in Elementary School Children: A Report of Research* (New York: John Wiley & Sons, 1960).

TABLE 6 *Percentage of Pupils at Various Ages Selecting "Easy," "Challenging," and "Hard" Unknown Tasks in Normative Level of Aspiration (by IQ and Type of Presentation of Task)*

				Box			Envelope		
Grade	IQ	N	Easy	Chal-lenging	Hard	N	Easy	Chal-lenging	Hard
K	Low	56	88%	5%	7%				
	Moderate	65	89%	5%	6%				
	High	35	80%	9%	11%				
1	Low	55	71%	18%	11%	114	82%	7%	11%
	Moderate	34	56%	32%	12%	138	73%	15%	12%
	High	37	59%	22%	19%	85	78%	13%	9%
2	Low	66	56%	29%	15%	100	61%	27%	12%
	Moderate	56	48%	29%	23%	86	45%	28%	27%
	High	33	48%	24%	27%	78	28%	46%	26%
3	Low	43	30%	12%	58%	118	40%	38%	22%
	Moderate	42	38%	36%	26%	108	24%	49%	27%
	High	50	26%	48%	25%	93	18%	58%	24%
4	Low	43	23%	35%	42%	74	28%	35%	36%
	Moderate	41	30%	49%	21%	84	19%	58%	23%
	High	31	0%	65%	35%	78	15%	60%	24%
5	Low	46	22%	43%	35%	52	29%	41%	25%
	Moderate	48	21%	50%	29%	63	19%	59%	22%
	High	65	22%	48%	31%	80	7%	59%	34%
6	Low					65	18%	55%	26%
	Moderate					92	13%	59%	28%
	High					104	9%	48%	43%

trends we saw in Table 5, but now controlling for IQ. These results are in Table 6.

What is clear from Table 6 is that the interest in challenge or moderate difficulty does show some increments in the middle elementary school years for children at all IQ levels. Significant F tests emerged for the age variation using IQ as a covariate in an analysis of variance ($F_{(age)} = 140.00$, $df = 2/1933$, $p < .001$). The peak of this interest is in the 4th grade for the high IQ group (when children are 9 or 10 years of age) but it comes later for the lower IQ groups. Some dramatic shifts in interests in social comparison occur at all IQ levels in the 1st, 2nd, or 3rd grades, when children are 7, 8, and 9 years old. The ages 6 to 9 have been cited by McClelland,[38] by Kagan and Moss,[39] and by Veroff[40] as perhaps being particularly critical in the evolution of achievement motivation and behavior. Our results suggest that this age may be a particularly ripe time for social

---

[38] *Op. cit.*
[39] J. Kagan and H. A. Moss, *Birth to Maturity* (New York: John Wiley & Sons, 1962).
[40] "Studying Human Motivational Disposition."

comparison. It is a time when placing oneself in comparison to peers may generate automatically. It is perhaps a time when parental concern about a child's performance vis-à-vis other children can be particularly effective in inducing either an interest in achievement competition or a strong sense of failure. In previous studies of the childrearing antecedents of achievement motivation, many of the items used to assess maternal orientation to achievement training are of the social comparison variety, in that they asked the mother to state at what age she expects a child to perform a certain behavior—do well in school, come out on top in sports and games. In fact, the latter two items were the most effective in the Veroff study.[41]

With continued social comparison, there may be some adaptation to particular social groups, rather than groups of children at large. Bright children compare themselves to other bright children. It should be noted that many more of the high IQ children were selecting "hard" choices than the other groups combined at Grade 6 ($\chi^2 = 7.98$, 1 df, $p < .01$). "Hard" may be a misnomer for this group; they may be selecting the most realistic challenges. At any rate, for all IQ groups, there should be a slackening in the child's anxiety about social comparison as he finds a relevant group, a group in which his ability will not be overtaxed. Using Atkinson's formulations about anxiety, one would guess that a generally anxious child might find a group in which he was not even moderately challenged. This could be a very unskilled group or a very skilled group. For the unanxious child, it might mean seeking a challenging reference group. A piece of evidence for this assertion comes from the fact that the General Anxiety scores shift downward at around Grades 5 and 6, a time when there may be this reorientation to more specific reference groups.[42] Table 7 presents General Anxiety scores at different grades. It can be seen that the effect of diminution of general anxiety is especially dramatic in girls. It is as if after a period of intense social comparison there may be a rebirth of autonomous striving for achievement. However, if there is no easily obtained reference group for a child, or if it is not easy to live up to the achievement standards of the reference group, the child could remain anxious. But, past Grades 3 or 4, I suspect the incapacitating anxiety about social experiences should diminish for most children. They seem to begin to settle into an appropriate reference group, they begin to become aware of their general standing on given abilities within that group, and, if allowed,

---

[41] *Ibid.*
[42] This downward shift in anxiety between 4th and 5th grade has been confirmed in studies of Test Anxiety in Connecticut schools by Hill and Sarason, *op. cit.*, in their sample of boys but not their sample of girls.

TABLE 7   *Mean General Anxiety Score at Different Grades (by Sex)*

Sex	Grade	Mean General Anxiety	SD	N
Boys	3	7.47	6.03	192
	4	7.37	6.34	160
	5	7.05[a]	5.93	126
	6	6.29[a]	6.27	177
Girls	3	14.31	9.48	205
	4	14.25	7.85	172
	5	11.00[a]	6.82	131
	6	10.24[a]	8.10	184

[a] Mean is significantly lower than mean at Grade 3 or at Grade 4 by *t* test comparisons (at least at the .05 level).

should begin to let their more autonomous achievement interest blossom once again.

ASSERTION 2: *Autonomous achievement motivation begins early, becomes less critical in school years devoted to social comparison and more critical in later school years, when the child tries to integrate both social and autonomous achievement motivations.* Using the same nursery school children Callard and I separately investigated, we find some significant and interesting results relating measures of maternal expectations about achievement to variations in autonomous achievement motivation. Mothers of middle-class nursery-school-age girls with high measured autonomous achievement motivation report earlier ages of achievement training than do a comparable set of mothers whose daughters have low autonomous achievement motivation. This finding replicates previous research attempting to relate maternal reactions to achievement motivation in children. The results for the other groups are not all readily understandable, and we will discuss them in detail in another context. But the fact that 4-year-old's scores on the measure do relate to significant aspects of maternal reactions suggests that we have tapped a very important feature of the 4-year-old's emotional life.

In the Normative Study there is an apparent peak in the development of autonomous achievement interests in 2nd to 4th grades (cf. Table 8) with some decline in the later grades of elementary school, perhaps attesting to the negative impact that unsuccessful social comparison might have on autonomy strivings. (Analysis of variance yields significant $F_{(age)}$ at 3.93, $df = 5/2061$,[43] and $p < .01$). My guess is that one would find that increases in this measure of autonomy would occur again at adolescence

---

[43] Based only on the administration given in 1966, which had the largest sample; parallel results were obtained with the 1965 scores.

TABLE 8   *Mean Autonomous Achievement Motivation Score at Various Grade Levels (by Sex)*

	Boys			**Girls**		
Grade	Mean Autonomous Achievement Motivation	SD	N	Mean Autonomous Achievement Motivation	SD	N
K	2.30	1.21	115	2.06	1.22	130
1	2.73	1.11	288	2.79	1.13	286
2	2.70	1.08	237	2.89	1.15	246
3	2.81	1.14	261	2.94	1.12	260
4	2.59	1.21	226	3.00	1.10	218
5	2.36	1.28	184	2.82	1.15	201
6	2.49	1.31	178	2.67	1.05	134

when the issues of autonomy become paramount again. I should note here that boys start out higher than girls on this measure of autonomous achievement motivation, but are consistently lower at the older ages (Analysis of variance yields significant results: $F_{(sex)} = 7.36$, $df = 1/2061$, $p < .001$). At Grade 6, boys seem to be on the rise again. My only suggestion about the meaning of these results is that boys may relinquish a rather well-developed autonomy orientation in order to adapt successfully to the stress of social comparison. At kindergarten boys are higher in autonomy motivation than girls, but not so in the later grades. I would contend that boys more than girls adapt successfully to social comparison. We see that boys more than girls do select the most difficult choices, as if they were seeking out the limits of their appropriate group for social comparison. Once reached, an appropriate reference group can help the child integrate autonomy and social comparison orientations. Boys *appear to have lower autonomous achievement motivation* during grade school because they are struggling more directly with the problem of social comparison.

ASSERTION 3: *Integration of appropriate autonomous and social achievement orientations occurs gradually after a child has learned some success at social comparison.* Looking at Table 9, we see that fantasy achievement motivation scores for boys and girls at various stages in the Normative Study show progressive increase with age, unlike the autonomous or social comparison achievement motivation measures. (Analyses of variance show that $F_{(age)} = 18.55$, $df = 5/2061$, $p < .001$.) We might tentatively conclude that integrated achievement motivation develops slowly over the elementary school years. Should we draw this conclusion with some caution? We know that story length and fantasy achievement moti-

75

TABLE 9 *Mean Fantasy Achievement Motivation Scores at Various Age Levels (by Sex)*

| | Boys | | | Girls | | |
Grade	Mean Fantasy Achievement Motivation Score	SD	N	Mean Fantasy Achievement Motivation Score	SD	N
1	1.89	1.02	187	1.78	.99	193
2	2.02	1.16	173	1.87	1.06	169
3	2.29	1.21	198	2.09	1.09	204
4	2.34	1.17	161	2.13	1.21	171
5	2.56	1.17	128	2.23	1.20	130
6	2.65	1.12	178	2.41	1.20	184

vation scores are correlated significantly even if at a low level. We also know that story lengths increase with age (in itself a potential reflection of increased integrated achievement orientation in older children). However, analyses of covariance on the fantasy scores yielded highly significant age effects, with story length as a covariate. Thus, the findings do not seem to be dependent on story length.

Does the fantasy measure truly reflect integration of achievement orientations? Slight corroboration of this set of assumptions comes from Table 10 where the fantasy achievement motivation scores are correlated with autonomous and social motivations in boys and girls at various ages. We find that in the youngest age group (1st grade) those high in fantasy achievement motivation are those most oriented to autonomous achievement motivation. Furthermore, the boys in the 1st grade who are high in fantasy achievement motivation are low in social comparison orientation. Thus, fantasy achievement motivation in the youngest group does seem to reflect the motivation appropriate to the age—autonomy. We have viewed the fantasy measure as a reflection of integration of autonomous and social comparison achievement motivation. At this young age little such integration can take place. And so the fantasy measure picks up what is most integrative for that age—autonomous achievement motivation. In the 3rd and 4th grade boys, there is some indication that high fantasy achievement motivation reflects the motivation appropriate to and integrative for that age—social comparison. There is a significant correlation between fantasy achievement motivation and choosing challenging tasks in normative level of aspiration, but only for boys. The results do not hold for girls. Finally, in Grades 5 and 6 the boys again show some slight provocative trends with their fantasy achievement motivation at that age

TABLE 10   *Relationship (Gamma) of Fantasy Achievement Motivation to Autonomous Achievement Motivation and to Normative Level of Aspiration (by Grade, Sex)*

Grade	Autonomous Achievement Motivation				Selection of "Challenge" in Normative Level of Aspiration			
	Boys		Girls		Boys		Girls	
	gamma	(N)	gamma	(N)	gamma	(N)	gamma	(N)
1	.13*	188	.17**	192	—.19**	186	.05	192
2	.02	173	.10	171	.04	123	.13	171
3–4	—.02	363	—.01	327	.16**	361	.07	375
5–6	.10	303	.02	318	.11	301	—.06	318

* $p < .10$
** $p < .05$

associated with both high autonomous and high social comparison motivations. At this later age, then, we have our first indications that the fantasy measure reflects an integration of both autonomy and social comparison as we originally suggested.

Results: Sex Differences and Achievement Types

We have examined some of the results that lend some substantiation to a few of the assertions I have made about the developmental sequence in achievement motivation. Now let us turn to some of the results in some of our studies that may help us see how such an analysis of different types of achievement orientations might help explain differences in children's behavior. Again, let us view the results as vehicles for backing up certain assertions. First, some assertions about sex differences in achievement motivation.

ASSERTION 4:   *In our society, boys are generally able to master autonomy striving more easily than are girls.* To back up this statement, let me first tell you about results of the study done by Lahtinen[44] under my direction. By using a puppet in a gamelike atmosphere, Lahtinen aroused kindergarten boys and girls to be concerned either about mastery of performance or about being rejected for bad performance. She presented a series of tasks for children to do. In mastery arousal, the puppet indicated it wanted the child to be concerned only about how well he did. In rejection arousal, the puppet oriented the child to perform in order to be

---

[44] Pirkko Lahtinen, "The Effect of Failure and Rejection on Dependency" (Unpublished doctoral dissertation, University of Michigan, 1964).

liked by the puppet. After one or the other arousal procedure, children were given measures of persistence, both in fantasy and in behavior. The fantasy measure entailed selection of story endings of doing something alone in a situation where a child can persist at an activity or turn to others for support. In the behavioral measure the child was asked to untie difficult knots and lift heavy weights. These are both motor tasks, and so may be more figural for their demands for competence in boys than in girls. Nevertheless, these motoric skills are relevant to the mastery of both sexes. Persistence was measured by the amount of time the child continued to try the task without asking for help. In the behavioral and the fantasy measures the boys reacted with endings reflecting persistence rather than dependency to both the pressures for mastery and social approval, while the girls reacted with these endings only to the social approval condition. It is as if at a very early age girls respond only to social rejection cues in the mastery domain, while boys can respond to simple mastery pushes as well as to social approval concerns. In these early years, it is apparent that autonomous achievement orientations are more easily found in boys' life experience than in girls'.

With this viewpoint it is indeed curious to find in Table 8 that except for the kindergarten year, girls are higher than boys on autonomous achievement motivation. To make this result consistent with my proposed difference between boys and girls and with other results, I would have to reiterate what I said earlier about these results: Boys master autonomy early, go on to engage in social comparison during grade school, *perhaps temporarily lower their autonomous achievement strivings,* and eventually work out an integration of the two. Girls start out with lower autonomous achievement motivation but are socially responsive to school pressures to be autonomous. Our best guess is, however, that girls rarely successfully integrate autonomous and social comparison motivation because their underpinnings for autonomy are weaker. I would predict that in junior high school or high school boys would be higher in autonomous achievement motivation as proposed in this report.

In Table 9 we can also see that girls have *lower* fantasy achievement motivation scores than boys. (Analyses of variance yielded a significant $F_{(sex)} = 15.52$, $df = 1/2061$, $p < .001$.) We must remember that the scores were based on stories written about males. Nevertheless, it is very provocative to think that this may be a general result for this age group. Do boys have higher achievement motivation fantasy scores at this age because they can more easily integrate autonomy strivings with social demands for achievement? We have no direct evidence of this, but interesting differences do appear when fantasy scores for boys and girls are examined according to different achievement orientations. The consistent differences between boys and girls at Grades 5 and 6 occur for those who are *low* in social achievement motivation. Those 157 boys who are low in social motivation have consistently higher scores in fantasy achievement motivation ($M = 2.75$) than the 136 girls who are low in social motivation ($M = 2.23$). This difference is significant at the .01 level ($t = 3.98$). It is important to note that it is the boys who are high in autonomy but low in social motivation who have the highest mean fantasy score (2.91). Perhaps boys at this age can master their autonomy strivings and integrate them without any person around to compare their standings with, while girls may ultimately be dependent on social comparison to facilitate their achievement behaviors. It is as if girls need the social orientation to translate their achievement interests into active tendencies, at least those tendencies that underlie fantasy behavior.

Let me take a sidetrack at this juncture. The foregoing analysis suggests an important methodological implication about sex differences in the fantasy measure of achievement motivation. Can it be that the fantasy measure of achievement motivation might reflect an orientation to social comparison among females and an orientation to autonomy in males? Over the years of research on the fantasy measure of achievement motivation, we have emerged with puzzling inconsistencies when we compare male and female scores. Perhaps this is one of the keys to the problem. I would contend that a reanalysis of fantasy scores of adults in terms of autonomy and social comparison may cast some light on the perplexing effects that different arousal conditions have on these scores. Such reanalysis might also help us understand why the relationships between fantasy achievement motivation scores and other achievement behaviors are different for the two sexes.

To return to our main theme, let us look at further evidence for our assertion that boys master autonomy striving more easily than do girls. Some evidence comes from a study of the measure of autonomous achievement motivation. In that study we found that boys and girls in nursery school or in 2nd grade, when especially aroused to think about doing well before performing the task, differed considerably from a group of boys and girls who were not aroused to think about achievement. The results are reported in Table 11. We find a large interaction effect, with 2nd grade boys tending to respond to achievement arousal with *increased* autonomous achievement motivation, while girls respond to this arousal with decreased autonomous achievement motivation. (The latter result is significant at the .05 level.) In the 2nd grade we thus have evidence for the sex difference we have asserted—with girls responding with anxiety to

TABLE 11 *Analysis of Variance of Autonomous Achievement Motivation Scores (by Age, Sex, and Arousal Condition)*

		Boys			Girls		
	Condition	Mean	SD	N	Mean	SD	N
Nursery School							
	Nonaroused	1.81	1.07	42	1.44	1.10	36
	Aroused	1.50	1.00	40	1.75	1.12	28
2nd Grade							
	Nonaroused	2.91	1.14	45	3.27	.70	49
	Aroused	3.04	1.08	51	2.73	1.02	44

Analysis of Variance	SS	df	MS	F
Age	37.57	1	37.57	28.68*
Sex	.01	1	.01	
Condition	.20	1	.20	
Age × Sex	.08	1	.08	
Age × Condition	.46	1	.46	
Sex × Condition	.11	1	.11	
Age × Sex × Condition	28.65	1	28.65	21.87*
Error	428.46	327	1.31	

* $p < .001$

pushes for achievement, while boys tend to respond with further increased autonomous achievement motivation.

But what about the younger group—at nursery school age? We found the opposite pattern. We found boys generally scoring lower on the measure of autonomous achievement motivation with increased concern about achievement, while girls' scores increased on the measure. Boys in nursery school react badly to social pressure for achievement; girls react well. These results are understandable if we assume that boys and girls at nursery school age are reacting to their autonomous achievement tendencies in different ways. As was suggested in the theoretical speculations outlined earlier, girls more than boys may be more ambivalent about their autonomy. Even at this early age they may react with autonomous achievement strivings only when the social world explicitly demands it of them. Such an interpretation is also appropriate to some further data coming from the Callard study. Let us examine these data in some detail.

Callard correlated mothers' expectations for independence and achievement in nursery school children with their children's scores on the autonomous achievement motivation measure. She used the Parental Developmental Timetable designed by Torgoff[45] and based on Winterbottom's

[45] I. Torgoff, "Parental Developmental Timetable: Parental Field Effects on Children's Compliance" (Paper read at the meeting of the Society for Research in Child Development, Pennsylvania State University, 1961).

TABLE 12 *Relationship (Taus) Between Autonomous Achievement Motivation Scores of Nursery School Children to Maternal Expectation for Achievement and Independence*[a]

Mothers of	N	Achievement Expectations	Independence Expectations
Middle-Class Girls	(20)	—.37[b]**	+.21
Working-Class Girls	(20)	+.03	+.14
Middle-Class Boys	(20)	+.25*	.00
Working-Class Boys	(20)	—.18	—.10

* $p < .05$
** $p < .01$

[a] After Callard, op. cit.
[b] The higher the tau, the stronger the relationship between age of expectation and strength of achievement motivation. A negative tau means that the younger the age of expected achievement, the higher the achievement motivation.

technique.[46] It asked a parent to think of the appropriate age to expect, or begin to expect, certain behaviors in the average child. The parent is asked not to think of his own child necessarily. In this timetable Torgoff[47] distinguishes between achievement-inducing attitudes, in which the parent explicitly trains for achievement or doing well (e.g., begin to teach their child that he will have to work hard if he is to reach his goals in life) and independence-granting attitudes, in which the parent allows the child to behave independently of the parent (e.g., begin to allow the child to use sharp scissors without adult supervision). In both scales, the assumption is that the earlier the mean age set, the stronger the parental attitude in this domain. When these two scores were related to the measure of autonomous achievement motivation, there were differences depending on the sex and social status of the child (cf. Table 12).

Let us consider the middle-class group first—the one similar to the Veroff nursery school study. The findings confirmed Winterbottom's results only in the case of middle-class girls. For these girls the earlier the achievement expectations, the higher the autonomous achievement motivation scores. It was negative in middle-class boys. The earlier the achievement demands for middle-class nursery school boys, the lower the autonomous achievement motivation. So again, at least in the middle-class sample, we have some evidence that girls at nursery school age react with stronger achievement striving to a positive achievement demand from the social world—the demand in this case residing in the mother's setting an earlier

[46] Marian Winterbottom, "The Relation of Need for Achievement to Learning Experiences in Independence and Mastery," in J. W. Atkinson (ed.), *Motives in Fantasy, Action, and Society* (Princeton: D. Van Nostrand, 1958), 453–378.
[47] *Op. cit.*

age for achievement. The result suggests that these girls at nursery school age are oriented to *others* as a means of establishing their achievement interests, while the boys, in fact, react negatively to such outside demands.

These exact results were not confirmed in the working-class sample. However, Callard did find that nursery-school-age girls from working-class background do have higher autonomous achievement motivation scores if their mothers set *moderate* achievement or independence ages. These results were also obtained by De Pree[48] on a middle-class sample of 2nd grade girls. Comparing extreme and moderate levels of maternal expectations for these girls, Callard found Mann Whitney U equals 21.5 ($p < .05$) in the case of achievement expectations and Mann Whitney U equals 15 ($p < .01$) in the case of independence expectations. These results do not pertain to the boys from the working class. So again we see that girls, and not boys, at nursery school age are responsive to an external demand. Callard does not have a clear explanation for the class differences. There are no mean or variance differences in scores that would provide clues. For our purposes, however, all that is important is the fact that at very young ages girls more than boys seem to turn to *social pressures* for achievement. Boys seem to react negatively to such pressures. I would argue that girls at this early age come to rely on the social world for setting the conditions for achievement because they continually feel uncomfortable with autonomy. At this age mothers are generally more tolerant of autonomy strivings in boys who, consequently, may be able to master such strivings more easily. The mastery of autonomy strivings may make the very young boy less susceptible and even resistant to social demands for achievement. Such a conclusion is not out of keeping with other observations about sex differences in childrearing. In particular it fits well with Barry, Bacon, and Child's cross-cultural observations[49] that in childrearing there seems to be more autonomy training for boys and more responsibility training for girls. Furthermore, Baumrind and Black[50] have recently shown that mothers of nursery school girls have higher expectations for their daughters' maturity and are more controlling of them than are mothers of boys. Baumrind and Black also find that there are significant correlations between maturity demands and independence and assertiveness for boys but not for girls. These results may indirectly suggest that mothers pace

---

[48] Suzanne De Pree, "The Influence of Parental Achievement Expectations and Role Definitions on Achievement Motive Development in Girls" (Unpublished honors thesis, University of Michigan, 1962).

[49] H. Barry, Margaret K. Bacon, and I. L. Child, "A Cross-Cultural Survey of Some Sex Differences in Socialization," *Journal of Abnormal and Social Psychology*, 55 (1957), 327–332.

[50] Diana Baumrind and A. E. Black, "Socialization Practices Associated with Dimensions of Competence in Preschool Boys and Girls," *Child Development*, 38 (1967), 291–328.

the autonomy of boys appropriately, but often inappropriately pace the autonomy of girls.

Given an initial headstart in solving the task of mastering autonomy strivings, boys can come to the task of social comparison with more ease and with less potential disruption than girls. If ever the task of social comparison becomes problematic, boys can more easily fall back on their firm autonomy orientations. Girls have no strong base of autonomy to retreat to. They often turn to social comparison defensively.

One important social implication of these suggested sex differences in achievement development is that there may be a greater potential in educational settings to enhance the autonomous achievement orientations of boys and to disrupt the social comparison orientations of girls. Girls from working-class backgrounds in particular have such overriding responsibilities at home either as mother's assistant or as mother surrogate that the autonomy orientation may have little chance to blossom. Furthermore, girls from both working-class and middle-class backgrounds, in turning to social comparison defensively, often do not like to stand out in a group. Thus, whenever a girl lacks a comfortable reference group, a peership in which she is not too deviant, she can become quite anxious and unable to master social comparison strivings as well.

It is with such a notion in mind that some recent results on the effects of desegregation on the achievement motivations of male and female Negro children seem to make sense. In the Normative Study we had two major samples of lower-status Negro children—one from a predominantly Negro school, who were transferred by busing arrangements to a predominantly white receiver school, and one from a school of about 50 per cent Negro who remained in that school setting. Let us call the first group the Transferred Group and the second the Non-Transferred Group. Assuming that the lower social class standing in family background and achievement orientations of the children from these two samples are relatively comparable (and all the evidence thus far accumulated seems to suggest that), one can look at the effect of desegregation as a little naturalistic experimental study in the shifts of reference groups for social comparison. For the Negro children who were one or two or three in a class of white children in the Transferred Group, the standard of excellence for achievement shifts from the Negro norm to the white norm. This is not necessarily so for the Negro children in the Non-Transferred Group, where the population was 47 per cent Negro. Since the white children generally perform better on the average, one might say that this study represents a partial answer to the question of what happens to children's achievement orientation when a shift to a very high standard of excellence in social comparison occurs. From my speculations about different male and female development of achievement orientation, my hypothesis is three-pronged, slightly different for three ages. In the youngest group males should react more favorably to desegregation. Boys should have a relatively strong autonomous orientation to achievement to begin with, an orientation that can anchor the child in any unfavorable social comparison. Thus, the generally strong achievement orientation of the white school setting could facilitate the development of achievement motivation of these Negro boys. Girls may not have this anchor of autonomy, being more oriented to the social world. The desegregation thus should bring about more confusing reference group problems for young Negro girls than for young Negro boys. If Negro girls have not resolved autonomy issues as well as Negro boys, then they should be more overwhelmed by new and not too clear norms presented from the outside on which they are so dependent. I would predict, however, that in the middle grades of elementary school, when social comparison motivation is so strong for both sexes, Negro boys as well as Negro girls would react poorly to desegregation. The older boys in 5th and 6th grade again might react better than the girls, since boys might have begun to establish an integration of autonomous and social motivations, while girls would likely be finding such an integration more difficult.

These ideas tend to be confirmed in Table 13, where we compared the percentage of Negro children in a transferred as opposed to a non-transferred school setting (controlling for grade level and sex) who scored high on measures of achievement motivation for the grade level being examined. In one case high achievement motivation is defined either by being above the median on the autonomous *or* the social comparison measures. In another case high achievement motivation is defined by being above the median fantasy achievement motivation score. In both cases the median was calculated for the distribution of subjects combining race, sex, and transferral status within each age level, because we were interested in absolute differences within each of these categories. For boys in all but one of the comparisons there is evidence of a positive effect of desegregation on achievement motivation at all grade levels, but the difference is significant only for the older groups. For girls in all but one of the comparisons there is evidence of negative effect of desegregation, but the effect is significant only in the older children. The results can be taken as tentative corroboration of the idea that the positive effect of desegregation presupposes a sufficient autonomy orientation in children. Following these findings, Negro boys, especially during periods of their development

TABLE 13   *High Achievement Motivation Among Negro School Children in Study of Desegregation: Transferred and Non-Transferred School Setting Compared (by Sex and Grade)*

	Boys				Girls			
Grade	% High Achievement Orientation (Autonomous or Social)[a]	(N)	% High Fantasy Achievement Motivation[a]	(N)	% High Achievement Orientation (Autonomous or Social)[a]	(N)	% High Fantasy Achievement Motivation[a]	(N)
1–2								
Transferred	47%	(17)	13%	(16)	35%	(23)	0%	(22)
Non-transferred	25%	(20)	19%	(21)	47%	(27)	8%	(24)
3–4								
Transferred	36%	(14)	61%	(13)	30%	(23)	43%	(23)
Non-transferred	33%	(18)	38%	(19)	55%	(31)	42%	(31)
5–6								
Transferred	65%**	(17)	63%	(16)	30%*	(10)	40%	(10)
Non-transferred	27%**	(26)	42%	(26)	69%*	(23)	61%	(23)

N = Total in each group (includes both high and low motivation subjects)
* p < .05 (Exact Test)
** % high vs. % low comparisons for transferred vs. non-transferred groups significant at p < .01 (Exact test)

[a] Percentage of a group (at a given age in either a transferred or non-transferred setting) scoring above the median achievement motivation, calculated from the distribution of subjects combined across sex, race or segregation status within a given age level.

when social comparison is not paramount, can be thought to have a better chance of immediate survival in a desegregated setting than Negro girls. The desegregation situation, at least initially, does not seem to foster the development of girls' achievement motivation, perhaps because the original Negro school setting did push primarily for a social approval orientation; or perhaps because the new situation is too confusing for them socially. The non-transferred school setting seems to permit a girl's achievement motivation to increase, perhaps because she is comfortable in that social setting and, hence, responsive to any achievement demands in it.

ASSERTION 5: *When boys do not master autonomy, they are likely to develop impulsive achievement motivation, but when girls do not master autonomy, they are likely to develop a cautious "fear of success" or "fear of failure" motivation.* To present evidence for this assertion, we compared the relationship that the measure of autonomous achievement motivation had with cautious kinds of behavior—selecting the "easiest" choice in the measure of autonomous achievement motivation, or with impulsive kinds of behavior—selecting the "hardest" choice. These correlations are pre-

TABLE 14 Relationship Between Autonomous Achievement Motivation Scores and Tendencies to Select "Very Easy" and "Hardest" Choices (by Sex)

| | Correlation with Number "Easiest" | | | | Correlation with Number "Hardest" | | | |
| | Testing Time 1 | | Testing Time 2 | | Testing Time 1 | | Testing Time 2 | |
	r	(N)	r	(N)	r	(N)	r	(N)
Boys	—.43	(638)	—.28	(1038)	—.68	(678)	—.82	(1038)
Girls	—.64	(676)	—.41	(1066)	—.55	(636)	—.78	(1066)
	Diff. = .21		Diff. = .13		Diff. = .13		Diff. = .04	
	p < .001		p < .01		p < .01		n.s.	

TABLE 15 Percentage of Students High and Low in Autonomous Achievement Motivation Selecting the "Hard" Choice in the Normative Level of Aspiration (by Sex)

Sex	Level of Autonomous Achievement Motivation	N	% Selecting "Hard" Choice
Boys	High	658	22%
	Low	388	48%
Girls	High	681	17%
	Low	368	32%

sented in Table 14.[51] The question we hope these correlations can help answer is: Do males who have low scores on autonomous achievement motivation get low scores because they are more likely to select high risks or low risks? And if so, how do these behaviors compare with the girls? Table 14 suggests that boys with low scores in autonomous achievement motivation tend not to select the easier alternative as often as the girls with low scores in autonomous achievement motivation. Furthermore, the boys' low scores correlate with number of hardest chosen more strongly than they do with number of easiest chosen.

Another and perhaps more direct way of pointing to the same result is to compare the normative risk-taking behavior of boys and girls who are high and low in autonomous achievement motivation. This is done in Table 15. All boys and girls regardless of race were divided into "high" and "low" autonomous achievement orientation groups, and the responses of each sex to the normative level of aspiration were ascertained. It was quite

---

[51] Since we had two different samplings of these behaviors in the Normative Study (prior to desegregation and after desegregation), we can look for replications of any effects found.

TABLE 16   *Percentage of Negro and White Children Choosing at Least One "Most Difficult" Choice in the Measure of Autonomous Achievement Motivation (by Sex and Age)*

| | Choosing at Least One "Most Difficult" Choice | | | |
| | Boys | | Girls | |
	%	N	%	N
Negro	66%	143	44%	167
White	52%	883	49%	886

χ^2 comparing Negro boys with white boys $= 4.82$
$p < .05$, 1 df.

clear that the boys who were low in autonomous achievement motivation not only selected high risks in autonomous achievement standards but also were taking more "overaspiring" risks in the social comparison measure. Particularly important to note is that they were taking more "overaspiring" risks than the girls who were low in autonomous achievement orientation ($\chi^2 = 14.55$, $p < .001$). This latter comparison is most relevant to our present discussion. This result is obtained for each race. Boys are generally more overaspiring than girls in both autonomous and social comparison orientations. These results corroborate Crandall's findings reported in Chapter 2. One could say that boys who are low in autonomous motivation tended to be low because they were overaspiring in general and so it is of no special importance that they are also overaspiring in social comparison. This consistency for boys, however, bears upon the present discussion because I have contended that boys handle autonomy or social comparison difficulties by overaspiration and that girls handle the same issues by cautiousness. They follow certain sex stereotypes.

This conclusion could help us explain an important difference between Negro and white boys that we find. In Table 16 we report a result that comes up time and time again in comparing Negro and white males in our study.[52] The Negro males are more impulsive than the white males in their setting of aspiration. Our previous analysis suggested that impulsivity is associated with low autonomous achievement motivation. Table 16 suggests that Negro males in our society are particularly disrupted by unresolved autonomy aspirations. One could reason that Negro males compared to white males are deprived of an early sense of mastery in dealing with the environment. The economically and culturally deprived homes of

---

[52] For a full discussion of racial difference in different schools at different ages, see Veroff and Pearlman (in press).

so many Negro boys are not good settings for preschool children to learn about their effectiveness in dealing with the environment. They arrive at school with lower IQ's than the white children, and thus find it difficult to master autonomy in the school setting. Thus, when Negro boys are pressed to achieve, it is no wonder that they may become anxious and adopt the customary masculine way of handling achievement anxiety—defensive overaspiration.

Results: Achievement Types and Their Reactions to Success and Failure

Let me tell you now about two other studies that demonstrate the usefulness of the typology I have described. Both of these studies describe children's reactions to success or failure.

ASSERTION 6: *Generally, reactions to success or failure by children depend on their achievement orientation.* The study that bears on this assertion was initiated in a slightly different context, but as I began thinking about the typology of achievement orientations, it made good sense to interpret it in that context. It is an interesting experiment in itself, so let me present it in detail. This study, by Veroff, Goldsmith, and Taylor,[53] represents an attempt to replicate and clarify results attained by Gerwitz[54] on young boys. Gerwitz's study demonstrated that, following reinforcement of performance on a puzzle, differential preference rankings for other puzzles (arranged along a dimension of similarity) defined marked and consistent generalization gradients. As an aside let me say that I find this study to be one of the most intriguing experimental paradigms for discovering potential developmental processes underlying the growth of achievement motivational dispositions in children. In this experimental paradigm, one asks what are the effects of success and failure on orienting children to approach or to avoid certain situations more or less relevant to the class of cues associated with the original success or failure.

In thinking about the development of achievement motivational dispositions, a researcher ought to look for the determinants of generalization capacities. He ought to look for the determinants underlying the tendencies to approach or avoid a new achievement situation where potential success or failure is not explicit, but is implied by applying information from a previous experience with a similar situation. An easy assumption to make in such a paradigm is that the more important success or failure

[53] J. Veroff, R. Goldsmith, and Linda Taylor, "Effects of Achievement Motivation and Self-Esteem on Generalization of Children's Preference" (USPHS Final Report [MH 10554], 1966).
[54] Hava B. Gerwitz, "Generalization of Children's Preferences as a Function of Reinforcement," *Journal of Abnormal and Social Psychology*, 58 (1959), 111–118.

might be, the more likely is the child to have such information available to him for generalization purposes.

Gerwitz found that while negative reinforcement generated avoidance gradients uniformly, positive reinforcement generated approach gradients in some children, and avoidance gradients in others. The latter children tend to have superior IQ's and to verbalize preference for difficult tasks. It is for these reasons that Gerwitz suggests that following success, high achievement motivated subjects will prefer puzzles that are less similar to the ones in which they succeeded, and would thus indicate avoidance generalization gradients.

Since all of Gerwitz's subjects were high in measures of intelligence (the median being equal to 130), research was undertaken by Goldsmith, Taylor, and myself to replicate and to extend results on a less homogeneous sample. Gerwitz's subjects were not only highly intelligent, but very likely highly achievement-motivated with an integrated orientation, as I have called it in the present context. The psychological significance of the uniform negative gradients following failure, and either positive or negative gradients following success, may be applicable only to her sample of children. Other results may be found in a more heterogeneous sample. In fact, we did find other results, and it is this set of results that I would like to interpret within the present context of an achievement typology.

We attempted to extend the Gerwitz study in two other ways. First, we used direct measures of achievement orientation. Second, we allowed the child to choose a *very different* puzzle from the original in addition to the ones Gerwitz used. We thereby allowed novelty interest to be ascertained separately from avoidance interest.

Following success, failure, or no feedback regarding performance on puzzle A (pieces that had to be arranged into diamond shape), 105 boys, 6 to 7 years old, were asked to perform paired comparisons for preferences among six puzzles: Puzzle A, four puzzles more or less similar to A in shape, and one puzzle very different from A. These puzzles are assumed to be all of the same apparent difficulty. Except for including a sixth puzzle very different from the others, this procedure is identical to Gerwitz's.

The subjects covered a wide range of boys—some university school children, and some summer camp children who were from lower-middle-class homes. Although the sample still overrepresents the middle-class population in general, it is not as homogeneously upper-middle-class as Gerwitz's sample is. Two measures were obtained for each child in addition to the puzzle preference: the autonomous measure of achievement motivation and the Embedded Figures Test for children. Both these tests were given prior to the puzzle preference and administered individually to children.

Children were assigned randomly to either a success, a failure, or a no-feedback condition. Under success conditions, a puzzle was easily completable. Under failure conditions, the pieces were cut in a way so that they were not completable, and under no-feedback condition, the subjects did not experience any success or failure at it.

Many different measures of preferences for puzzles were attempted, since it is possible to look at gradients of preferences in many different qualitative ways. We will confine our analysis to two types of measures of preferences. First, we will assess whether or not a child's pattern of response showed approach gradients (greatest preference for the most similar, next greatest preference for the next most similar, and so on), avoidance gradients (greatest preference for the most dissimilar, and so on), or random gradients, using only the five puzzles Gerwitz used in her original study. This is a replication of Gerwitz's assessment procedure. Second, we will assess how many times a subject preferred puzzles one, two, or three (same or similar to previously experienced ones) to four, five, and six (dissimilar to previous experience). We will look at puzzle preferences within different types of combinations of autonomous and social comparison orientations to achievement.

To assess autonomous achievement motivation we used the measure of autonomous achievement motivation described earlier which involves the choice of repeating one among a series of tasks of varying difficulty. High scores on the Embedded Figure Test were taken as an approximation to having a high social achievement orientation. At this age (6–7), however, social orientation would seem to be a *precocious* development. Therefore, social orientation or social comparison interest perhaps indicates anxiety about one's own capacity vis-à-vis other children. With this in mind, children who are high in autonomous achievement motivation, but *low* in social achievement motivation, are those who will most likely be best equipped to cope with success or failure. Those high in both orientations we will assume are potentially anxious types, either because they are precociously sensitive to social comparison or not at all capable of it. Those high in social comparison and low in autonomy we will designate "fear of success" types, because they are not only precociously aware of social comparison but also they lack autonomy strivings. Those low in both are assumed to be low achievement types who may be potentially impulsive, as previously discussed.

It is important to note first of all, that we had few findings that paralleled Gerwitz's findings (see Table 17). The only result in the present study that replicated Gerwitz's findings is that in comparing "no-feedback"

TABLE 17   *Percentage of Types of Gradients in Different Conditions of Reinforcement (Present Study and Gerwitz Study Compared)*

Type of Gradient	Present Study			Gerwitz Study		
	Condition of Reinforcement			Condition of Reinforcement		
	No Feedback	Success	Failure	No Feedback	Success	Failure
Approach	29%	22%	24%*	15%	45%**	0%**
Avoidance	21%	26%	42%*	10%	20%**	75%**
Random Gradient	50%	52%	34%*	75%	35%**	25%**
N	100%	100%	100%	100%	100%	100%
	(20)	(40)	(41)	(20)	(40)	(40)

* χ^2 testing distribution comparison to no feedback significant at .025.
** χ^2 testing distribution comparison to no feedback significant at .01.

and "failure" groups in either study, there is a significantly greater frequency of avoidance gradients in the failure condition.

The following differences between Gerwitz's study and the present one can be noted in Table 17: (1) The "no-feedback" group in the present study did not make as many random gradients; (2) following success, children in the present study did not give as many approach gradients and gave more random gradients; (3) following failure, children in the present study did not give as many avoidance gradients, but did give approach gradients. Thus, one might conclude that the effects Gerwitz obtained were striking only because she was dealing with a highly achievement-oriented population to begin with. There is also the possibility that the results are due to the inclusion of a very novel choice, but it is difficult to see what bearing this would have on the pattern of results.

Now let us look at results by types in separate conditions. These are reported in Table 18.

Following success, the "fear of success" group (those low in autonomous motivation and high in field dependence) tend to repeat similar tasks and to avoid generalizing to new tasks. Those high in autonomy and low in social motivation tend to avoid similar tasks and to prefer new tasks when success occurs. These two groups are significantly different from one another by median test ($p < .05$), but the overall F in a simple Analysis of Variance is not significant, as can be seen in Table 18. Thus, we can see that there is some trend indicating that the "fear of success" type does consist of those people who may not profit by success. They do not seem to be interested in new tasks following success. Those high in autonomy and low in social motivation at this age may be those who can profit by

TABLE 18　*Preferences for Similarity after Success and Failure in Four Types of Achievement Orientation*

Achievement Motivation Orientation		Following Success		Following Failure	
Autonomous Achievement Orientation	Social[a] Achievement Orientation	N	Mean Preference for Similar	N	Mean Preference for Similar
High	High	11	−1.00	10	.00
High	Low	14	−2.00	12	−2.92
Low	High	8	.88	10	− .90
Low	Low	8	− .12	8	−6.00

Analysis of Variance	Following Success	Following Failure
Between ss (df)	79.47 (3)	186.58 (3)
Within ss (df)	897.75 (37)	795.82 (36)
F	1.09, n.s.	2.81 $p < .05$

[a] A high Social Achievement Orientation is defined by low scores on the Embedded Figure Test.

success in that they turn to new tasks following success. Thus, the possibility of mastering new and various tasks is facilitated. I would like to suggest that it is such a preference for new tasks following success that enhances further success, and, in fact, promotes further development of achievement motivation.

Following failure, all types tend to avoid similar tasks. But some types avoid it more than others, as can be seen in Table 18, where a significant F accounting for mean differences in groups emerges. Those children who are low in both autonomous and social achievement motivation tend to be those who avoid similar tasks more than other groups. It is the type that is presumably "in phase" with appropriate development—those who are high in autonomy and low in field dependence at this age—who seem to take a relatively "moderate" stand on which type of task they would prefer following failure. That is, relative to other groups, they choose tasks that are moderately similar to the ones with which they experienced failure. From these results, one might conclude that the high autonomy-low social orientation type at this age describes a group of children who profit best by failure. After failure they do not repeat similar tasks and yet do not become interested in totally new tasks. Instead, they turn to tasks that are moderately dissimilar from those tasks on which they experienced failure. It is the group that is low in autonomy motivation and low in social achievement motivation who are most likely to turn to dissimilar tasks, who in a sense avoid repeating any tasks that are similar to those in which failure occurred, and who do not allow, therefore, for any possibility for recouping their failures.

From this study one might conclude that it is the high autonomy-low social orientation type in the early grades who seems to profit most from success and failure. Perhaps whatever accounts for this type of person's reacting profitably to success and failure would also help account for how he got to be this motivational type to begin with. It may be that at this age it is only the high autonomy-low social motivation type who can ignore the positive social reinforcement value of a *particular* success and go on to a new level of difficulty to define success. A socially oriented motivation for achievement in the early years can lead a child to *repeat* successes for their specific reinforcement value. This is admittedly a gross speculation, but seems a potentially provocative basis for understanding the development of achievement aspirations at this age.

Finally, let me demonstrate the usefulness of this typological approach to achievement in another large study, done by Feher[55] under my direction. Feher's study deals with the seventh assertion.

ASSERTION 7: *Taking account of different types of achievement orientation will aid in understanding those subjects who will respond to internalized standards of excellence applied to their performance, as opposed to those who will respond to social comparison standards of excellence applied to their performance.* Feher reasoned that children of different motivational orientations will react to the type of standards used to elicit aspirations and performance that are congruent with their motivational type. Autonomously-oriented children will react better to standards of performance that are specific to the self, while children with predominantly social orientations will react better to standards of social comparison. To test this, Feher designed a study which used measures of both social (normative level of aspiration) and autonomous achievement motivations (repetition task). Children were not allowed to meet the standards set for them either in competition with others or in competition with themselves. The particular question Feher was interested in was: What effect did these two types of failure have on subsequent aspiration settings and performance output for the various achievement types? We will be concerned only with performance. Raynor and Smith's dot-to-dot task[56] was used with 3rd grade boys. On the first four trials of the connect-the-dot task, all children had the same experiences. They were allowed to com-

[55] B. Feher, "Children's Reactions to Social Comparison" (Unpublished master's paper, University of Michigan, 1967).
[56] J. O. Raynor and C. P. Smith, "Achievement-Related Motives and Risk Taking in Games of Skill and Chance," *Journal of Personality*, 34 (1966), 176–198.

plete 25, 30, 35, 40 dots on trials one through four respectively. Before the fifth trial, experimental conditions were introduced. There were two conditions, the *self condition* and the *social comparison condition*. In the self condition the child was instructed in the following way: "On the next puzzle you should be able to do forty-five in a minute if you're doing your best, judging from what you've done in the first few trials." In the social comparison condition, the child was told: "Many boys in your grade have done the next puzzle. That means I know how many you should be able to do in one minute. These boys did forty-five on this puzzle when they were trying their best." On trial five, subjects were allowed to complete 35, which represented a failure experience. Before trial six, the same norm was repeated.

There were many different performance measures used in this study, but the important measure that we will consider here is the amount of time that it took each child to reach a specified criterion on the sixth trial. This measure was expressed as a ratio to his base rate established in the first four trials. This ratio should give some indication of the amount of effort after a failure to meet a norm of self or social comparison that was presented to him. What emerges significantly in the Analysis of Variance comparison (cf. Table 19) is a triple interaction between autonomous achievement motivation, social comparison orientation, and norm orientation. In that interaction the result that stands out is the following: Children who are high in both autonomous and social comparison motivations are the ones least disrupted by failure in meeting a norm of social comparison. All other groups show a decrement in their performance after such failure. It is important to note that following failure in *self* comparison there is much higher performance in general than following failure in social comparison. It would seem that most boys at this age have a backlog of experience in meeting autonomous pressures which can elicit confidence in spite of failure for most of them. Such confidence undoubtedly is not there with regard to failure in social comparison at this age. From the earlier developmental speculations, I would predict that children of this age are especially sensitive to social comparison. It is an aspect of achievement evaluation about which they are most concerned. Only those children who were high in both autonomy and social achievement motivation are in the process of mastering the social comparison orientation, and, hence, they, being those least affected by failure in the social comparison situation, can respond effectively to it. This is a *post hoc* explanation of the results, but using the developmental speculations about these types, these findings have very provocative implications for understanding why failure may facilitate the growth of achievement strivings in some children and inhibit

TABLE 19 *Mean Rate of Performance*[a] *Following Failure by Typology and Norm Orientation*[b]

Typology		Norm Orientation	
Level of Autonomous Achievement Motivation	Level of Social Achievement Motivation	Self	Social Comparison
High	High	1.05	1.10
High	Low	1.06	.97
Low	High	1.15	.89
Low	Low	.97	.86

Analysis of Variance

Source	MS	df	F
(A) Autonomous Achievement Motivation	1457	1	5.49*
(B) Social Achievement Motivation	1213	1	4.57**
(C) Norm Orientation	2414	1	9.09***
A × B	87	1	
A × C	9	1	
B × C	1542	1	5.81*
A × B × C	1155	1	4.35**
Error	266	80	

* $p < .025$
** $p < .05$
*** $p < .005$

[a] Ratio of number of seconds to criterion on Trial 6 to average number of seconds to criterion on Trials 1–4.
[b] After Feher, op. cit.

it in others. Or, again, it may very well be that whatever enables children to react effectively to failure in social comparison also accounts for why they have been able to develop both a social and an autonomous achievement motivation.

CONCLUSIONS

In the last two studies we have noted how considering both the autonomous and social orientations to achievement in types aided us in understanding the effects of success or failure on generalization of experiences as well as on performance output. Such a refined look into the achievement orientations of young children is perhaps time-consuming, but it is my guess that it will be the only means by which we can illuminate the complicated effects that particular life experiences in the school setting or at home have on different children. Thinking about the effects of school desegregation, for example, it now seems critical to account for the particular achievement orientation of the different children that the educator is dealing with. Desegregation can positively affect children with sufficiently strong feelings of competence, but could have drastic consequences for those who do not, or who are in the throes of unmastered social comparison. New social comparison, new groups to refer to, could be very potent tools to implement the growth of achievement orientations. But to use such tools without attending to a child's particular pattern of achievement development would be an oversight.

We have seen how achievement motivations vary with younger and older children, with boys and girls, with different social groups. To disregard these patterns of achievement orientation in social engineering would be very shortsighted. But, more important, to disregard such complexity in social research is to discount what we have known for a long time intuitively, but failed to implement in our research. The developmental process is a continuing one. Achievement training builds on achievement training. An achievement typology will necessarily be complex. We should begin to differentiate types of achievement motivation, based both on autonomy and on social comparison, and then we should explicate these types in our research. In the present paper I have attempted to show why such distinctions are developmentally meaningful. Empirical results showing age, sex, and race differences in these different types of achievement orientations tend to confirm the usefulness of such developmental speculations. Much more refined empirical research is required—particularly some careful longitudinal studies—to see whether the reported trends will hold up under more rigorous scrutiny.

SUMMARY

Two types of achievement motivation are discernible: autonomous and social comparison motivations for achievement. A theory of how these motivations develop suggests that autonomous achievement motivation occurs initially followed by social comparison motivation if autonomy is mastered. Both autonomous and social comparison motivations for achievement can be active in people if, in turn, the social comparison motivation for achievement is mastered. A typology of achievement motivation is suggested from this basic position.

Critical to the evidence offered in support of this general scheme are two new assessment devices, one to measure autonomous achievement motivation and the other to measure social comparison motivation for achievement, each especially adapted for research with young children. These measures are based on Atkinson's thinking about risk-taking propensities in people with high achievement motivation. These measures, along with evidence for their validity, are described in detail.

There are three major sets of results stemming from many different pieces of research: results supporting developmental assertions; results suggesting important sex differences in types of achievement motivation; results highlighting the usefulness of the proposed typology of achievement motivation in understanding children's reactions to success and failure.

From the first set of results supporting developmental assertions, the following were major findings:

1. Social comparison motivation for achievement is apparently absent from most preschool children but gradually becomes more evident in older children until it reaches a peak among 7–9-year-olds.

2. Autonomous achievement motivation is apparent in preschool children, but again with some peaking among 7–9-year-olds.

3. A fantasy measure of achievement motivation purported to assess an integration of both autonomous and social comparison orientations to achievement shows a gradual increase with age.

Major results pointing to important sex differences in achievement types are:

1. Second grade boys respond to achievement arousal with increased autonomous achievement motivation; while the girls respond with decreased autonomous achievement motivation.

2. Correlating maternal attitudes and children's achievement motivation, studies suggest that mothers pace the autonomy of boys more appropriately than the autonomy of girls. A study showing more positive effects of school desegregation on Negro boys' achievement motivation than on Negro girls' is interpreted in the same context.

3. Boys are generally more overaspiring than girls in both autonomous and social comparison motivations for achievement.

The third major set of results come from two experimental studies. In 6–7-year-old boys being high in autonomous achievement motivation coupled with low social comparison motivation describes those who seem to profit most from success or failure. In 8–9-year-old boys, being high in both autonomous and social comparison orientation to achievement describes those who react least unfavorably to failure.

APPENDIX MATERIALS

Instructions for Administering Measure of Autonomous Achievement Motivation

Bead Task

Materials. "snap-it" beads. Six strings of beads of varying shape and color as below: (Y = yellow; P = purple; R = red; B = blue; LB = light blue; DB = dark blue; G = green; PK = pink; O = orange).

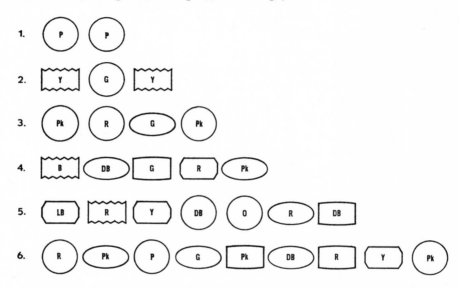

Instructions. The first thing we're going to do is with these beads. You see they are all different colors. Also they are different otherwise. Some of them are round (shows); this one has these funny lines like an accordion; and this one looks like a lantern. Now, we can put them together and make different things out of them. This is the game: I'll show you something put together already. You'll look at it carefully, because I'm going to hide it behind my back and then you'll make one just like it. And then we'll see whether yours looks just like mine.

(Show Item I—be sure the child's beads are not within his reach.)

Look at this carefully. (After five seconds hide them behind your back.)

Now make one just like mine. (Offer child assortment of beads.)

(Wait until the child shows he is through. If there is any doubt about it, ask) Are you finished?

(To get the child's evaluation, present the model and ask noncommittally) Does yours look just like this one?

(If the child says yes or no too hastily, add) Look very carefully.

Possible situations

1. (If the child says yes to a string that is correct, indicate agreement.) Yes, it does look just like this one.

2. (If the child says yes to a string that is incorrect, show your disagreement.) No, it does not look just like this one because . . .

3. (If the child says no to a string that is incorrect, say) That's right. Your beads don't look just like this one because . . .

4. (If the child says no to a string that is correct, say) Yes, your beads do look just like this one. Look at them both again.

(Take the beads from the child, take his apart, and put them back into his box. Hide your own beads. Take the following string of beads and say) All right. Let's try this one, etc. . . .

(Every time the child is successful, go to the next bead design. After the child has failed twice, show him the first item, the last success, the first failure and the second failure. Say) Now let's make one more string of the beads. You may try one of these things. Remember, this one was quite easy for you to do; this one was not so easy, but you got it right; this one was hard for you, and this one was very hard for you. Now, which one would you like to try again?

(After the child chooses let him try; then whether successful or not say cheerily) Okay.

Basket Throw Task
Materials. Laundry pail-whiffle ball (or poker chip); plastic carpet marker with black, one-inch tape at two-foot intervals. Carpet is placed next to pail. Child stands behind taped lines. The poker chip can be used for older subjects more skilled at ball throwing.

Instructions. The next thing we'll do is one that many children in school like to play. You are to throw this ball into the basket from behind these lines. Let's start up real close to the basket.

(Bring the child behind the first line with his toes behind it.) Now try to get the ball in.

(When the ball does not go into the basket, just say) Okay (or) That's it.

(Point out the second line.) Now stand right here and try to get the ball in, etc. . . .

(After the child has failed twice, take him away, aside from the lines, and say) Stand away here and listen to what I have to say. Let's throw the ball once more. You may try from behind one of these lines. Remember, from here it was quite easy for you to get the ball in; this line was not so easy, but you got the ball in all right; from behind this line it was hard for you, and from here it was very hard for you. Now, from which of these lines would you like to try again?

(After the child chooses, let him try as before.)

Picture Memory Task
Materials. Eight sheets of paper with two, three, five, seven, nine, thirteen, sixteen, and twenty objects pasted on them. Objects should be readily identifiable to subject.

Instructions. Now let's play a different game. On the other side of each paper there are pictures of different things. When I turn the paper over, you look at the pictures carefully, and try to remember them, because soon I am going to turn the paper so you can't see the pictures. Then you tell me what pictures you saw. Okay? Let's look at this paper first.

(Point to the pictures individually on the paper, say) This is a . . .

(Let the child finish the sentence. If he hesitates, supply a name. After he has named all the objects, say) Now look carefully, because soon I'm going to turn the paper over.

(After five seconds do so.)

Now tell me what pictures you saw. (You may wish to write down the objects the child names. Let him have ample time to finish the recall. If there is any doubt about him being through, ask) Are you finished?

(Turn the card over for the child's evaluation and say noncommittally) Did you name all the pictures?

(Agree or disagree as on the Bead Task. If the child says yes to a card when he failed to name all the pictures, say) No, you did not name them all, because there is . . . and . . . and . . .

Okay. Now let's try this piece of paper, etc. . . .

(After two failures show the child the first item, the last success, the first failure and the second failure. Say) Let's try one more of these again. Remember, these pictures were easy for you to remember; this paper was not so easy, but you got it right. This paper was hard for you, and this one was very hard for you. Which one would you like to try again?

(After the child chooses, let him try as before.)

Drawing Task

Materials. Blank paper, a china pencil, and seven designs to draw. The simplest one embedded in the next most simple, the latter embedded in the next one, and so on.

Instructions. Here is something children like to do when they are learning about things. Children who are —— years old learn how to draw, make pictures, and all kinds of things with crayon on paper. I would like to see what kind of things you do with crayon on paper. Let's try this red crayon.

(Show the first model.) Can you draw this one? Try to make one just like mine.

(Wait until he is finished. If there is any doubt about it, ask) Are you finished?

(For the child's evaluation present the model and ask noncommittally) Now tell me, does your drawing look just like this one? (If necessary, say) Look very carefully.

(For possible situations, see Bead Task instructions.)

All right. Now let's try another one. Can you draw this one, etc. . . .

(After the child has failed twice, say) Now let's make one more drawing. You may try one of these that you have done. Remember, this one was quite easy for you. This one was not so easy, but you got it right. This one was hard for you, and this one was very hard for you. Now, which one of these drawings would you like to try again?

(Let him reproduce it, as before. Praise him for this task and the rest of the performance.)

100

Instructions for Measure of Social Comparison Interest

Materials. Three identical containers (e.g., 3″ × 5″ × 2″ boxes or 5″ × 7″ envelopes) with tasks to do inside.

Instructions. Here are three boxes (envelopes). They all look alike on the outside, don't they? Well, there's something inside (rattle them) for you to do. In this box (pointing to one on child's right) there is something—How old are you? Four years old? Well this is very easy for boys (girls) four years old.

In this box (pointing to middle box) there is something that some boys (girls) four years old can do and some can't do.

In this box (pointing to box on child's left) there is something that's hard for boys (girls) four years old to do.

You may do just one. Which one would you like to try? Remember, this one is easy—this one some boys (girls) your age can do and some can't—and this one is hard.

(Wait for an answer and then give him the box he chooses, with instructions for whatever task experimenter thinks is appropriate.)

CHAPTER FOUR

The Origin and Expression of Achievement-Related Motives in Children[1]

CHARLES P. SMITH

INDIVIDUAL differences in concern about achieving or doing well at things are well established by the age of 10 or 11. The responses of two 5th grade boys who were asked to tell a story about "a group of children playing" illustrate this differing preoccupation with achievement:

Subject A. They are having a game of baseball and it is a championship game. And one team gets ahead 5 to 3 and it is the ninth inning and one team has the bases loaded.

Both teams were champions of two leagues and they were playing for the title.

[1] This project was supported by Public Health Service Research Grants No. MH–08065 and 7–RO1–MH–13028. The research made use of computer facilities supported in part by National Science Foundation Grant NSF–GP579. Grateful acknowledgment is made for the help of the school officials and teachers whose cooperation and support made the study possible. Special thanks are due to Dr. John J. McKenna, Jr., formerly Superintendent of Princeton Township Schools and Mrs. Alice Packard, Principal. A research conference on Learning and the Educational Process at Stanford University, Summer, 1964, under the direction of R. C. Atkinson, Lee J. Cronbach, Fred L. Strodtbeck, and others contributed to the formulation of the research. Major contributions to the computer analysis of the data were made by Roald Buhler, Roy Lilly, and Richard Pargament. Finally, the author wishes to thank the following persons for their valuable contributions to the collection and analysis of the data: Cynthia Aronson, Judith Bergman, Janice Gibson, Barry Goldstein, Helena Halperin, Robert E. Lee, III, Susan London, Joel Raynor, Lois Teagarden, and Joan Terhune.

They are pretty nervous and are just hoping they can win the game.

Well, the guy up at bat, with the bases loaded, hits a home run and wins the game for his team.

Subject B. They are out on the playground in school and there are a set of seesaws and the one girl falls off and so she goes in to the nurse, and blames another boy for what happened.

The boy and girl were seesawing and having a nice time and then she fell off.

Well, the girl knows it wasn't his fault but she is blaming him anyway. The boy is worried about what is going to happen.

Well, finally the girl admits that it wasn't his fault.

While the first story is filled with achievement imagery, the second deals with entirely different concerns.

Children at this age also differ greatly in the extent to which they are apprehensive about failure. For example, on the thirty-item Test Anxiety Scale for Children[2] which includes questions such as: "Do you worry about being promoted . . . at the end of the year?" "When the teacher asks you to get up in front of the class and read aloud, are you afraid that you are going to make some bad mistakes?" some children in the present study endorsed as many as twenty-seven such items, while others endorsed none.

Since differences in concern about success and failure influence performance level, persistence, and aspiration and also the way a person views himself and the extent to which he can effectively express and develop his capacities, it becomes important to investigate the sources of the differential strength of the "achievement-related" motives, that is, the motive to achieve success and the motive to avoid failure. Motivation to achieve success is conceived as an approach tendency—a disposition to strive for the satisfaction that comes from successful performance. It is assumed to be aroused in situations that offer the possibility of pride in accomplishment, and is assessed by a projective measure of Need for Achievement. Motivation to avoid failure is conceived as a disposition to avoid the unpleasant consequences of failure. It is assumed to be aroused in situations where negative evaluation of performance is possible, and is assessed by means of the Test Anxiety Scale for Children.[3]

The present study deals with four major questions: (1) How do child-rearing practices and values contribute to the development of these in-

---

[2] S. B. Sarason *et al., Anxiety in Elementary School Children* (New York: John Wiley & Sons, 1960).
[3] *Ibid.*

dividual differences? (2) What is the relationship between these two achievement-related motives? Are they opposite ends of the same dimension, or are they independent dispositions? (3) What other personality characteristics are related to these motives, develop concomitantly with them, and interact with them in determining thought and action? (4) How are the achievement-related motives expressed in classroom behavior?

Concerning the first question there exists a provocative body of theory and research on the influence of childrearing practices on the development of the Need for Achievement or the achievement motive, and a promising but less extensive set of ideas and findings about the origins of test anxiety (regarded here as indicative of motivation to avoid failure). Relevant background material on the development of the achievement motive in children will be briefly reviewed; then a similar review will be made of literature on the sources of test anxiety.

Writing on the origins of the achievement motive, McClelland and his colleagues stated a general theory which has guided most research on the subject:

All motives are learned, . . . they develop out of repeated affective experiences connected with certain types of situations and types of behavior. In the case of achievement motivation, the situations should involve "standards of excellence," . . . and the behavior should involve either "competition" with those standards of excellence or attempts to meet them which, if successful, produce positive affect, or if unsuccessful, negative affect.[4]

In other words, the achievement motive is learned from a wide range of mastery experiences which are accompanied by strong positive affect. Once developed the disposition is considered to be relatively stable, and is assumed to be aroused when the person expects that a situation offers the possibility of mastery and the accompanying positive affect.

This theory and the early research it fostered focused attention on several aspects of childrearing: How early did parents begin to encourage achievement behavior in their children? How did they reinforce such behavior? What general attitudes toward and aspirations for their children did parents hold which might foster the growth of the motive? A discussion of the *ages* at which parents encourage achievement behavior in their children raises issues concerning (a) the nature of the relationship between age of demands and strength of achievement motivation; (b) the relationship between demands for achievement behavior and demands for

---

[4] D. C. McClelland *et al.*, *The Achievement Motive* (New York: Appleton-Century-Crofts, 1953), 275.

independence behavior; (c) the direction of causality—that is, whether parental demands precede or follow evidences of achievement behavior; and (d) whether parental demands can be measured accurately.

Regarding the ages at which achievement behavior is encouraged, an early study by Winterbottom[5] indicated that earliness of maternal demands for independence and mastery was related to strong achievement motivation in 8- to 10-year-old boys. However, later studies by McClelland[6] and Moss and Kagan[7] suggest that the relationship between the age at which parental demands are made and the strength of the achievement motive may be curvilinear rather than linear, with very early and very late demands producing low achievement motivation and intermediate demands producing high achievement motivation. Studies with groups other than middle-class Protestants have not revealed either linear or curvilinear relationships between age of demands and strength of achievement motivation.[8]

Winterbottom[9] did not distinguish between demands for achievement and for independence. For example, one of her items asked the age at which the mother expected her son "to do well in school [achievement] on his own" [independence]. In commenting on the Winterbottom items, which deal with independence, mastery, and caretaking, McClelland says: "In the middle-class American families with which Winterbottom initially worked, the three types of attitudes tend to hang together as a unitary syndrome."[10]

A set of items, similar to those of Winterbottom, which were developed by Torgoff,[11] include separate scales for achievement and independence. Torgoff reports that the correlation between the two scales is only .20. This indicates that when demands for achievement are early, demands for independence may be either early or late; so the two types of demands do *not* appear to be as closely related as Winterbottom[12] and McClelland[13] have

[5] Marian R. Winterbottom, "The Relation of Need for Achievement to Learning Experiences in Independence and Mastery," in J. W. Atkinson (ed.), *Motives in Fantasy, Action and Society* (Princeton: D. Van Nostrand Co., 1958), 453–478.

[6] D. C. McClelland, *The Achieving Society* (Princeton: D. Van Nostrand Co., 1961).

[7] H. A. Moss and J. Kagan, "The Stability of Achievement and Recognition Seeking Behavior from Childhood to Adulthood," *Journal of Abnormal and Social Psychology*, 62 (1961), 543–552.

[8] Cf. E. W. Bartlett and C. P. Smith, "Childrearing Practices, Birth Order and the Development of Achievement-Related Motives," *Psychological Reports*, 19 (1966), 1207–1216; McClelland, *The Achieving Society*, 343 ff.

[9] *Op. cit.*

[10] *The Achieving Society*, 342.

[11] I. Torgoff, "Parental Developmental Timetable" (Unpublished paper presented at the 1958 American Psychological Association meetings).

[12] *Op. cit.*

[13] *The Achieving Society.*

assumed. Furthermore, studies by Child, Storm, and Veroff[14] and by Rosen and D'Andrade[15] indicate that achievement training (setting standards of excellence) is more closely related to the child's achievement motivation than is independence training (emphasis on self-reliance and autonomy).

Behavioral evidence concerning whether persons having strong achievement motivation are more independent is not consistent. Winterbottom found that boys with high Need for Achievement less frequently requested help when solving problems than boys with low Need for Achievement. However, Koenig[16] in a later study with college students found that subjects with high achievement motivation were more likely to ask for help than subjects with low achievement motivation if the task was especially difficult. Also, Krebs[17] found no significant relationship between Need for Achievement scores and age of independence training as reported by college males.

The relationship between independence training and the development of achievement motivation is, therefore, not clear. It would appear that a certain amount of independence in performing a task would be necessary in order for the child to feel a sense of accomplishment. On the other hand, insistence on a high degree of independence might mean that the parent was willing to settle for poorer performance so long as no supervision was required. The latter situation would not appear to be especially conducive to the development of a desire to do well at things.

A further complication arises concerning these relationships—are child-rearing practices a cause of the child's personality characteristics or a response to them? Siss[18] reports that earlier demands are reported for children of higher intelligence, and a similar trend is found by Bartlett and Smith.[19] It seems entirely possible that the more intelligent children are ready for achievement training sooner, and that the parents' demands may simply be a response to this readiness. Feld[20] has emphasized the need for a view of the parent-child interaction as reciprocal, with the parent both

---

[14] I. L. Child, T. Storm, and J. Veroff, "Achievement Themes in Folk Tales Related to Socialization Practice," in J. W. Atkinson (ed.), *Motives in Fantasy, Action and Society* (Princeton: D. Van Nostrand Co., 1958), Chap. 34.

[15] B. Rosen and R. D'Andrade, "The Psychosocial Origins of Achievement Motivation," *Sociometry*, 22 (1959), 185–218.

[16] K. Koenig, "Social Psychological Correlates of Self-Reliance" (Unpublished doctoral dissertation, University of Michigan, 1962).

[17] A. M. Krebs, "Two Determinants of Conformity: Age of Independence Training and *n* Achievement," *Journal of Abnormal and Social Psychology*, 56 (1958), 130–131.

[18] R. Siss, "Expectations of Mothers and Teachers for Independence and Reading and Their Influence upon Reading Achievement and Personality Attributes of Third Grade Boys" (Unpublished doctoral dissertation, Rutgers University, 1962).

[19] *Op. cit.*

[20] Sheila C. Feld, "Longitudinal Study of the Origins of Achievement Strivings," *Journal of Personality and Social Psychology*, 7 (1967), 408–414.

influencing and reacting to the child's personality and behavior. In studying the relationship between childrearing demands and motivational development, therefore, it is important to try to establish the direction of causality, or alternatively, whether or not reciprocal influence exists.

It should also be noted that it is difficult to determine for older children the age at which early demands were made since most parents do not recall early events accurately.[21] The procedures employed by Torgoff[22] of asking about demands while the children are still of preschool age appear to be an improvement in this respect; likewise, the methods employed by investigators at the Fels Research Institute which involve visits to the home and observer recordings of parent-child interaction appear to be superior approaches to the problem of determining the ages at which demands are made and the extent to which demands precede and foster the growth of particular personality characteristics.

To sum up, the existing evidence regarding the influence of the age of demands on the development of achievement motivation does not clearly confirm or disconfirm the McClelland *et al.*[23] theory. The research to date points up a need for a refinement of the theory, but does not provide an adequate test of the theory. The age at which demands for achievement and independence are made is probably an important variable the effects of which need to be better conceptualized and measured.

The present writer suspects that the parent who produces high achievement motivation in his child is one who gears his demands to the child's current level of performance. No absolute age of training would be expected to be especially effective; rather, "early" and "late" are defined with reference to the particular child and his abilities. Holding up realistic but challenging goals and responding positively to successful accomplishment become more important in this view than the specific age at which demands are made.

A second relevant aspect of childrearing is parental attitudes toward and reactions to the child's performance and accomplishment. Winterbottom[24] found that mothers of boys with high Need for Achievement reported responding more often with physical affection in reaction to their sons' attainment of independent accomplishments than mothers of boys with low Need for Achievement. This finding was not replicated, however,

---

[21] Cf. L. C. Robbins, "The Accuracy of Parental Recall of Aspects of Child Development and of Child Rearing Practices," *Journal of Abnormal and Social Psychology*, 66 (1963), 261–270.
[22] *Op. cit.*
[23] *The Achievement Motive.*
[24] *Op. cit.*

in a similar study by Bartlett and Smith[25] using subjects with higher social-class membership.

Studies by Winterbottom[26] and by Rosen and D'Andrade[27] report that parents of children with high achievement motivation have a more positive evaluation of their sons' competence than the parents of boys with low motivation to achieve. Rosen and D'Andrade[28] also found that the parents of boys with high Need for Achievement held higher aspirations for their sons' performance and displayed more warmth and involvement toward their sons' performance than the parents of boys with low Need for Achievement. Another study found that nursery school children displayed more achievement behavior in free play if their mothers responded at home with approval of the children's achievement efforts.[29] These investigators found that maternal affection and independence training were not predictive of achievement behavior but that direct maternal reward of achievement efforts was. In still another study,[30] mothers of academically competent girls were found to be less affectionate and less nurturant than mothers of less proficient girls.

These findings concerning parental attitudes and reactions are again not entirely consistent with each other or with the McClelland *et al.*[31] theory that early and intense affective rewards for achievement should foster the development of strong achievement motivation. Several factors complicate the interpretation of the results—the relationships may be somewhat different for boys and girls, for different social classes and ethnic groups, for children of different ages (since a hug for accomplishment means something different to a boy of 5 and a boy of 15), for the training methods of mothers and fathers, and for the prediction of high achievement *behavior* instead of high achievement *motivation*.

Somewhat less information is available on the relationship of childrearing practices to the development of anxiety about testing situations. Sarason *et al.*[32] theorize that test anxiety develops when parents criticize and punish a child who fails to perform satisfactorily. Because he fears that his own angry reaction to their criticism may bring further punishment and rejection, the child stifles his anger, becomes highly dependent on parental

---

[25] *Op. cit.*
[26] *Op. cit.*
[27] *Op. cit.*
[28] *Ibid.*
[29] V. J. Crandall, Anne Preston and Alice Rabson, "Maternal Reactions and the Development of Independence and Achievement Behavior in Young Children," *Child Development,* 31 (1960), 243–251.
[30] V. Crandall *et al.,* "Parents' Attitudes and Behavior and Grade-School Children's Academic Achievements," *Journal of Genetic Psychology,* 104 (1964), 53–66.
[31] *The Achievement Motive.*
[32] *Op. cit.*

aid in achievement activities and self-deprecating about his abilities. According to this theory the highly test-anxious child should be less aggressive, more dependent, and have a less favorable self-image than the child with low test anxiety. Sarason et al.[33] report some evidence supporting these expectations. Bartlett and Smith[34] report a positive relationship for boys between high test anxiety and high teacher ratings of dependence. Feld[35] found that high test anxiety in adolescent boys was associated with relatively late maternal demands for independence and mastery, and Bartlett and Smith[36] report a similar finding. Sarason et al.[37] and Feld, Owen, and Sarason[38] found that parents of boys with high test anxiety showed more signs of defensiveness in an interview than parents of boys with low test anxiety, and the former group tended to describe their sons in less favorable terms on an adjective check list. Mothers of boys with high test anxiety more often sought to impress the interviewer as being good parents. Fathers of sons with high test anxiety more frequently reported punishing their sons for a poor report card than fathers of sons with low test anxiety.

In summary, past research and theory leads to the expectation that strong achievement motivation in boys should be associated with (1) relatively early demands for accomplishment, (2) affectively intense rewards for accomplishment such as physical affection or praise, (3) relatively high goals set for children by parents, (4) a favorable parental view of a son's competence, and (5) interest and involvement in a son's achievement endeavors. Theory and research on test anxiety leads to the expectation that high test anxiety should be associated with (1) relatively late demands for independence, (2) criticism and punishment for failure, and (3) an unfavorable view of a child's abilities.

It appears that different combinations of childrearing practices are possible which would produce various combinations of achievement and anxiety motive strengths. For example, a parent could make early achievement demands and late independence demands, and could reward achievement but punish failure, thus producing high achievement motivation and high anxiety. Or, the practices of one parent might foster high achievement motivation while those of the other parent might produce high anxiety. Various combinations of motive strengths might be produced, for

[33] Ibid.
[34] Op. cit.
[35] Op. cit.
[36] Op. cit.
[37] Op. cit.
[38] S. Feld, W. Owen, and S. B. Sarason, "Interviews with Parents of Anxious and Defensive Young Boys" (Unpublished manuscript, National Institute of Mental Health, 1963).

example, one motive strong and one weak, both strong, or both weak. The two motives are not conceived as opposite ends of the same motivational continuum but rather as two relatively independent dispositions that are both aroused in situations in which performance will be evaluated in terms of some standard of excellence.

Such situations also arouse other kinds of personality processes, but most research on the relationship of achievement-related motives to performance has ignored the total personality context in which these motives operate. According to the most explicit theory of the relationship of these motives to performance,[39] the person sizes up a task, estimates his likelihood of succeeding at it, and the motive forces aroused then combine to contribute to the determination of behavior. In a sense this formulation is saying "other relevant things being equal" certain predictions about behavior can be made on the basis of information about motives, expectancies, and incentives.

Perhaps the time has come to try to specify some of the other personality factors that are relevant to performance in achievement situations. When a person faces a difficult task he may also consider the effect that success or failure will have on his feelings of competence and self-worth. In other words, higher-order personality systems such as self-esteem may be involved in the internal processes which intervene between the arousal of motivation and the initiation of behavior. A girl, for example, might consider that failure at a masculine activity would not be harmful to her self-esteem. She might not become "ego involved" regardless of the challenge presented by the task.

It is assumed here that "self concept" is a relevant personality factor which interacts with motives in determining performance in achievement situations. The term "self concept" is used to refer to attributes one assigns to oneself and the values attached to these attributes. Some previous research has dealt with the relationship between Need for Achievement and self concept[40] and between test anxiety and self concept.[41]

It is of interest to ask to what extent the self concept is influenced and developed by the same childrearing practices that promote the growth of achievement motivation and anxiety about failure. It has been noted already that a negative relationship between test anxiety and self-esteem is

---

[39] J. W. Atkinson and N. T. Feather (eds.), A *Theory of Achievement Motivation* (New York: John Wiley & Sons, 1966).
[40] Cf. S. Coopersmith, "Self-Esteem and Need for Achievement as Determinants of Selective Recall and Repetition," *Journal of Abnormal and Social Psychology*, 60 (1960), 310–317; J. G. Martire, "Relationships Between the Self Concept and Differences in the Strength and Generality of Achievement Motivation," *Journal of Personality*, 24 (1956), 364–375.
[41] Cf. Sarason *et al.*, *op. cit.*

expected. The child who is criticized comes to devalue himself. To the extent that parents view the child's competence favorably, the child with high achievement motivation should have relatively high self-esteem. However, to the extent that ever higher standards are set for performance, he may feel a discrepancy between his actual self concept and ideal self concept. These variables can be taken into consideration in conceptualizing the determinants of performance and in the prediction of performance.

A final concern of the present investigation is the expression of achievement-related motives in the classroom and on paper-and-pencil measures of level of performance and level of aspiration. Extensive research and theory[42] indicates that under achievement-oriented or testlike conditions, achievement motivation is expected to be positively related to performance and test anxiety negatively related to performance. Reading performance was selected as a classroom activity to be given special study primarily because of research on elementary school children by Sarason, Hill, and Zimbardo[43] showing a negative relationship between test anxiety and reading with defensiveness partialed out. In the present study, in addition to the standard reading curriculum, a program of self-directed reading was introduced which minimized the threat of teacher evaluation. It was thought that test anxiety would be less debilitating to reading performance under such conditions. A positive relationship was expected between Need for Achievement and reading performance on the standard teacher-evaluated reading program, though Crandall, Katkovsky, and Preston[44] found no significant relationship between Need for Achievement and a reading achievement test. No prediction was made in the present study concerning the expected relationship between Need for Achievement and performance on the self-directed reading materials.

Goal setting. The expected relationships between achievement-related motives and goal setting are taken from Atkinson's model for risk-taking behavior.[45] Briefly, subjects with strong motivation to achieve and weak motivation to avoid failure are expected to set goals of intermediate difficulty while subjects with weak motivation to achieve and strong motivation to avoid failure are expected to set goals that are either extremely easy or extremely difficult. McClelland[46] obtained data consistent with this

[42] Cf. Atkinson and Feather, *op. cit.;* Sarason *et al., op. cit.*
[43] S. B. Sarason, K. T. Hill, and P. G. Zimbardo, "A Longitudinal Study of the Relation of Test Anxiety to Performance on Intelligence and Achievement Tests," *Monographs of the Society for Research in Child Development,* Serial No. 98, Vol. 29 (1964), No. 7.
[44] V. J. Crandall, W. Katkovsky, and A. Preston, "Motivational Determinants of Young Children's Intellectual Achievement Behaviors," *Child Development,* 33 (1962), 643–661.
[45] Atkinson and Feather, *op. cit.*
[46] D. C. McClelland, "Risk Taking in Children with High and Low Need for Achievement," in J. W. Atkinson (ed.), *Motives in Fantasy, Action and Society* (Princeton: D. Van Nostrand Co., 1958), Chap. 21.

model in a study in which young children played a game of ring toss. In the present study a paper-and-pencil puzzle task is used to investigate the relationship between achievement-related motives and goal setting.

Aims of the research. In the present research, the development of motives and other personality characteristics in the child is related both to the origins of these characteristics in the home and to their expression in the form of classroom behavior, as shown in the diagram below:

(A)		(B)		(C)
Parental Influence	$\rightleftarrows$	Personality Development of the Child	$\rightarrow$	Classroom Behavior of the Child

The design permits the investigation of relationships from A to B to C sequentially, and also between A and C, A and B, and B and C separately. It may be, for example, that a particular form of parental influence is not related in the expected manner to personality measures but is related in a meaningful way to the child's classroom behavior. In such a case a reconceptualization of the relationship of such parental behavior to the child's personality development might be called for.

METHOD

Subjects

All of the 4th and 5th grade boys ($N = 148$) in two public schools in Princeton, New Jersey, and their parents were subjects in the present study. The mean Kuhlmann-Anderson IQ for all boys is 115.5 ($SD = 14.2$). The number of boys in each class, grade, and school is presented in Table 1. Fewer children are included in some analyses because (a) some moved away during the school year, (b) some were absent at later data collection sessions, and (c) data (e.g., IQs) obtained from the school records were occasionally missing. The number of subjects will, therefore, be specified separately for each analysis to be reported.

The two elementary schools were attractive new buildings in which the latest equipment and educational methods were employed. The teachers were pleasant, competent, and cooperative. Class size varied from 16 to 29. The schools were located in attractive residential neighborhoods, and the students came almost exclusively from white middle- and upper-middle-class families. No attempt was made to control for race since there were only three Negro children in the entire group. These schools were intentionally selected because of their homogeneous populations, since it was beyond the scope of the study to vary socioeconomic class and race in addition to the other variables investigated.

112

TABLE 1   *Number of Boys in Each Class, Grade, and School*

School	Grade	Teacher	No. of Boys
A	4	K	16
A	4	T	17
B	4	B	12
B	4	B	14
B	4	D	13
B	4	D	14
		Total 4th Grade =	86
A	5	M	17
A	5	V	12
B	5	C	9
B	5	C	8
B	5	O	8
B	5	O	8
		Total 5th Grade =	62
		Total Sample =	148

Procedure

The experimenter obtained approval of the research proposal from the local Board of Education. He then had a series of meetings with the principals and teachers of the participating schools to explain the study and to make arrangements for data collection.

Projective storytelling.   Early in October each child was called from the classroom for an individual interview of approximately thirty minutes in length. The interview consisted of a few warmup questions dealing with the child's attitude toward school matters, followed by a projective storytelling measure.

Three women who were themselves mothers of elementary school children conducted the interviews. They had previously attended a series of training seminars and had practiced the interview procedures on children in another nonparticipating school. The interview materials were pretested and revised during this period of interviewer training.

The interviewer began by saying that she was "interviewing the members of your class to get some ideas about your reactions to the kinds of things you do in school. What you tell me may help us to improve our school system." The child was then asked what subjects he liked best and least and how his parents reacted when he got good grades and bad grades. Then the interviewer gave the following instructions for the projective measure of motivation:

What I have for you next is a sort of game. I'm interested in storytelling and I'd like you to tell some stories. I'm going to tell you what to make up a story about —I'll give you an idea, and you tell me a story about it. Make up a story with a beginning and an end just like the ones you read. As you tell me the story, I'll ask you some questions to guide you. Let's try one for practice. Tell me a story about a boy who has just left his house. (Pause.) (1) What is happening in the story? (2) What happened before? How did the story begin?[47] (3) What is he thinking about and how does he feel? (4) What will happen? How will the story end?

After the child had completed the practice story, the interviewer said:

Now you have the idea. You can tell me the rest of your stories in the same way. I'll ask you what is happening, how the story began, how the people think and feel, and how the story ends. You can tell the story by answering my questions and I'll write down what you say.

Stories were then obtained in response to the following topics:

1. Tell me a story about a little boy who is in school.[48]
2. Tell me a story about a group of children playing.
3. Tell me a story about a boy at home who is making something.
4. Tell me a story about two children on a rainy day.

The wording of the practice story topic was taken from Winterbottom.[49] The other topics were composed for this study and were selected from a larger number of pretested topics because they appeared effectively to sample a variety of situations in which achievement-related behavior was possible.

Nearly all of the children took the interview in stride, answered the introductory questions with little probing, and told reasonably sustained and coherent stories which averaged about a hundred words in length. An occasional nondirective probe (e.g., "Anything else?" or a recapitulation of the first part of the story) was all that was necessary to obtain satisfactory stories from most of the children. Three children were apprehensive about the interview and had to be seen a second time to obtain complete protocols.

Stories were scored for Need for Achievement by two independent scorers using the McClelland *et al.* scoring system.[50] A product-moment

---

[47] A suggestion for a more effective storytelling procedure is to omit the second prompt question (i.e., "What happened before?") since most children seemed unable to extend the story back in time to some earlier inception. Instead, they nearly always repeated, almost verbatim, their response to the first question. As a result, virtually no new scorable material was produced by the second question. The omission of this question from each story would speed up the procedure and allow time to collect more stories.

[48] The word "little" was unintentionally included in this topic and should be omitted in future research. It apparently caused some of the 4th and 5th graders to tell stories about kindergarten children. For this reason, this topic probably did not elicit as much achievement imagery as might have been desired, although a good many achievement-related stories about older school children were also told to this cue.

[49] *Op. cit.*

[50] J. W. Atkinson (ed.), *Motives in Fantasy, Action and Society* (Princeton: D. Van Nostrand Co., 1958), Chap. 12.

correlation of .85 was obtained between the two sets of scores. Differences were discussed and resolved to arrive at a final set of scores.

Test anxiety, defensiveness. Early in December measures of test anxiety and defensiveness developed by S. B. Sarason and his colleagues[51] were administered in the classrooms following the procedures described in Sarason *et al.*[52] The teacher introduced to her class one of the women who had conducted individual interviews with the children. She told the children that they would be asked some questions about how they thought and felt about school and about some other things and that their answers would not be seen by their teacher, principal, or parents. The instructions, which were taken with minor changes from Sarason *et al.*[53] emphasized that there were no right or wrong answers to any of the questions. Answer sheets were distributed which contained "yes" and "no" next to each item number. The tester then read each item aloud (e.g., "Do you worry when the teacher says that she is going to ask you questions to find out how much you know?") and the children circled "yes" or "no" for each item. The thirty items of the Test Anxiety Scale for Children (TASC) are given in Sarason *et al.*[54] These items were followed by asking the children to draw a picture of a person on a blank piece of paper for two minutes. This task was employed primarily as an intervening activity and data derived from it will not be reported here. Following the human figure drawing, the tester read aloud the forty items from the Defensiveness Scale for Children (DSC) as given in Sarason, Hill, and Zimbardo[55] which included eleven "lie scale" items, and the children once again circled "yes" or "no" in answer to each item (e.g., "Do you sometimes dream about things you don't like to talk about?"). These measures took about thirty minutes to administer.

The TASC was employed as a measure of the motive to avoid failure in activities in which performance will be evaluated in order to avoid the negative emotional feelings produced by failure. The DSC is intended by Sarason *et al.*[56] to be a measure of the tendency to deny the experience of negative feelings such as anxiety, hostility, and inadequacy. Since some children do not admit to anxiety on the TASC it is useful to have a measure of defensiveness with which to attempt to detect children who may be unwilling or unable to report their anxiety. A separate score may be ob-

---

[51] Sarason *et al.*, *op. cit.*; Sarason, Hill, and Zimbardo, *op. cit.*
[52] *Op. cit.*, Appendix B.
[53] *Ibid.*, 306–309.
[54] *Ibid.*, 307–308.
[55] *Op. cit.*, Appendix A.
[56] *Op. cit.*

tained for "lie" and "defensiveness" items. Sarason, Hill, and Zimbardo[57] conceive of "lying" as conscious censoring or distortion of negative feelings. "defensiveness" as unconscious censoring or distortion of negative feelings. However, these authors report that the two scales correlate between .64 and .72 on different groups of subjects. Also, the effects on the correlation between test anxiety and IQ are the same with the lie score partialed out as with the defensiveness score partialed out. In the present study, therefore, a single defensiveness score was obtained, namely, the total number of lie and defensiveness items endorsed.

Level of aspiration, puzzle performance, and self concept. Early in June two male testers administered several additional measures in the classrooms. Level of aspiration and performance level were assessed by means of a set of puzzles that were adapted for children from a task constructed for college students.[58] Each puzzle consisted of a page containing numbers from 1 to 80 arranged nonconsecutively in rows. The subject's task is to connect the numbers consecutively with a pencil line. He must spot the next number in a nearby row or column and draw a line to it. The task is surprisingly interesting and becomes moderately challenging when fast completion is attempted.

The subjects were told that the first task was a game called "Connect the Numbers" and were asked to work a sample puzzle. Then they were asked to turn to the first puzzle and write "the number you will try to reach in one minute at the top of the page. This is just an estimate of what you will try to do. If you can do more before time is up keep working and try to do as many as you can." Subjects were given twenty seconds to look at the puzzle and to write down their estimates (levels of aspiration). Then they were given one minute to work on the puzzle itself. This procedure was repeated for five puzzles. The last number reached on each puzzle was regarded as the performance score (P) for that puzzle. This procedure yielded levels of aspiration (LA) for five puzzles, performance scores for five puzzles, and four goal discrepancy scores ($GlDs = LA$ minus past performance, e.g., $LA_2 - P_1$).

Next the subjects were asked to fill out a questionnaire designed to assess "actual" and "ideal" self concept. They were given the following instructions:

The purpose of the first page is to have you describe yourself. All you have to do is circle a number beside each adjective showing the degree to which you are like that. For example, for the quality of being friendly, if you circled 5 it

[57] *Op. cit.*
[58] Cf. J. O. Raynor and C. P. Smith, "Achievement-Related Motives and Risk Taking in Games of Skill and Chance," *Journal of Personality,* 34 (1966), 176–198.

116

would mean that you think of yourself as being very friendly, 3 means moderately friendly, and 1 means only slightly friendly. You can circle any number along the scale to show how friendly you are. Do the same thing for each adjective. Try to describe yourself as honestly as you can.

The first page contained a list of adjectives headed by the words "I am." The tester read and defined each adjective and the subjects then circled the appropriate scale value for that term. The list contained the following ten words selected for their relevance to the content of the study: independent, lazy, intelligent, responsible, nervous, competent, cooperative, realistic, competitive, resourceful, and four additional "filler" words (friendly, stubborn, curious, creative) for which data will not be reported.

The subjects were then asked to turn to the second page which contained the same list of adjectives headed by the words "I would like to be." The tester then said:

On this page you should do the same thing except this time describe how you would *like* to be. Think of the degree to which you would like to possess each quality and then circle a number for each adjective to show how you would *like* to be.

The words were again read aloud and defined.

Teachers' ratings of dependence and classroom behavior. At the end of May, the eight participating teachers were asked to rate each of their pupils on thirty-one items which were intended to assess behaviors reflecting dependence-independence (e.g., "ability to work at tasks independently after directions are given"), achievement motivation (e.g., "desire to do well in school work"), and other forms of classroom behavior such as aggressiveness and friendliness. A copy of the teacher rating form is also included in the Appendix of this chapter. Some of the items were taken from a teacher rating form devised by Siss.[59]

The teachers were asked to give thoughtful and objective ratings of their students. They had had a year of classroom experience with the children, but they had no access to any data collected in the present investigation, so such information could not have influenced their ratings. The teachers were each given a ten dollar honorarium for their efforts in filling out the forms. There is every evidence that they did so conscientiously, and they reported few difficulties in using the scales provided.

Reading performance. Two kinds of reading performance scores were obtained—one based on conventional classroom exercises, and the other based on the use of semi-programed reading materials. The conventional reading curriculum involved assignments in selected basic readers, class

---

[59] *Op. cit.*

117

discussion, workbook exercises, silent reading in the library, and book reports. The measure of performance for these reading activities was simply the reading grade assigned by the teacher at the end of the year.

The semi-programed materials (SRA Reading Labs[60]) were introduced into the 4th and 5th grades especially for the purposes of the present investigation. They were intended to permit self-directed learning, to eliminate competition and concern about evaluation, and to individualize learning by permitting each child to work at his own level and pace.

The SRA Reading Labs contain short reading selections at twelve different levels of difficulty (e.g., for 4th graders the levels range from 2nd grade to 7th grade). The booklets at each level have a distinctive color and there are twelve different selections at each color level. At the outset the child is given a brief reading test to determine his starting level. Then he is told what color to start with and is allowed to choose any of the twelve selections in that color level each time he starts a reading exercise. Each exercise consists of a short reading selection (e.g., "Davy Crockett," "Going Skin Diving") followed by questions on comprehension, word meanings, letter sounds, compound words, etc. Each exercise is designed to teach certain skills. When the child gets a score of 90 to 100 per cent correct on each of a series of eight to ten exercises at one level, he is ready to move to the next level. Other aspects of the materials are designed to improve reading rate, concentration, and retention.

After a child reads a selection, he answers the questions in his record book. Then he gets an answer key for that exercise and marks his own paper, writing out corrections for incorrect answers. Finally, he gives himself a grade (excellent, good, fair, poor) and marks his score on a chart which shows his progress over time. The measure of reading performance obtained from these materials is the number of correct answers for each exercise.

The teachers were given an extensive briefing on the use of the materials by an SRA representative in mid-September. They used the materials in a standardized way three days each week during October and November. Each daily session lasted approximately forty-five minutes. In introducing the materials to the students, the teachers emphasized (as suggested in the SRA procedure) that performance on the SRA materials would not be graded.

Data from school records.   At the end of the year, information was ob-

[60] The author wishes to acknowledge the helpful cooperation of Science Research Associates in the present research. Reading materials for research purposes were provided at a discount, and an SRA representative, Mr. Richard Noyes, was most helpful in his consultations with the investigator and the teachers concerning the use of the materials.

tained from the school records on each child's Kuhlmann-Anderson IQ, his grades, and his scores on the Iowa Tests of Basic Skills.

Questionnaire on childrearing practices. In April the children took home a questionnaire on childrearing practices to their parents. An accompanying letter explained that the questionnaire was part of a study of reading and parental attitudes and expectations toward their child's development. Mothers and fathers were asked to fill out the questionnaires independently without discussing the content with each other.

The questionnaire included six items which described independence behaviors a child might carry out (e.g., "call a friend on the telephone without your help") and three "caretaking items" ("dress himself," "put his clothes away," and "do some regular tasks around the house"). The parent was asked to fill in the ages at which the behaviors were first allowed or encouraged. Because of the necessity to keep the questionnaire brief, items describing achievement behaviors (e.g., "doing well at school") were omitted as were a number of other questions of interest. Parents were also given a list of characteristics and asked to rate their children on the degree to which they possessed each one (e.g., "being obedient to parents," "doing his best at tasks"). Then they were asked, on the following page, to indicate for each of the same characteristics "the extent to which you feel it is important for your child to possess each of the qualities listed." Next the parents were given a list of ways in which they might react when their child succeeded at something difficult (e.g., "tell him how proud you are of him") and a list of possible reactions "when your child fails to do a good job at something you have expected of him" (e.g., "show disappointment"). The parent was asked to use a scale to indicate how frequently he or she reacted in each of the ways listed. Finally, parents were asked to indicate on a seven-point scale how overtly affectionate they are toward their child. Some of the questionnaire items concerning age of independence demands, characteristics possessed by the child, and parental reactions to the child's successes and failures, were adapted from Winterbottom,[61] McClelland,[62] and Bartlett and Smith,[63] while others were newly composed for the present investigation.

Questionnaires were not available from families who had moved away during the school year and fathers in ten families were deceased. Questionnaires from stepmothers were not used. Taking these factors into account, the return from mothers was 87 per cent, and from fathers was 78 per cent.

---

[61] *Op. cit.*
[62] *The Achieving Society.*
[63] *Op. cit.*

RESULTS

Independence Training, Motivational Development, and Independence Behavior

Age of independence training. Two indexes were used to represent the ages at which mothers and fathers allowed or encouraged independence. (See items in Appendix.) The ages for each item were transformed into standard scores. The "age of independence training" index is the sum of the standard scores of each mother or father for the first six items (e.g., "call a friend on the telephone without your help"). The "age of caretaking" index is the sum of the standard scores for the last three items (e.g., "dress himself"). The first group of items represents behaviors that will be of value to the child for his own sake. The caretaking items represent behaviors that will relieve the mother of troublesome chores, but they can also be regarded as legitimate demands for independence and responsibility. Since some parents omitted some items, it was not possible to get index scores for all parents. As a result, the Ns vary for the two indexes.

The independence and caretaking indexes are correlated with each other .49 ($N=95$) for mothers and .45 ($N=81$) for fathers. The independence indexes of mothers and fathers are correlated .54 ($N=74$) and the caretaking indexes of mothers and fathers are correlated .50 ($N=86$).

There is a nonsignificant relationship between achievement motivation and the independence index for mothers ($r=-.15$, $N=101$) and for fathers ($r=-.15$, $N=83$). The correlations indicate that early independence training tends to go with high achievement motivation and are in the direction expected by McClelland and Winterbottom. There is a significant relationship between achievement motivation and the caretaking index for mothers ($r=-.194$, $N=112$, $p<.05$, two-tailed test)[64] and a similar but nonsignificant relationship for fathers ($r=-.159$, $N=91$). This relationship indicates that the earlier the caretaking demands, the higher the achievement motivation—a relationship not expected by McClelland[65] who regards the caretaking items as possible indications of rejection or indifference. There are no curvilinear relationships between achievement motivation and either the independence or caretaking indexes.

In previous studies the largest correlations between independence training and achievement motivation were obtained for middle-class Protestant boys.[66] Data for Protestant boys in the present sample were, therefore,

---

[64] Probability levels for all statistical tests are two-tailed.
[65] *The Achieving Society.*
[66] Cf. *ibid.*, 343–344.

analyzed separately. The correlations between sons' achievement motivation and parents' independence training ages were still nonsignificant ($r=-.21$ for age estimates of both mothers and fathers). However, the correlations between sons' achievement motivation and Protestant parents' caretaking ages were stronger than for the total sample (for mothers, $r=-.42$, $N=57$, $p<.01$; for fathers, $r=-.34$, $N=47$, $p<.02$). These data provide further evidence of the desirability of controlling for religion in the investigation of the relationship between childrearing and the development of achievement motivation.

Contrary to expectation, there are no significant linear or curvilinear relationships between TASC scores and the age of independence or caretaking demands for either mothers or fathers. (A subanalysis for Protestant boys also reveals no such relationships.) However, the child's self-rating on the "actual self" rating form of the extent to which he possessed the quality of being "nervous" was related to the mothers' independence index ($r=.30$, $N=96$, $p<.05$), the mothers' caretaking index ($r=.21$, $N=106$, $p<.05$) and the fathers' independence index ($r=.18$, $N=80$, $p<.10$) indicating that the later the training, the more likely the child was to rate himself as highly nervous. If the self-rating of "nervous" is indicative of anxiety, this finding is consistent with the expectation that later independence demands are associated with higher anxiety.

The next relationship pertaining to the "actual self" data is somewhat surprising, however, since late demands also tend to be positively associated with self-ratings of competence. The correlation for the mothers' independence index is .175 ($N=96$, $p<.10$), for the mothers' caretaking index is .21 ($N=106$, $p<.05$), and for the fathers' independence index is .20 ($N=80$, $p<.10$). Finally, the father caretaking index was significantly related to the boys' self-ratings of the quality of being "responsible" ($r=-.22$, $N=88$, $p<.05$). The earlier the demands, the higher the self-rating of the term "responsible."

Finally, there is a near-significant relationship between IQ and the caretaking index for mothers ($r=-.157$, $N=108$, $p<.10$) indicating a tendency for early demands to go with higher intelligence.

Some idea of the association between reported ages of independence training and independence *behavior* can be gained from the relationships between the training indexes and teacher ratings of classroom behavior. Two teacher rating items of dependence were related to the fathers' independence index. "Desire for praise" was correlated .187 ($N=83$, $p<.10$) and "need for affection" was correlated .23 ($N=81$, $p<.05$), that is, the later the reported independence training, the greater the observed need for praise and affection. "Standing up for his own rights with other children" was correlated with the mothers' independence index ($r = -.26$, $N = 100$, $p < .01$) and with the fathers' independence index ($r = -.17$, $N = 82$, *n.s.*), that is, the later the reported independence training, the less a child was observed to stand up for his own rights. These correlations provide weak evidence that reports of late independence training are related to observed dependent behavior.

Achievement-related motives and teacher ratings of dependence and independence. The relationship between achievement-related motives and early demands for independence has been examined. Now it is of interest to determine the relationship of these motives to independence behavior in the classroom. The ratings of their pupils made by each teacher were converted to standard scores in an attempt to reduce differences between classes. All teacher-rating items were then intercorrelated, and the following four items appeared to constitute a cluster representing *dependent* behavior:

1. Desire for praise by adults.
2. Need for affection from teacher.
3. Need for emotional support.
4. Frequency of asking for help with schoolwork.

These items are intercorrelated between .51 and .75. A sum of the z scores on these items was used as a teacher-rating index of dependent behavior.[67]

Six additional items were regarded as representing *independent* behavior:

1. Ability to work at tasks independently after directions are given.
2. Initiative and resourcefulness.
3. Ability to carry out reasonably difficult tasks on his own without assistance or guidance.
4. Being explorative and curious.
5. Being able to make his own decisions.
6. Trying new things on his own.

These items are intercorrelated from .58 to .92 with each other. A sum of these items was used as a teacher-rating index of independence behavior. (The item "standing up for his own rights with other children" was not closely related to any of the other items and was not included in either index.)

---

[67] Since the first three items indicate emotional dependence, the inclusion of the last item indicating task dependence may seem surprising. The decision was made purely on the basis of the obtained correlations. "Asking for help with schoolwork" was correlated .75 with "Need for emotional support," whereas "Asking for help" was not so strongly related to any of the items included in the "independence" index.

All items of the independence index correlate less highly with the dependence items than with each other. The correlation between the independence index and the dependence index is $-.33$ ($N=140$). This surprisingly low correlation indicates, as has been pointed out before,[68] that rated dependence is not necessarily the opposite of rated independence. In the present data Need for Achievement scores are unrelated to both teacher ratings of dependence ($r=.10$) and independence ($r=.01$). Test anxiety scores are not related to dependence behavior ($r=.11$),[69] but are significantly related to teacher ratings of independence ($r=-.23$, $N=143$, $p<.01$). This finding, that boys with high test anxiety manifest a low degree of independence behavior in the classroom, is consistent with earlier research and with the theoretical notion that dependency is a way of coping with anxiety. The strongest correlate of rated dependence and independence behavior, however, is IQ, which is related to rated dependence $-.29$ ($N=138$, $p<.01$) and to rated independence .55 ($N=138$, $p<.01$). In other words, highly intelligent boys are rated as more independent and less dependent than boys with low intelligence (though part of this relationship may be attributable to a positive bias in teacher ratings for pupils with high intelligence).

The relationship between independence training and achievement training. One set of data obtained from the questionnaire on childrearing practices is relevant to the question of whether achievement and independence training tend to occur together. Each parent indicated on a five-point scale the extent to which he felt that it was *important* for his child to possess each of a number of characteristics (e.g., obedience, resourcefulness, competitiveness). (See items in Appendix.) These ratings will be regarded as indications of a parent's childrearing *values*, that is, expressions of the qualities he wishes to see his son possess.

A principal components factor analysis was carried out on the scores for the twenty traits for the mothers ($N=119$) and also for the fathers ($N=106$). Three first-order factors were obtained for each set of parents, and the equamax method of rotation was employed to arrive at orthogonal factors. The results are presented in Table 2.

---

[68] Cf. W. W. Hartup, "Dependence and Independence," in H. W. Stevenson (ed.), *Child Psychology* (The 62nd Yearbook of the National Society for the Study of Education [Chicago: University of Chicago Press, 1963]), 333–363.

[69] It is possible that a bias in teacher ratings could be reducing the size of this correlation. J. W. Barnard, P. G. Zimbardo, and S. B. Sarason, "Bias in Teacher's Ratings of Student Personality Traits Due to IQ and Social Desirability" (Unpublished study, 1965), found teacher ratings of subjects with high test anxiety who were also high in intelligence to be *favorably* biased, that is, these subjects were characterized by their teachers as "independent" when they were rated by impartial observers as quite *dependent*. In the present study, therefore, children with high test anxiety and high intelligence may also have been rated as less dependent than they really are.

TABLE 2 *Factor Loadings of Items from Factor Analysis of Parents' Childrearing Values (Parents of Boys)*

	Mothers (N = 119)			Fathers (N = 106)[a]		
	Factors			Factors		
Item	I	II	III	II	I	III
1. doing well in competitive games	.78*	.06	—.02	.74*	.11	.08
2. being skillful at athletic activities	.70*	—.03	—.03	.79*	.06	.13
3. being a leader with other children	.59*	.08	.03	.50*	.15	.43*
4. standing up for his own rights with other children	.56*	.12	.27	.45*	.25	.28
5. being friendly with other children	.48*	.07	.03	.58*	—.10	.38
6. being obedient to parents	.36	—.10	.18	.25	—.20	.52*
7. taking pride in doing things well	.31	.11	.64*	.33	.44*	.09
8. trying to *improve* his performance at skills he has learned	.23	.21	.61*	.32	.40*	.13
9. sticking with a task within his range of ability until he completes it	.14	.16	.59*	.15	.42*	.20
10. controlling his emotions and impulses	—.14	.08	.57*	.31	.14	.58*
11. being able to make his own decisions	.01	.30	.41*	.04	.43*	.40*
12. being resourceful	.09	.69*	.15	.12	.65*	.11
13. being self-reliant	.06	.59*	.32	.11	.61*	.44*
14. being explorative and curious	—.13	.58*	.09	.02	.62*	.11
15. being creative	.12	.52*	—.06	.10	.66*	.05
16. trying new things on his own	.02	.51*	.34	.25	.67*	.08
17. being able to carry out reasonably difficult tasks on his own	—.07	.46*	.29	.12	.70*	.17
18. thinking of things to do without asking for suggestions	.14	.36	.25	.28	.50*	.15
19. doing his best at tasks	.03	.30	.30	—.02	.21	.60*
20. being stubborn	.08	.12	.09	.30	.20	.04

* indicates loadings of .40 or higher.

[a] The three father factors are presented out of order (i.e., II, I, III) to facilitate comparisons with the similar factors obtained for mothers.

It is apparent, first, that the factors obtained for mothers (M) and fathers (F) correspond quite closely, though the order of the factors was slightly different. The following congruence coefficients were obtained between factors: MI and FII = .91, MII and FI = .95, MIII and FIII = .68.

An examination of the item loadings for each factor reveals that the factors are meaningful, and that the independence items are primarily represented on one factor (MII and FI), while the items intended to represent achievement characteristics are divided between the other two factors.

Regarding the independence items, all items loading above .40 on factor MII have to do either with independence or with curiosity or creativity. The item with the highest loading is "being resourceful." Only two items which apparently have to do with independence are more highly loaded on other factors for mothers. "Standing up for his own rights with other children" (which was also not grouped with the independence-dependence items by the teachers) is loaded most highly on factor *MI*, a factor which appears to be defined by activities involving social assertiveness. "Being able to make his own decisions" has a slightly higher loading on factor *MIII* than on factor *MII*. Hence, *for mothers, independence values appear to be essentially orthogonal to achievement values.* Almost the same pattern emerges for fathers with respect to the loadings of the independence items on factor *FI*. However, factor *FI* is not so purely an independence factor as the comparable factor for mothers (*MII*), since factor *FI* also includes loadings from several achievement items (e.g., "taking pride in doing things well," and "trying to improve his performance at things he has learned").

To some extent, therefore, for both parents, but especially for mothers, it appears that *values* for achievement and independence do not necessarily go together. Apparently parents can hold a high value for both kinds of behavior, for neither, or for one and not the other. Although such values do not necessarily have to be reflected in the parent's behavior toward the child, it seems likely that they would have some influence on parental childrearing practices. These results lend further support, therefore, to the notion that it is important to study the effects of achievement training independently of the effects of independence training.

A second finding of interest is the separation of the "achievement" items into different factors. One of these factors (*MI* and *FII*) appears to represent what might be called "assertive achievement." The two highest loadings on this factor are "doing well in competitive games" and "being skillful at athletic activities." The other factor (*MIII* and *FIII*), on which there is the least agreement between mothers and fathers, may be tentatively characterized as "conscientious" or "responsible achievement." The highest loading item on *MIII* is "taking pride in doing things well." The highest loading item on *FIII* is "doing his best at tasks." The item "controlling his emotions and impulses" loads highly on both *MIII* and *FIII*.

The separation of the achievement items into different factors may indicate a distinction in the mind of the parent between individual or autonomous achievement and achievement involving social comparison.[70] These results suggest that it is possible for a parent to emphasize one kind of achievement behavior and not another, such as doing well in competitive games but not on tasks which call for individual performance in isolation,

---

[70] Cf. Veroff, Chap. 3.

or vice versa. For example, many academically oriented parents explicitly downgrade the importance of competitive sports as compared with intellectual pursuits while others emphasize the opposite values.[71] These results call into question the assumption underlying much research on achievement motivation that such motivation is general across situations. It should be noted that researchers at the Fels Institute working on achievement behavior typically have not made such an assumption.[72]

The next relationships of interest are those between parental values and the achievement-related motives. None of the parental value scores are significantly related to achievement motive scores. This may be due in part to the fact that the areas of achievement that are separated in the factors are combined in the Need for Achievement score. A scoring system that distinguishes between "assertive" achievement and "conscientious" achievement may be necessary in order to obtain scores related to parental value factors.

Test anxiety scores are related to two maternal values items: "being skillful at athletic activities" from factor MI ($r=.16$, $N=119$, $p<.10$) and "trying new things on his own" from factor MII ($r=.23$, $N=119$, $p<.05$). That is, the higher the child's test anxiety, the more important the mother felt it was for the child to possess these characteristics. Test anxiety is also related to the following paternal values items: "being explorative and curious" from factor FI ($r=.19$, $N=106$, $p<.10$), "taking pride in doing things well" from factor FI ($r=.27$, $N=106$, $p<.01$), and "standing up for his own rights with other children" from factor FII ($r=.19$, $N=106$, $p<.10$). In other words, the more important these qualities of independence, assertiveness, or pride in accomplishment were to the parents, the higher was the test anxiety of their sons. The direction of causality is not clear, however. These parental values may have preceded and caused the child's high test anxiety, or alternatively they may represent a dissatisfied reaction to the child's dependence and lack of assertiveness.

Achievement-Related Motives and Parental Reactions to Success and Failure

There are some weak but interesting relationships between the achievement-related motives and the reactions of mothers and fathers to their

[71] Cf. J. Coleman, *The Adolescent Society* (New York: Free Press, 1961).
[72] Cf. V. J. Crandall, "Achievement," in H. W. Stevenson (ed.), *Child Psychology* (The 62nd Yearbook of the National Society for the Study of Education Part 1 [Chicago: University of Chicago Press, 1963]), 416–459.

sons' successes and failures. High Need for Achievement is associated with *infrequent* maternal use of kissing or hugging in response to success ($r=.17$, $N=114$, $p<.10$), frequent maternal use of "telling him he should be very proud of himself" in response to success ($r=-.17$, $N=115$, $p<.10$), frequent maternal use of "encourage him to keep trying" in response to failure ($r=-.20$, $N=116$, $p<.05$), and *infrequent* paternal use of "getting angry and shouting at him" in response to failure ($r=.17$, $N=100$, $p<.10$).

High test anxiety is associated with frequent maternal use of the following reactions to success: "tell him how much you love him" ($r=-.16$, $N=114$, $p<.10$), "show him you expected it of him" ($r=-.17$, $N=116$, $p<.10$), and "show him how he could have done better" ($r=-.16$, $N=116$, $p<.10$). High anxiety is also associated with frequent maternal use of the following reaction to failure: "encourage him to keep trying" ($r=-.17$, $N=116$, $p<.10$). The only paternal reaction related to high test anxiety was the frequent use of "tell him how much you love him" in response to success ($r=-.17$, $N=101$, $p<.10$).

All of the maternal and paternal reactions to success and failure that are related to high Need for Achievement seem to make sense except for the infrequent maternal response to success: "kiss or hug him to show how pleased you are." Winterbottom predicted, and found, the opposite relationship. It may be quite important, however, that many of her subjects were 8 and 9 years old, while most of the subjects in the present study were 10 and 11 years old. A hug for achievement at the age of 8 may produce pride in accomplishment; at 10 it may encourage immaturity. This result indicates the need to include the age of the child in any hypothesis about the effect of a specific reward on the development of a motivational disposition.

The relationships between parental reactions and test anxiety are not as easy to interpret, but they raise some provocative possibilities. Both mothers and fathers report that they frequently respond to the successful behavior of the high test anxiety child by telling him how much they love him. Bartlett and Smith[73] introduced this item into a list of maternal reactions to success in their study with the specific prediction that high test anxiety would be related to love contingent upon success. In their study this item was endorsed significantly more often by mothers of sons with low Need for Achievement than by mothers of sons with high Need for Achievement, but it was not significantly related to test anxiety. The

---

[73] *Op. cit.*

possibility that "conditional love" fosters the development of high test anxiety and/or low Need for Achievement warrants further investigation. The frequent maternal use of "show him how he could have done better" in reaction to the child's success might produce high test anxiety by giving the child a sense of failure after each accomplishment, thereby producing a tendency to avoid achievement activities and the unpleasant evaluation which accompanies them.

Achievement-Related Motives and Parental
Ratings of the Child's Characteristics

On the childrearing questionnaire parents also rated their children on the extent to which they possessed each quality listed. In general the relationships between Need for Achievement and parental ratings of their children are positive as expected, and those for test anxiety are negative as expected.

There were significant positive relations (r between .20 and .30, $N = 118$–119, $p < .05$) between Need for Achievement and maternal ratings of "being obedient to parents," "being skillful at athletic activities," "doing well in competitive games," and "trying to improve his performance at various skills he has learned." Only one maternal rating was negatively related to Need for Achievement, namely, "being explorative and curious" ($r = -.20$, $N = 119$, $p < .05$). All of the significant relationships (r between .20 and .30, $N = 105$–106, $p < .05$) between paternal ratings and Need for Achievement were positive: "doing his best at tasks," "being skillful at athletic activities," "doing well in competitive games," and "standing up for his own rights with other children."

In other words, mothers and fathers of children with high achievement motivation tend to see their sons as more competitive and assertive, more achievement-oriented, and more obedient than parents of boys with low Need for Achievement scores. In only one respect, "being explorative and curious," which might be considered a kind of independence behavior, did mothers of boys with high Need for Achievement give their sons lower ratings than mothers of boys with low Need for Achievement. These results are consistent with the findings of Winterbottom[74] and Rosen and D'Andrade[75] showing that parents of children with strong achievement motivation have a more favorable view of their sons' competence than parents of children with weak achievement motivation.

All significant relationships between parental ratings and test anxiety

---

[74] *Op. cit.*
[75] *Op. cit.*

were negative. Mothers gave lower ratings to sons with high test anxiety on the items "being obedient to parents" ($r=-.17$, $N=119$, $p<.05$), and "doing his best at tasks" ($r=-.16$, $N=118$, $p<.10$). Fathers gave lower ratings to sons with high test anxiety on the items "being self-reliant" ($r=-.25$, $N=106$, $p<.01$) and "controlling his emotions and impulses" ($r=-.26$, $N=106$, $p<.01$). It appears that parents of children with high test anxiety have a somewhat less favorable view of their children's characteristics, especially with reference to independence, obedience, and control of emotions.

Achievement-Related Motives and Self Concept

The relationship of Need for Achievement and test anxiety scores to actual and ideal self concept scores was examined. There were no significant correlations between achievement motivation and items on the actual self concept list. However, test anxiety was significantly related to several of the actual self items: Subjects with high test anxiety thought of themselves as more "nervous" ($r=.19$, $N=139$, $p<.05$) and more "lazy" ($r=.16$, $N=140$, $p<.10$) and as less "intelligent" ($r=-.20$, $N=140$, $p<.05$) and less "competent" ($r=-.31$, $N=139$, $p<.01$).

In contrast, there were no significant correlations between test anxiety and the items on the ideal self concept list. However, Need for Achievement scores were significantly related to two of the ideal self items. The higher the Need for Achievement, the higher the ideal ratings of "intelligent" ($r=.17$, $N=140$, $p<.05$) and "competent" ($r=.17$, $N=140$, $p<.05$).

These results are consistent with the expectation that subjects with high test anxiety would have a relatively low opinion of themselves, and with the expectation that the subjects with high Need for Achievement should have higher aspirations for how competent they would like to be. Ideal-actual discrepancy scores were obtained for each item and summed, disregarding the direction of the difference, to obtain a single index of ideal-actual discrepancy. These discrepancy scores were correlated $-.08$ with Need for Achievement ($n.s.$), .16 for test anxiety ($N=134$, $p<.10$), and $-.17$ for defensiveness ($N=134$, $p<.05$). These results are consistent with prior research on test anxiety indicating that subjects with high test anxiety tend to have lower self-esteem (i.e., a larger ideal-actual discrepancy). It is interesting to note the significant negative relationship between the ideal-actual discrepancy and defensiveness. This means that the discrepancy was smaller the higher the defensiveness—a finding consistent with the notion of defensiveness as unwillingness to admit unpleasant matters.

TABLE 3 *Relationship of Personality Variables to Reading Performance*

Personality Variable	Iowa[a] Reading Score		Reading[b] Grade		SRA[c] % Correct	
	r	N	r	N	r	N
Need for Achievement	—.07	143	.10	143	.08	132
Test Anxiety (TASC)	—.12	143	—.18*	143	—.06	132
Defensiveness	—.24**	143	—.17*	143	—.06	132
IQ	.66**	137	.55**	141	.09	128

* $p < .05$ two-tailed
** $p < .01$ two-tailed

[a] The "grade equivalent" score for reading from the Iowa Tests of Basic Skills.
[b] The reading grade assigned by the teacher for the standard classroom reading curriculum.
[c] The per cent of questions answered correctly on the first 16 "power builder" exercises from the SRA Reading Labs.

Achievement-Related Motives and Reading Performance

Table 3 presents the relationships between several personality variables and three different measures of reading performance. The first is an "achievement" test—the reading score from the Iowa Tests of Basic Skills; the second is the grade the teacher assigned at the end of the year for the regular school reading program; the third is the per cent of correct answers on the first sixteen "power builder" exercises of the SRA Reading Labs.

Need for Achievement scores are not significantly related to any of the indexes of reading performance, contrary to the expectation of a positive relationship. Relationships between test anxiety and reading performance are negative, as expected, but significant only in relation to the grade assigned by the teacher ($r = -.18$, $N = 143$, $p < .05$). Defensiveness is also negatively related to reading performance—significantly so in relation to the Iowa test ($r = -.24$, $N = 143$, $p < .01$) and in relation to the teacher's reading grade ($r = -.17$, $N = 143$, $p < .05$). IQ is positively related to reading performance, and the relationship is significant for the Iowa test and for the teacher's reading grade but not for SRA scores (see Table 3). Following Sarason, Hill, and Zimbardo,[76] the correlation between test anxiety and the teacher's reading grade was computed with defensiveness partialed out. The resulting partial correlation was $-.27$ ($N = 143$, $p < .01$). These results concerning the relationship between test anxiety and reading performance closely parallel those of Sarason, Hill, and Zimbardo.[77]

The absence of a significant relationship between test anxiety and SRA

---

[76] *Op. cit.*
[77] *Ibid.*

scores is suggestive, but not definitive. It was expected that the debilitating effects of anxiety on reading performance might be reduced with the self-directed reading materials because they substitute self-evaluation of performance for teacher evaluation. The low correlation between test anxiety and SRA performance ($r = -.06$) is, therefore, in the expected direction, but that correlation is not significantly smaller than the correlation between test anxiety and the teacher-assigned reading grade. Further research will be necessary to determine whether or not the programed reading materials effectively reduce the detrimental effects of test anxiety. It will be noted that the relationship between IQ and SRA performance is also minimal ($r = .09$). One reason for these low correlations may be that there is little variance in the SRA reading scores. The SRA exercises are so constructed that very few mistakes are made by any of the children.

One other variable is related in a meaningful way to the SRA scores, however, and that is the teacher-rating index of independence behavior ($r = .23$, $N = 128$, $p < .01$). Apparently those children who displayed the greatest degree of independence behavior in general also performed most successfully on the self-directed reading materials which require the child to teach himself. Since children high in test anxiety tend to be low in independence, the SRA materials may have conflicting characteristics from the point of view of the anxious child. As compared with the standard reading curriculum, the SRA materials may reduce anxiety because of the relatively easy self-administered tests and the self-evaluation, but they may also raise anxiety because the child is put on his own in doing the work and is encouraged to be independent.

Achievement-Related Motives and Goal Setting

A goal discrepancy score (i.e., level of aspiration minus past performance) was obtained for each pair of puzzles, namely, $LA_2 - P_1$, $LA_3 - P_2$, $LA_4 - P_3$, $LA_5 - P_4$, and these goal discrepancy scores were related to Need for Achievement and test anxiety. It should be noted that *the goal discrepancy score controls for differences in aptitude* since it is based not on the absolute level of a person's performance but on the distance of his goal from his performance. Thus, a person who connected 30 numbers and aspired to 35 on the next trial receives the same goal discrepancy score as a person who connected only 15 numbers and aspired to 20.

The Atkinson theory of achievement-related motives and risk taking[78] states that subjects with motivation for success (M_S) greater than motiva-

[78] J. W. Atkinson, "Motivational Determinants of Risk-Taking Behavior," *Psychological Review*, 64 (1957), 359–372.

tion to avoid failure (M_{AF}) will set goals of intermediate difficulty, while subjects with $M_{AF} > M_S$ will set extremely easy or extremely difficult goals. No direct measure of the perceived difficulty of the task was obtained in the present study. Therefore, following Raynor and Smith,[79] it was assumed that a goal of intermediate difficulty is represented by a level of aspiration somewhat above past performance while an easy goal is one that is below past performance and a difficult goal is one considerably above past performance. For purposes of data analysis subjects whose motive scores were above the median in Need for Achievement and below the median in test anxiety were regarded as the $M_S > M_{AF}$ group; subjects with low Need for Achievement and high test anxiety were regarded as the $M_{AF} > M_S$ group.

If the $M_{AF} > M_S$ group is expected to prefer either very easy or very difficult tasks, it follows that the variance of their goal dicrepancy scores should be considerably greater than that of the $M_S > M_{AF}$ group whose goals should more closely approximate past performance. It would also be expected that the mean of the goal discrepancy scores for the $M_S > M_{AF}$ group would be a relatively small positive discrepancy representing goals somewhat above past performance rather than greatly above or below past performance. No clear expectation can be stated regarding the mean of the goal discrepancy scores of the $M_{AF} > M_S$ group. Since some high positive scores and some high negative scores are expected in that group; the mean could be lower, higher, or the same as the mean for the $M_S > M_{AF}$ group.

Table 4 presents the relationships between the goal discrepancy scores of the two motivation subgroups. The expected relationships are present for both the 4th and 5th grade boys. The variance of the goal discrepancy scores is greater for the $M_{AF} > M_S$ group than for the $M_S > M_{AF}$ group in every instance. The largest differences between the two groups occur in the first few puzzles, then the size of differences diminishes, presumably because the reality determinants of the task are becoming so clear that little room is left for motivational effects on goal setting. That is, by the time the subject reaches the fifth puzzle, he can predict within a few points what his next performance will be and this knowledge apparently reduces the tendency to set extreme goals. The rapidity with which the differences between the two groups diminish suggests that for most activities in which performance can come to be predicted, motivational factors will not have a sustained influence on goal setting. That is to say, the "unrealistic" aspirations of the $M_{AF} > M_S$ group probably do not characterize a good portion of their goal-setting behavior, but only that portion concerning activities

---

[79] *Op. cit.*

TABLE 4 *Comparison of Goal Discrepancy (GlDs) Scores of $M_{AF} > M_S$ and $M_S > M_{AF}$ Subgroups*

Subjects	GlDs	Sub-group[a]	Mean	Variance	F* (Var.₁/Var.₂)	p (2-tailed)
4th Grade Boys	1	$M_{AF} > M_S$	17.66	537.45	2.62	.05
		$M_S > M_{AF}$	7.82	205.33		
	2	$M_{AF} > M_S$	13.38	521.35	2.59	.05
		$M_S > M_{AF}$	6.27	201.47		
	3	$M_{AF} > M_S$	8.67	409.22	2.69	.05
		$M_S > M_{AF}$	5.09	151.99		
	4	$M_{AF} > M_S$	7.89	316.21	1.62	n.s.
		$M_S > M_{AF}$	5.82	195.42		
5th Grade Boys	1	$M_{AF} > M_S$	7.20	73.76	4.13	.01
		$M_S > M_{AF}$	4.44	17.87		
	2	$M_{AF} > M_S$	4.73	61.40	1.95	n.s.
		$M_S > M_{AF}$	3.00	31.53		
	3	$M_{AF} > M_S$	.93	41.40	1.35	n.s.
		$M_S > M_{AF}$	3.18	30.73		
	4	$M_{AF} > M_S$	2.73	39.13	1.03	n.s.
		$M_S > M_{AF}$	.82	38.15		

* df for 4th grade boys = 17/21; df for 5th grade boys = 14/16.

[a] $M_{AF} > M_S$ or motive to avoid failure greater than motive to approach success = high in test anxiety (above the median) and low in Need for Achievement (below the median); $M_S > M_{AF}$ = high in Need for Achievement and low in test anxiety.

in which there is considerable ambiguity concerning the performance level they will be able to attain.

The results in Table 4 also show that, as expected, the mean of the goal discrepancy scores nearly always tends to be a more moderate positive discrepancy for the $M_S > M_{AF}$ group than for the $M_{AF} > M_S$ group. These data, therefore, are consistent with the predictions derived from Atkinson's theory and are closely parallel to results obtained by Raynor and Smith[80] using a similar task under both "relaxed" and "achievement-oriented" conditions with college males as subjects.

A more complete understanding of these results is provided by an analysis of the relationship of goal setting to Need for Achievement (M_S) alone, test anxiety (M_{AF}) alone, and defensiveness. Table 5 shows that the variances of the goal discrepancy scores are smaller for subjects high in Need for Achievement (above the median) than for subjects low in Need for Achievement (below the median). Following Atkinson's theory this result would be expected if one makes the additional assumption that on

---

[80] *Ibid.*

TABLE 5 *Comparison of Goal Discrepancy (GIDs) Scores of Subjects High and Low in Need for Achievement*

Subjects	GIDs	Sub-group[a]	Mean	Variance	F* (Var.$_2$/Var.$_1$)	p (2-tailed)
4th Grade Boys	1	High Ach.	8.28	167.20	2.03	.05
		Low Ach.	11.51	339.82		
	2	High Ach.	4.28	111.20	2.65	.01
		Low Ach.	8.62	294.72		
	3	High Ach.	2.71	91.51	2.52	.01
		Low Ach.	5.41	230.57		
	4	High Ach.	3.13	110.55	1.68	n.s.
		Low Ach.	3.86	185.63		
5th Grade Boys	1	High Ach.	4.68	43.86	3.03	.01
		Low Ach.	7.32	132.79		
	2	High Ach.	2.17	53.94	3.05	.01
		Low Ach.	6.75	164.76		
	3	High Ach.	2.28	32.61	3.68	.005
		Low Ach.	3.00	120.07		
	4	High Ach.	1.69	38.01	2.59	.025
		Low Ach.	4.04	98.46		

* df for 4th grade boys = 36/45; df for 5th grade boys = 27/28.

[a] High Ach. = above the median in Need for Achievement;
Low Ach. = below the median.

the average subjects high in Need for Achievement have $M_S > M_{AF}$, while subjects low in Need for Achievement have $M_{AF} > M_S$.

A comparison of subjects high and low in test anxiety, in Table 6, reveals mixed results. Fourth-grade boys behave in the expected manner, with those high in test anxiety having goal discrepancy scores with higher variances than those low in test anxiety. Quite unexpectedly, however, the reverse pattern occurs for 5th grade boys, with those low in test anxiety having goal discrepancy scores with larger variances. These findings explain the relatively weak results obtained for 5th grade boys in the lower half of Table 4 in which the differences, though in the expected direction, are not significant for the last three goal discrepancies. Apparently Need for Achievement scores are primarily responsible for the fact that the results are in the predicted direction for 5th grade boys in Table 4.

The key to the reversal in the role played by test anxiety from the 4th to the 5th grade is provided by an analysis of the influence of defensiveness on goal setting. Table 7 shows that for the 4th grade boys there is a highly significant tendency for subjects low in defensiveness to have goal discrepancy scores with a higher variance than subjects high in defensiveness, while the reverse is true for 5th grade boys. In other words, for 4th

TABLE 6 *Comparison of Goal Discrepancy (GlDs) Scores of Subjects High and Low in Test Anxiety*

Subjects	GlDs	Sub-group[a]	Mean	Variance	F* (Var./Var.)	p (2-tailed)
4th Grade Boys	1	High Anx. Low Anx.	12.55 6.83	325.34 149.65	2.17	.05
	2	High Anx. Low Anx.	7.14 5.27	264.98 126.93	2.09	.05
	3	High Anx. Low Anx.	4.02 3.80	206.50 102.79	2.01	.05
	4	High Anx. Low Anx.	3.76 3.15	159.75 127.98	1.25	n.s.
5th Grade Boys	1	High Anx. Low Anx.	6.22 5.79	76.99 102.16	1.33	n.s.
	2	High Anx. Low Anx.	3.07 5.63	74.59 145.63	1.95	.10
	3	High Anx. Low Anx.	.96 4.13	37.44 105.38	2.81	.025
	4	High Anx. Low Anx.	2.81 2.87	37.41 97.58	2.61	.025

* df for 4th grade boys = 41/40; df for 5th grade boys = 29/26.

[a] High Anx. = above the median in scores on the Test Anxiety Scale for Children;
Low Anx. = below the median.

grade boys unrealistic goal setting (i.e., large positive or large negative goal discrepancies) is associated with high test anxiety and low defensiveness, but for 5th grade boys unrealistic goal setting is associated with low test anxiety and high defensiveness. The results suggest that unrealism is associated either with high anxiety or with high defensiveness, depending on a subject's age, with defensiveness becoming more important as the children grow older. It is relevant to note that there are no differences between the means of the test anxiety scores for the 4th graders ($Mean = 9.8$, $SD = 5.96$) and the 5th graders ($Mean = 10.3$, $SD = 4.40$), or of the defensiveness scores for the 4th graders ($Mean = 13.2$, $SD = 5.61$) and the 5th graders ($Mean = 13.1$, $SD = 5.17$).

Another result that calls attention to changes which occur with age is that the goal-setting behavior of the 5th grade boys is considerably more realistic than that of the 4th graders. For example, the variance of the first goal discrepancy scores equals 249.74 for all 4th grade boys and only 91.71 for all 5th grade boys ($F = 2.72$, $df = 82/55$, $p < .005$). Apparently one year makes a considerable difference in the ability to appraise a task realistically and accurately estimate one's performance.

135

TABLE 7   *Comparison of Goal Discrepancy (GlDs) Scores of Subjects High and Low in Defensiveness*

Subjects	GlDs	Sub-group[a]	Mean	Variance	F* (Var./Var.)	p (2-tailed)
4th Grade Boys	1	High Def.	5.14	83.93	4.41	.001
		Low Def.	14.41	370.00		
	2	High Def.	2.67	46.89	6.95	.001
		Low Def.	9.85	325.98		
	3	High Def.	1.38	38.57	6.78	.001
		Low Def.	6.51	261.52		
	4	High Def.	1.57	38.34	6.39	.001
		Low Def.	5.39	245.17		
5th Grade Boys	1	High Def.	7.19	126.77	2.26	.05
		Low Def.	4.97	55.97		
	2	High Def.	5.81	191.78	4.80	.005
		Low Def.	3.17	39.94		
	3	High Def.	4.04	126.41	4.73	.005
		Low Def.	1.37	26.70		
	4	High Def.	4.22	103.88	3.01	.01
		Low Def.	1.60	34.51		

* df for 4th grade boys = 40/41; df for 5th grade boys = 26/29.

[a] High Def. = above the median in scores on the Defensiveness Scale for Children;
Low Def. = below the median.

DISCUSSION

Childrearing Practices and the Development of Achievement-Related Motives

One finding basic to the interpretation of the other results bears on the relationship of achievement training to independence training. Although McClelland[81] has assumed that the two types of training tend to go together, there is increasing evidence that they are independent. In the present study a factor analysis of parental childrearing values (i.e., the qualities a parent feels it is important for his child to have) reveals that values for achievement are essentially orthogonal to values for independence for mothers, and the two kinds of values are only modestly related for fathers. These results provide further evidence that the effects of achievement training and independence training should be studied separately.

Relationships between children's achievement motivation and age of demands for both independence and achievement have been reported in earlier studies, with recent studies placing greater emphasis on the role of specific demands for achievement. The lack of a significant relationship

[81] *The Achieving Society.*

in the present study between reported age of independence training and Need for Achievement scores of 4th and 5th grade boys is consistent with a minimizing of the role of independence training in the development of achievement motivation. It may be significant in this connection that the mothers of boys with high Need for Achievement rated their sons as good at athletic activities and competitive games (assertive achievement) but relatively lacking in explorativeness and curiosity (independence).

If early stress on independence does contribute to the development of Need for Achievement, it may be a necessary but not sufficient condition. For example, Child, Storm, and Veroff tentatively conclude that "training in self-reliance may somewhat discourage preoccupation with thoughts of achievement unless there is added to it specific training in achievement."[82] That is, it may be necessary for the parent to say "Do it well" in addition to saying "Do it on your own."

However, early "caretaking" demands reported by mothers are associated with high Need for Achievement in the present study. Since the caretaking items employed are highly similar to those used by McClelland,[83] the present findings are in clear contrast to those of McClelland who argued that early emphasis on caretaking skills tends to discourage the development of achievement motivation. It seems likely that the notion of "caretaking" needs reexamination, since the same behaviors (e.g., "learning to dress himself") can represent early *mastery* training as well as an attempt on the part of the mother to rid herself of responsibility.

The causal direction of the relationship between age of demands and motivational development is not clear, however, since in the present research, as in some previous studies, there is a tendency ($p < .10$) for early demands to be made of children with higher intelligence. Children who display intelligence and competence at an early age probably *elicit* earlier demands for independence and mastery from their parents. As Bell[84] has pointed out, studies of parent-child interaction tend to emphasize the influence of the parent on the child and ignore the possibility of the influence of the child on the parent. The important factor in the development of achievement motivation may be parental sensitivity to the child's current stage of development, and the setting of demands that are challenging rather than too easy or too difficult.

Parental ratings of their sons' characteristics are consistent with earlier findings that parents of sons with high Need for Achievement regard their

---

82 *Op. cit.*, 486.
83 *The Achieving Society.*
84 R. Q. Bell, "A Reinterpretation of the Direction of Effects in Studies of Socialization," *Psychological Review*, 75 (1968), 81–95.

sons as more competent than parents of sons with low Need for Achievement. In the present study parents of children with high achievement motivation tend to see their sons as more competitive and assertive, more achievement-oriented, and more obedient. The "obedience" finding may indicate that these children are more responsive to adult demands and have incorporated adult values to a greater extent than children with low Need for Achievement.

Parental reactions to the child's success and failure were only weakly related to boys' Need for Achievement scores, but mothers of boys with high Need for Achievement did more often respond to their sons' failures with "encourage him to keep trying" than mothers of sons with low Need for Achievement. This reaction to failure, which, incidentally also tended to be characteristic of mothers of children with high test anxiety, may indicate parental stress on the importance of doing well. For mothers of children with high Need for Achievement, however, success tends to be accompanied by "telling him he should be very proud of himself" while for children with high test anxiety success is often accompanied by the maternal reaction "show him how he could have done better." The latter reaction may give the child the feeling that "No matter how well I do, I'll never be able to please them."

The results also provide some information about factors associated with the development of high test anxiety. Although age of childrearing demands was not associated with test anxiety in the present study, there was a relationship between later independence and caretaking demands and high self ratings by the boys of "nervous"—a finding that is consistent with the expectation that later demands for independence would be associated with higher anxiety about achievement activities. There is also a tendency in the present study for later demands to be associated with high teacher ratings of the boys' dependent behavior in the classroom.

An interesting finding emerged from the correlations between parental values items and the boys' test anxiety scores. Parents of boys with high test anxiety indicated a greater value for independence, assertiveness, and pride in accomplishment than parents of boys with low test anxiety.

It is possible that these parents are simply giving "socially desirable" answers to the values items, but it seems more likely that the high test anxiety children, by the age of 10 and 11, have displayed dependent behavior, lack of assertiveness, and avoidance of achievement situations[85] and that their parents have reacted to these characteristics by wishing their sons were different in these respects.

---

[85] Cf. Feld, *op. cit.*

Parental ratings of their sons' present characteristics are consistent with this interpretation. The parents of boys with high test anxiety indicated a less favorable view of their son's independence, achievement, obedience, and control of emotions than parents of boys with low test anxiety.

Another finding of relevance comes from mothers' reports of their reactions to their sons' grades. The childrearing questionnaire permitted open-ended answers to the following sequence of questions: "What kind of grades, on the average, would you like your child to try for? Have you communicated your expectations concerning grades to your child? If so, how? What do you do if your child gets a good grade? What do you do if your child gets a bad grade?" Since the answers to these questions were often related, they were treated as a sequential unit and coded for the presence of achievement-oriented statements. These were defined as any explicit reference to standards of excellence (e.g., encouraging the child to do his best, perform well, strive for high grades, improve his grades, or aim for a long-term achievement goal). Two scorers agreed on 86 per cent of the coding decisions. The results indicate a highly significant difference between mothers of boys with high and low test anxiety. Mothers of boys with high test anxiety report making *more* achievement-oriented statements in response to their sons' grades than mothers of boys with low test anxiety ($t = 3.53$, $N = 129$, $p < .002$). This finding indicates that mothers of boys with high anxiety not only report a relatively low opinion of their competence, but they also report more attempts to motivate the child to achieve. Again, it is not possible in this study to determine whether these mothers behaved in this manner when their sons were younger, or whether they began to try to motivate the child to do well only after he had developed a stable pattern of behavior associated with high test anxiety.

Relationships between Achievement-Related Motives and other Personality Variables

Need for Achievement scores are not related to "actual self" items on the self concept measure, but they are related to two "ideal self" items: intelligence and competence. The higher the Need for Achievement, the higher the *ideal* self-rating of these two terms. Apparently boys with high Need for Achievement value competence highly. The attractiveness of success is probably great for such persons and they may feel that they could attain their desired goals more effectively if they possessed greater ability.

Whereas Need for Achievement scores are positively related to the *ideal* self items "intelligent" and "competent," test anxiety scores are negatively related to the *actual* self items "intelligent" and "competent." The greater the test anxiety, the less intelligent and competent the boys thought they

TABLE 8 *Intercorrelations Between Personality Variables and Intelligence*

	Test Anxiety		Defensiveness[a]		IQ[b]	
	r	N	r	N	r	N
Need for Achievement	—.09	148	.16*	148	.00	141
Test Anxiety (TASC)			—.40**	148	—.21**	141
Defensiveness					—.12	141

* $p < .10$
** $p < .01$

[a] Defensiveness scores include "lie" scale items (cf. Sarason, Hill, and Zimbardo, *op. cit.*).
[b] Kuhlmann-Anderson IQ.

were, and the more "lazy" and "nervous" they thought they were. There was also a tendency ($p < .10$) for subjects with high test anxiety to have greater ideal-actual discrepancy scores than subjects with low test anxiety. These findings support the theory that the highly anxious child develops a negative self-image, and suggest that the self-image is negative particularly with respect to achievement-relevant characteristics.

Defensiveness scores were also related to ideal-actual discrepancy scores, with higher defensiveness being associated with lower discrepancies. The tendency to deny unpleasant or unacceptable matters which the defensiveness scale was intended to measure is apparently reflected in a tendency not to find fault with one's self in the sense of seeing one's actual self as relatively close to one's ideal self.

The intercorrelations between test anxiety, Need for Achievement, defensiveness, and intelligence are presented in Table 8. There is a small negative correlation between Need for Achievement and test anxiety ($r = -.09$) indicating that the two personality dispositions, as assessed by these techniques, are essentially independent rather than opposite ends of the same continuum. It is not entirely clear, however, how a set of child-rearing practices could produce strong motivation to approach success and strong motivation to avoid failure at the same time. It is not possible, for example, for parents to have both a favorable and an unfavorable view of a child's competence. On the other hand, it is possible to reward success and punish failure, thereby making success desirable and failure undesirable, and it is possible for one parent to encourage achievement and to make achievement related activities interesting and rewarding while the other parent is overly critical and causes the child to turn away from such activities. It is also apparently possible for parents to make early demands for achievement (which may foster the development of achievement motivation) and late demands for independence (which may contribute toward

140

the development of anxiety about failure). Further clarification of the childrearing determinants of each motive may be necessary before it is possible fully to understand how the two motives can be so minimally correlated.

Motivation and Classroom Behavior

There are no significant relationships between Need for Achievement and various measures of reading proficiency. However, test anxiety is negatively related to the reading grade assigned by the teacher, and this relationship is strengthened when defensiveness scores are partialed out, as was the case in the study by Sarason, Hill, and Zimbardo.[86]

There is the provocative possibility in the present data that test anxiety is less debilitating for performance with self-directed reading materials than for a standard classroom reading program. (The difference between the two correlations suggests this possibility, but the difference is not significant.) This interpretation is consistent with the fact that teacher evaluation of performance is greatly played down with the programed reading materials and the reduced threat of evaluation should reduce the detrimental effects of anxiety in reading performance. The results also indicate, however, that subjects rated as most independent by teachers were the ones who performed best on the programed reading materials (which require independence performance). Since test anxiety is negatively correlated with teacher ratings of independence, the two properties of the programed materials—reduced teacher evaluation and independent performance—may counteract each other in determining the performance of subjects with high test anxiety. Another property of the materials is that they are constructed so as to insure that the child will make few errors. This feature should also reduce anxiety about failure, but by the same token, the materials may not be sufficiently challenging for subjects high in achievement motivation.

Goal-Setting Behavior

The obtained relationship between achievement-related motives and goal setting confirms the prediction derived from Atkinson's theory[87] of risk-taking behavior that subjects with $M_S > M_{AF}$ will tend to set goals of intermediate difficulty, and that subjects with $M_{AF} > M_S$ will tend to set either extremely difficult or extremely easy goals. (Since no direct measure of the perceived difficulty of the task was obtained in the present study, the re-

---

[86] *Op. cit.*
[87] "Motivational Determinants."

sults cannot be said to confirm or disconfirm that aspect of the Atkinson theory which states that the goals of the $M_S > M_{AF}$ group should cluster around a difficulty level defined by a subjective probability of success of .5. It seems reasonable to assume that the small positive goal discrepancies characteristic of the $M_S > M_{AF}$ group represent intermediate probabilities of success, but it is impossible from these data to say whether they are "intermediate" in the sense of .5, .7, or .3.) The similarity of these results to those obtained with college students by Raynor and Smith[88] gives further support to the general expectation that persons with $M_S > M_{AF}$ tend to select "realistic" goals and that persons with $M_{AF} > M_S$ tend to select "unrealistic" goals.

The fact that the predicted relationship was weaker in the 5th grade than in the 4th grade turned out to be due to the association of unrealistic goal setting with *defensiveness* rather than anxiety in the 5th grade. The notion of adopting a very high or a very low level of aspiration as an habitual defense against anxiety is certainly plausible. In this connection there is no particular indication that the "unrealistic" goals of the $M_{AF} > M_S$ group are produced by situational threat or stress, since similar findings have been obtained with college students under "relaxed" assessment conditions.[89] The idea that defensiveness operates under relaxed conditions appears to make more sense than the notion that anxiety produces unrealistic choices under relatively stress-free conditions. In any event, the results suggest that the prediction of goal setting in future studies may be improved by including defensiveness as a predictive variable.

One implication of these findings for classroom training is that subjects with high test anxiety might well profit from some explicit training in setting realistic goals and in estimating their own abilities and the difficulty-levels of training tasks accurately. This kind of training may not be as important as it first appears, however, in view of the fact that the $M_{AF} > M_S$ group tended to become more realistic as a function of age (i.e., 5th grade compared with 4th grade) and experience (i.e., goal setting on later puzzles as compared with the first few puzzles).

Several concluding comments are in order concerning methodology and the tenuous nature of some of the results. First, there are difficulties involved in the projective measurement of achievement motivation with 4th and 5th graders which probably adversely affect the reliability and validity of the measure. Fourth and 5th grade children tend to write slowly, and their written stories tend to be more primitive than their oral stories,

---

[88] *Op. cit.*
[89] *Ibid.;* C. P. Smith, "Achievement-Related Motives and Goal Setting under Different Conditions," *Journal of Personality,* 31 (1963), 124–140.

hence, oral stories were obtained in individual interviews. This procedure introduces unwanted variation due to differences between interviewers, time of day, the degree of the subject's foreknowledge of the interview, and the difficulty of standardizing the length of the stories. Clearly a less time-consuming and more satisfactory way of measuring young children's achievement motivation is needed. Some of the measures devised by Joseph Veroff (see Chapter 3) are particularly welcome in this regard.

Although some of the findings are clear-cut and strongly support the theories outlined earlier, in other instances relatively small relationships were obtained between variables. From the point of view of "accounting for variance" some of the results are clearly ineffectual. Several comments are in order concerning this problem. Part of the difficulty is undoubtedly due to the low reliability of some of the personality measures employed, particularly the projective measure of Need for Achievement. Another problem may be that uncontrolled factors such as differences between schools, teachers, grades, and religious background introduced unwanted variation. To some extent it may be excusable in personality research to have modest goals concerning the size of expected relationships. One of the best predictive variables which psychologists employ is IQ. If relationships between intelligence and performance rarely exceed correlations of .40 and .50, as in the present study, it is probably not reasonable to expect that less established measures of more subjective variables will reveal relationships of even that humble magnitude. Despite this perspective, however, it is clear that major advances in measurement, experimental design, and conceptualization remain to be made if a more complete understanding of the development of achievement-related motives is to be obtained.

In conclusion it may be said that the present research attempts to explore some issues deriving from earlier theory and research and also attempts to extend the purview of earlier concerns to include some new socialization variables (e.g., parental childrearing values), some relatively unexplored personality variables (e.g., self concept, defensiveness), and some novel performance variables (e.g., self-directed learning). A characterization of the origin and expression of achievement-related motives emerges which is complex and inchoate but at the same time provocative and promising. It is a realistic aspiration that the next ten years of research will bring the picture into focus.

APPENDIX MATERIALS

TEACHER RATINGS

Please fill out a form like this one for each child in your class. Circle a number for each item to indicate the extent to which the child possesses the quality described.

Child _____ Teacher _____ Date _____

1. Ability to work at tasks independently after directions are given.

   | very independent | 5 | 4 | 3 | 2 | 1 | not independent |

2. His (or her) estimation of own abilities.

   | very realistic | 5 | 4 | 3 | 2 | 1 | unrealistic |

3. Ability to react constructively to frustration.

   | very constructive | 5 | 4 | 3 | 2 | 1 | not constructive |

4. Desire for praise by adults.

   | high desire | 5 | 4 | 3 | 2 | 1 | low desire |

5. Ability to postpone gratification.

   | not demanding of immediate satisfaction | 5 | 4 | 3 | 2 | 1 | demands immediate satisfaction |

6. Need for affection from teacher.

   | great need | 5 | 4 | 3 | 2 | 1 | slight need |

7. General competitiveness.

   | very competitive | 5 | 4 | 3 | 2 | 1 | not competitive |

8. Ability to concentrate and maintain attention on work.

   | very good concentration | 5 | 4 | 3 | 2 | 1 | poor concentration |

9. Popularity with fellow students.

| very popular | 5 | 4 | 3 | 2 | 1 | not popular |

10. Initiative and resourcefulness.

| develops own ideas, projects and goals | 5 | 4 | 3 | 2 | 1 | does not develop own ideas, projects and goals |

11. Desire to do well in schoolwork.

| strong desire to do well | 5 | 4 | 3 | 2 | 1 | no desire to do well |

12. General aggressiveness toward other children.

| frequently aggressive | 5 | 4 | 3 | 2 | 1 | rarely aggressive |

13. General aggressiveness toward the teacher.

| frequently aggressive | 5 | 4 | 3 | 2 | 1 | rarely aggressive |

14. Pride in accomplishment.

| very pleased when he does something well | 5 | 4 | 3 | 2 | 1 | indifferent when he does something well |

15. Need for emotional support.

| seeks reassurance when in difficulty | 5 | 4 | 3 | 2 | 1 | almost never comes to me for reassurance |

16. Frequency of asking for help with schoolwork.

| very frequently | 5 | 4 | 3 | 2 | 1 | infrequently |

17. Ability in written assignments to use language in a fresh and imaginative way.

| very imaginative | 5 | 4 | 3 | 2 | 1 | unimaginative |

18. How does this child respond to failure? (Check as many as apply.)

_____ with anger
_____ with shame
_____ with indifference
_____ with a desire to improve
_____ by avoiding the activity the next time
_____ other (please describe) _____

19. How does this child respond to criticism by adults?

_____ with anger
_____ with shame
_____ with indifference
_____ with a desire to please
_____ with a desire to improve
_____ by avoiding the activity the next time
_____ other (please describe) _____

Please circle a number for each item below to indicate the extent to which the child possesses the quality described.

	Extent Child Possesses the Quality				
	very great		moderate		very slight
20. being friendly with other children	5	4	3	2	1
21. being a leader with other children	5	4	3	2	1
22. being able to carry out reasonably difficult tasks on his own without assistance or guidance	5	4	3	2	1
23. being explorative and curious	5	4	3	2	1
24. being able to make his own decisions	5	4	3	2	1
25. sticking with a task within his range of ability until he completes it	5	4	3	2	1
26. trying to improve his performance at various skills he has learned	5	4	3	2	1

27.	being stubborn	5	4	3	2	1
28.	trying new things on his own	5	4	3	2	1
29.	standing up for his own rights with other children	5	4	3	2	1
30.	controlling his emotions and impulses	5	4	3	2	1
31.	being well organized	5	4	3	2	1

INDEPENDENCE AND CARETAKING ITEMS FROM
THE CHILDREARING QUESTIONNAIRE[a]

At what age did you first allow (or encourage) your child to do the things described below? (If your child doesn't yet do some of these things, please *estimate* the age when you expect him to do them.)

Age	Behavior
(a) _____	call a friend on the telephone without your help
(b) _____	select some of his own clothes at the store
(c) _____	go to the movies by himself
(d) _____	earn some of his own spending money outside the home
(e) _____	play away from home for long periods of time during the day without first telling his parents where he will be
(f) _____	ride a two-wheel bicycle in streets where there is only light traffic
(g) _____	dress himself
(h) _____	do some regular tasks around the house
(i) _____	put his clothes away

[a] Items a through f were intended to assess independence demands; items g, h, and i have been characterized as "caretaking" demands (cf. McClelland, *The Achieving Society*; Winterbottom, *op. cit.*).

QUESTIONS ON CHILDREARING VALUES

Parents have different ideas about how important it is for a child to have each of the qualities described on the previous page. Would you indicate for the items below *the extent to which you feel it is important* for your child to possess each of the qualities listed.

		Degree of Importance				
		very im- portant		moder- ately im- portant		very unim- portant
(a)	being friendly with other children	5	4	3	2	1
(b)	being obedient to parents	5	4	3	2	1
(c)	doing his best at tasks	5	4	3	2	1
(d)	being a leader with other children	5	4	3	2	1
(e)	being resourceful	5	4	3	2	1
(f)	being able to carry out reasonably difficult tasks on his own without assistance or guidance	5	4	3	2	1
(g)	being creative	5	4	3	2	1
(h)	being self-reliant	5	4	3	2	1
(i)	being explorative and curious	5	4	3	2	1
(j)	being skillful at athletic activities	5	4	3	2	1
(k)	being able to make his own decisions	5	4	3	2	1
(l)	sticking with a task within his range of ability until he completes it	5	4	3	2	1
(m)	trying to *improve* his performance at various skills he has learned	5	4	3	2	1
(n)	being stubborn	5	4	3	2	1

		Degree of Importance				
		very im-portant		moder-ately im-portant		very unim-portant
(o)	trying new things on his own	5	4	3	2	1
(p)	taking pride in doing things well	5	4	3	2	1
(q)	doing well in competitive games	5	4	3	2	1
(r)	standing up for his own rights with other children	5	4	3	2	1
(s)	thinking of things to do without asking for suggestions	5	4	3	2	1
(t)	controlling his emotions and impulses	5	4	3	2	1

CHAPTER FIVE

The Assessment of Achievement Anxieties in Children[1]

SHEILA C. FELD AND
JUDITH LEWIS

THE research reported in this chapter grew out of a general interest in the development and manifestations of achievement strivings and anxieties about achievement in young children. There were a number of interesting, substantive questions in this area, but a priority appeared to exist concerning the measuring instruments. A method for measuring achievement motivation in young children was not firmly established, although the research reported by Joseph Veroff in Chapter 3 changes that situation. The Test Anxiety Scale for Children (TASC), developed by Sarason and his colleagues, appeared to be a valid method for measuring school achievement anxiety and had proved to be a heuristic tool.[2] However, continued progress in research using this instrument seemed to hinge on certain unresolved methodological problems that had been considered in the early development of the Test Anxiety Scale for Children and later left in abeyance because the scale did seem to yield fruitful results.

[1] The authors conducted this research at the Mental Health Study Center and are indebted to their colleagues for their help throughout this project. We especially wish to express appreciation to our dedicated project clerks, Mrs. Niel Solomon and Mrs. Jesse Stern; research assistants, Galen Alessi, Alvin Danenberg, Robert Edmondson, Jean Kavanaugh, Youngja Kim, Abbas Mirrashidi, and Stephen Shevitz; and our colleagues who assisted in the data collection: Mary Lou Bauer, Eleanor Fay, Anita Green, Sandra Hansen, Julie Kisielewski, Janet Moran, Gretchen Schafft, Juliana Schamp, Esther Solomon, and Elizabeth Unger. The comments of Dee N. Lloyd and Edna R. Small on an earlier draft of this paper are gratefully acknowledged. Finally, the authors wish to thank the school officials, children, and parents who so generously participated in this project.
[2] Sarason *et al.*, *Anxiety in Elementary School Children* (New York: John Wiley & Sons, 1960).

HOW IMPORTANT IS RESPONSE SET AND MULTI-DIMENSIONALITY IN THE TEST ANXIETY SCALE FOR CHILDREN?

As with any self-report device, the major methodological question was whether the self-reports elicited by the scale are accurate reflections of conscious feelings. Two specific issues seemed crucial to answering this question for the Test Anxiety Scale for Children. The first issue concerned defensive distortion used to hide one's unpleasant or undesirable qualities. The second issue was the problem of response set, posed by the fact that the scale was scored by counting the number of "Yes" answers.

Defensive distortion can result from the suppression of reports about consciously experienced feelings, or the operation of defense mechanisms that prevent conscious recognition of one's feelings. In an attempt to control the former type of distortion, a Lie Scale concerning general anxiety reactions in and out of school was developed during the course of early work on the Test Anxiety Scale for Children.[3] It consisted of questions about experiences that everyone presumably has at one time or another. Questions were worded in extreme forms to insure that their denial more likely reflected a distortion (e.g., Have you ever been afraid of getting hurt?). Subjects who denied many experiences of this type were presumed to be lying, and their scores on the Test Anxiety Scale for Children were discounted as invalid. More recently, the Defensiveness Scale for Children (DSC) has been used to measure the tendency to deny the experience of unpleasant feelings in a variety of life situations.[4] Like the Lie Scale items, the questions on the Defensiveness Scale for Children were assumed to concern very common feelings, but they were not phrased in such absolute terms, and they did not stress anxiety reactions (e.g., Do you feel cross and grouchy sometimes?). They seemed to be more relevant to the kind of distortion that could be viewed as a general style of defense. The Lie Scale and the Defensiveness Scale for Children are positively correlated, and each is negatively correlated with the Test Anxiety Scale for Children. Since both the Lie Scale and the Defensiveness Scale for Children are based on summing replies of "No" to a series of items, the use of either of them to "correct" for distortion on the Test Anxiety Scale for Children is confounded with the influence of response set bias due to acquiescence or negativism.

Only two studies have directly investigated the influence of acquiescence or negativism on the Test Anxiety Scale for Children or the Defensiveness

---

[3] *Ibid.*, Chap. 5.
[4] B. K. Ruebush, "Children's Behavior as a Function of Anxiety and Defensiveness" (Unpublished doctoral dissertation, Yale University, 1960).

Scale for Children. Sarason and his colleagues[5] developed a measure of response acquiescence based on the number of "Yes" answers to a balanced scale of good descriptions and bad descriptions of the self and others. The descriptions did not concern anxiety, and the questions concerning good and bad characteristics had different content. Correlations between the Test Anxiety Scale for Children and this measure were not significant for either boys or girls in the 5th grade. Lunneborg and Lunneborg[6] also employed a measure of acquiescence with heterogeneous content that did not specifically include questions about anxiety. The scale was balanced for social desirability. This measure of acquiescence and the Defensiveness Scale for Children were significantly and *positively* correlated for children in Grades 4 through 6. This surprising result is difficult to interpret in a response set framework, since it seems to indicate that being acquiescent on the Lunneborgs' measure is associated with being negativistic on the Defensiveness Scale for Children. Although both these studies failed to show the expected relationship of acquiescent or negativistic response set to the Test Anxiety Scale for Children and the Defensiveness Scale for Children, their relevance to that issue rests on the assumption of a general acquiescent style rather than a test-specific response bias. Since this assumption is disputable, the importance of response set on these scales remains an open question.

The assumption that the Test Anxiety Scale for Children measures a unidimensional class of anxiety reactions was the other major methodological issue. Although the scale had been developed by means of item analyses, further investigation of the appropriateness of a single total score seemed necessary in view of the theoretical importance attached to the specific type of anxiety being measured. After the present study was begun, two reports on the factor structure of the scale were published.[7] Both indicated a fairly stable multidimensional structure for the Test Anxiety Scale for Children when comparing 4th through 9th graders, and even mentally retarded children. These studies emphasized the need to investigate several questions about the implications of the multidimensional structure of the scale, for example, which components of the scale accounted for previously found relationships with the entire scale score? Would theoretical conceptions of the test anxious child be affected by considering the separate com-

[5] *Op. cit.*, Chap. 5.
[6] P. W. Lunneborg and C. E. Lunneborg, "The Relationship of Social Desirability to Other Test-Taking Attitudes in Children" (Paper presented at the meeting of the American Psychological Association, Philadelphia, September, 1963).
[7] J. A. Dunn, "Factor Structure of the Test Anxiety Scale for Children," *Journal of Consulting Psychology*, 28 (1964), 92; and "Stability of the Factor Structure of the Test Anxiety Scale for Children Across Age and Sex Groups," *Journal of Consulting Psychology*, 29 (1965), 187. See also A. B. Silverstein and P. J. Mohan, "Test Anxiety or Generalized School Anxiety?" *American Journal of Mental Deficiency*, 69 (1964), 438–439.

ponents of the scale? Would a rescoring of the scale in terms of its factor structure be feasible and useful?

The third general issue concerned a further specification of the broad social background correlates of the scale. Since the initial validation studies, most of the research with the Test Anxiety Scale for Children has been done with subjects from white middle-class backgrounds. There is some evidence that the test anxiety scores of boys are negatively associated with the socio-economic status of their parents.[8] On the other hand, there have been repeated findings that achievement motivation is positively related to social class.[9] Therefore, it seemed important to reassess the demographic correlates of scores on the Test Anxiety Scale for Children in a more heterogeneous sample than had previously usually been used.

The issues discussed above led to the development of a two-stage program of research. This chapter reports on the first stage of the research program, which was designed to deal with the general methodological and normative problems cited above. There were three general purposes in the first phase: (1) consideration of the methodological issues of response set and multidimensionality, which might lead to refinement of the measuring instruments; (2) investigation of the social background and school achievement correlates of test anxiety and defensiveness in a more heterogeneous sample of children than had previously been done; and (3) establishment of a pool of subjects with measured levels of test anxiety and defensiveness from which subjects could be selected for further studies that required certain levels of these variables. The present chapter focuses on these issues in relation to the Test Anxiety Scale for Children. Similar data concerning the Defensiveness Scale for Children will be reported elsewhere. More detailed substantive studies are planned for the next stage of the research program.

Because of the sizable negative correlation typically found between scores on the Test Anxiety Scale for Children and the Defensiveness Scale for Children, initial collection of data from a large sample was necessary in

---

[8] W. D. Abelson, "Differential Performance and Personality Patterns among Anxious Children" (Unpublished doctoral dissertation, Harvard University, 1961); E. B. Adams and I. G. Sarason, "Relation Between Anxiety in Children and Their Parents," *Child Development*, 34 (1963), 237–246; J. A. Dunn, "School Approach-Avoidance Values: A Differential Study of Children's Affect and Value Patterns for the Academic as Contrasted to the Social Aspects of School" (Paper presented at the meeting of the American Psychological Association, New York, September, 1966); S. Feld, W. Owen, and S. B. Sarason, "Interviews with Parents of Anxious and Defensive Young Boys" (Unpublished manuscript, National Institute of Mental Health, 1963); Sarason *et al., op. cit.*, Chap. 8.

[9] S. Feld, Studies in the Origins of Achievement Strivings (Doctoral dissertation, University of Michigan [Ann Arbor: University Microfilms, 1960], No. 60–1759); B. C. Rosen, "The Achievement Syndrome: A Psychocultural Dimension of Social Stratification," *American Sociological Review*, 21 (1956), 203–211; and "Race, Ethnicity, and the Achievement Syndrome," *American Sociological Review*, 24 (1959), 47–60. J. Veroff *et al.*, "The Use of Thematic Apperception to Assess Motivation in a Nationwide Interview Study," *Psychological Monographs*, 74 (1960), 12, Whole No. 499.

154

order to provide a sufficient pool of subjects with extreme scores on both measures. With the typically found negative correlations between these two scales of around — .50, it was estimated that to obtain 100 subjects in the extreme quartiles on both measures, a total pool of 6,000 subjects would be required.[10] Because of this estimate and an interest in studying children from heterogeneous backgrounds, the sample used was the entire 2nd grade population of the county school system where the research laboratory is based. Second-graders were chosen because it was desirable to work with children as young as possible.

A major decision concerned the manner of assessing the influence of acquiescent response set on the Test Anxiety Scale for Children (or the Defensiveness Scale for Children). Three interrelated considerations were used as guidelines. The first concerned the need to reassess the validity of *these particular* measuring instruments. The second was Cronbach's early definition of response set, "A response set is any tendency causing a person consistently to give different responses to test items than he would when the same content is presented in a different form."[11] Lastly, the authors were not convinced that a *general* acquiescent response style had been demonstrated to exist.[12]

These three considerations required a method of assessing acquiescent response set that could directly determine whether revising the form of the questions on the Test Anxiety Scale for Children would change a subject's position on the scale. A further requirement was that high scores on the measure of acquiescence would be based on contradictory responses. This requirement was especially important because of the assumption made in the present study that the Test Anxiety Scale for Children was not uni-dimensional. In studies where subjects are not required to be contradictory to get high acquiescence scores, it is difficult to eliminate the possibility that the self-descriptions are accurate. Therefore, it was decided to investigate acquiescence by reversing the items on the scale itself, and giving both versions of the same item to the same subjects, although not consecutively.

Because of the assumptions that acquiescence could only be inferred from contradictory replies and that the different items were not necessarily equivalent, the assessment of response set had to be made at the item level. The factor analysis of an expanded Test Anxiety Scale for Children that

---

[10] Donald N. Morrison, then of the Biometrics Branch of the National Institute of Mental Health, very kindly provided this estimate.

[11] L. J. Cronbach, "Response Set and Test Validity," *Educational and Psychological Measurement*, 6 (1946), 475–494.

[12] For similar conclusions, see R. K. McGee, "Response Style as a Personality Variable: By What Criterion?" *Psychological Bulletin*, 59 (1962), 284–295; or L. G. Rorer, "The Great Response Style Myth," *Oregon Research Institute Research Monograph*, 3 (1963), No. 6.

included matched pairs of original and reversed items seemed to meet this condition, as well as to provide desired data on the factor structure of the scale. The use of reversed items to measure response set in this manner rests on two assumptions: (1) that the psychological content of the original and reversed items are polar opposites, and (2) that giving the same answer to both the original and reversed versions of an item is psychologically and logically contradictory. Accepting these assumptions, for the time being, how would response set influence the nature of the factor structure? If response set has no influence, the matched original and reversed items should load on the same factor, with opposite signs for their factor loadings. The "ideal" factor to interpret as a refutation of the influence of response set would be one where for every original item with a high positive factor loading, there is a reversed version of the item that has an equally high negative factor loading, and vice versa. On the other hand, if response set strongly influences replies, a response set factor should occur. This factor would be one where the loadings for matched original and reversed items have congruent signs. If replies to the Test Anxiety Scale for Children are primarily due to response set, this would be a large and general factor, with all the original and reversed items having factor loadings with the same signs. Alternatively, there could be both content and response set dimensions underlying replies to the Test Anxiety Scale for Children. The proportions of variance accounted for by the two types of factors would then be of interest.

If the basic assumption of totally adequate reversal of the items is not valid, then other factor patterns may occur that would obscure the interpretation of content versus response set factors. If the reversal process changes the psychological meaning of a question, rather than only its form, the two versions of a question may load on different factors. This would leave unresolved the issue of content versus response bias determination of replies. Shifts in meaning could also occur that would result in the two versions of a question reflecting the same underlying dimension of meaning to varying degrees. This would be revealed in factor loadings of different size on the same factor. This pattern would also be equivocal since it could be attributed either to the inadequate reversal of psychological meaning or to the influence of response bias.

These then were the major outlines of the study: (1) to develop reversed versions of the questions on the Test Anxiety Scale for Children and the Defensiveness Scale for Children; (2) to determine the multidimensional structure of each of these expanded scales in order to specify content versus response set dimensions; (3) to reassess the relationship between the two scales in terms of their multidimensional structures; (4) to develop revised versions of the scales that controlled for response bias and multi-dimensionality; (5) to relate scores on the original and revised versions of the scales to various social background, school history and school achievement characteristics in order to consider these relationships in a heterogeneous population, and to compare these relationships for the original and revised versions of the scales.

This chapter specifically deals with the factor analyses of revised versions of the Test Anxiety Scale for Children, and sex and race comparisons using a simplified rescoring of the original Test Anxiety Scale for Children based on its multidimensional structure.

METHODS AND PROCEDURES[13]

The Sample and Research Site

The site of the study was a rapidly growing suburban county adjacent to one of the larger and older metropolitan areas in the eastern part of the United States. The county has been shown to be typical of the residential suburbs that have developed since World War II.[14] Its rapid population growth reflected the suburban movement of relatively affluent families with young and school-age children. The county school population can be viewed as a sample from the school populations of these rapidly growing suburban areas that have relatively high socioeconomic status.

Despite this overall characterization, there was considerable diversity in occupational, educational, and financial status among the county residents. In 1960, 17 per cent of the county population (and 30 per cent of the U.S. population) lived in rural areas. The proportion of Negroes in the county was slightly less than in the United States (9 per cent versus 10.5 per cent in 1960). Proportionately, the Negroes were mostly concentrated in the rural areas (they were 26 per cent of the population in the county rural areas) and least likely to be resident in the fastest growing suburban areas of the county (3 per cent of that population). Selected socioeconomic population characteristics of the county are compared with those for the total United States in Table 1. Higher proportions of white-collar workers (especially professional, clerical, and kindred workers) were found among the employed males in the county (49 per cent) than in the United States (36 per cent). Unlike the nation as a whole, the county's modal occupation was skilled blue-collar workers (26 per cent in the county and 20 per

---

[13] More complete descriptions of the methodology are available from the authors upon request for Working Paper #3 from Mental Health Study Center, Project 27.

[14] H. F. Goldsmith and E. G. Stockwell, "Socio-Demographic Characteristics of Rapid Growth Counties in the United States: Some Preliminary Considerations" (Laboratory paper #12, Mental Health Study Center, National Institute of Mental Health, August, 1965).

TABLE 1 *Percentage Distributions of Selected Demographic Characteristics of County and United States Populations in 1960*

Occupational distribution of employed males[a]

Occupational level	County	U.S.
Professional, technical, kindred workers	19.98	10.80
Farmers and farm managers	1.24	5.76
Managers, officials, proprietors (not farm)	10.80	11.16
Clerical, kindred workers	11.45	7.27
Sales workers	6.92	7.18
Craftsmen, foremen, kindred workers	26.17	20.46
Operatives, kindred workers	11.99	20.83
Private household workers	0.04	0.15
Service workers (not private household)	6.36	6.26
Farm laborers and foremen	0.94	2.90
Laborers (not farm and mine)	4.10	7.23

Educational attainment of persons 24 years and over[b]

Educational level	County	U.S.
No School	0.72	2.29
Elementary School:		
1–4 years	2.99	6.06
5–7 years	10.70	13.83
8 years	10.43	17.54
High School:		
1–3 years	20.89	19.22
4 years	31.52	23.59
College		
1–3 years	11.10	8.79
4 years	11.64	7.67

Family income in dollars in 1959[c]

Income level	County	U.S.
< 1000	1.76	5.57
1000–1999	2.05	7.48
2000–2999	3.50	8.34
3000–3999	5.09	9.49
4000–4999	8.32	10.99
5000–5999	11.10	12.33
6000–6999	12.75	10.70
7000–7999	11.51	8.58
8000–8999	9.94	6.63
9000–9999	8.31	4.85
10,000 and >	26.66	15.05

[a] Base N for U.S. = 41,480,039, for County = 83,307 persons.
[b] Base N for U.S. = 99,438,084, for County = 179,698 persons.
[c] Base N for U.S. = 45,128,393, for County = 87,453 families.

Source: Tables 83, 84, and 86 in U.S. Bureau of the Census, *U.S. Census of Population: 1960. General Social and Economic Characteristics, Maryland,* Final Report PC (1)–22C (Washington, D.C.: Government Printing Office, 1961); U.S. Bureau of the Census, *U.S. Population: 1960. General Social and Economic Characteristics, United States summary,* Final Report PC (1)–1C (Washington, D.C.: Government Printing Office, 1961).

cent in the U.S.). The median level of educational attainment also was higher (12.1 years) than the average for the United States (10.3 years). Even so, 25 per cent of the county adult population had no high school education (as compared with 39 per cent for the U.S.). Family income level in the county clearly surpassed that of the United States. About 26 per cent of the county families earned at least $10,000 in 1959 (as compared with 15 per cent for the U.S. and only 20 per cent of them earned less than $5,000 in 1959 (as compared with 41 per cent of the U.S. families).

The total sample was defined to include all children enrolled in the 2nd grade classes of the county public school system on the day that the testing was done at their particular school. This included 8,875 subjects enrolled in 111 schools. Not all children in the total sample were administered the classroom procedures: 7.9 per cent were absent, and 2.6 per cent had parents who refused permission for participation. Subjects who omitted answers to *more than one* question on either the expanded Test Anxiety Scale for Children or the expanded Defensiveness Scale for Children were also excluded from the sample used in this chapter (4.3 per cent).

A check was made for bias in the final sample, which included about 85 per cent of the original subjects. The subjects excluded for any reason tended to be lower in IQ and reading readiness scores, and those whose parents refused permission for participation tended to come from families with lower socioeconomic status. Thus, the subjects used in the present paper included a slight overrepresentation of the upper status and high-ability 2nd graders. The mean first grade IQ of the final sample was about 101, with a standard deviation of 14.6. A fuller description of the characteristics of the final sample is available in Table 2.

Instruments

Expanded forms of the Test Anxiety Scale for Children and the Defensiveness Scale for Children were developed, which included original and reversed questions. It was difficult to write questions where alternate responses of "Yes" and "No" to original and reversed versions would indicate consistent feelings. Logically, this could be handled by "reversing" one feeling state by its negative, for example, worry and not worry, fearful and not fearful. However, 2nd grade children could not be asked to answer "Yes" or "No" to questions such as, "Are you not afraid of tests in school?" Instead an attempt was made to write reversed items so that if a subject said "Yes" to the original question, it would be logically and psychologically inconsistent to say "Yes" to its reversed version, for example, "Are you afraid of tests in school?" versus "Do you like tests in school?" "Do

Demographic Characteristics of the Final Sample (by Sex)

Variable	Item	Male (3867)[a]	Female (3684)[a]	Total (7551)[a]
Age[b]	M	88.105*	87.201	87.664
	SD	5.662	4.943	5.343
	N	3861	3674	7535
IQ (Grade 1)	M	100.215	100.965	100.587
	SD	14.815	14.320	14.576
	N	3043	2984	6027
RR (Grade 1)	M	0.960*	1.099	1.028
	SD	0.573	0.564	0.573
	N	3006	2943	5949
# Retentions	M	0.158*	0.086	0.123
	SD	0.375	0.285	0.336
	N	3497	3335	6832
School Stability[c]	M	2.338	2.382	2.360
	SD	0.928	0.911	0.920
	N	3819	3644	7463
# Siblings	M	2.483	2.485	2.484
	SD	1.661	1.638	1.650
	N	3780	3600	7380
Mother Absence[d]	M	1.035	1.029	1.032
	SD	0.184	0.168	0.176
	N	3681	3505	7186
Father Absence[d]	M	1.090	1.090	1.090
	SD	0.286	0.287	0.286
	N	3681	3505	7186
Education of Mother (yrs.)	M	12.142	12.174	12.157
	SD	1.961	2.038	1.999
	N	3698	3519	7217
Education of Father (yrs.)	M	12.505	12.487	12.496
	SD	2.604	2.587	2.595
	N	3649	3477	7126
Mother Not Working[d]	M	1.770	1.752	1.761
	SD	0.421	0.432	0.426
	N	3690	3506	7196
SES of Father's Occupation[e]	M	65.439	64.919	65.185
	SD	22.687	22.548	22.619
	N	3818	3652	7470

* Sex differences in final sample yielded t test with $p < .001$.

[a] Maximum N in each group. Variations in Ns for individual variables due to missing data in school records.

[b] Age in months (9/1/63) upon entry to Grade 2 during year research data were collected.

[c] Trichotomy: 1 = transfer; 2 = transfer due to new school construction; 3 = no transfer (stable).

[d] Dichotomous variable: 1 = named item not present; 2 = named item present.

[e] These are the socioeconomic status scores for detailed occupations developed by the U.S. Bureau of the Census ("Methodology and Scores of Socioeconomic Status," Working Paper No. 15 [Washington, D.C.: Government Printing Office, 1963]). They indicate the position of the average person in a given occupation, based on the education and income distribution for that occupation. The score range is 00–99.

you worry about being promoted?" versus "Do you feel sure that you will be promoted?" The difficulty with this approach was that replying "No" to both questions was not necessarily inconsistent; there is no contradiction in feeling neither worried nor optimistic, fearful nor confident, etc.

The second rule used in writing reversals was to avoid extreme statements. The original questions were not worded in the extreme; they asked whether the child felt afraid or *sometimes* worried. These items were reversed by asking if the child felt sure of himself or *usually* felt pleased. It would have been more logically correct to oppose sometimes being afraid with always feeling confident, but the psychological implications of reporting always feeling a certain way did not seem to be appropriately opposite to the original questions.

Several possible reversals were developed for most questions in consultation with teachers and elementary school principals, and were then pretested in order to choose those most meaningful to the children. The final set of items, listed in Table 3, included reversals for all but one item (Item 27). The reversed versions of two sets of items were not entirely satisfactory, however. The problematic questions were those that concerned dreams and waking fantasies about school while at home. A child who was anxious about school might have both anxiety-provoking dreams about school and pleasant dreams about school, the latter being more clearly wish-fulfillment dreams. The key element might be whether the child remembered having dreams about school. Similarly, it seemed possible that an anxious child could have both pleasant and unpleasant fantasies; or that the presence or absence of such thoughts about school might be the critical dimension underlying these questions. The original items that concerned anxiety dreams or unpleasant fantasies and thoughts about school while at home were revised to describe pleasant dreams or fantasies about school, but these were not considered adequate reversals. Two affectively neutral questions were also added to all forms of the expanded scale; they simply asked about the occurrence of these thoughts or dreams.

For example:

31. When you are at home, do you think about your school work?
32. Do you sometimes dream at night about school?

TABLE 3 *Original and Reversed Questions on the Expanded Test Anxiety Scale for Children*

Question Content

1. Do you worry when the teacher says that she is going to ask you questions to find out how much you know?
1R. Do you feel relaxed when . . . ?

2. Do you worry about being promoted, that is passing from the 2nd to the 3rd grade at the end of the year?
2R. Do you feel sure that you will be promoted, that is pass from . . . ?

3. When the teacher asks you to get up in front of the class and read aloud, are you afraid that you are going to make some bad mistakes?
3R. When . . . aloud, do you feel sure that you are going to get all the words right?

4. When the teacher says that she is going to call upon some boys and girls to answer arithmetic problems out loud, do you hope that she will call upon someone else and not on you?
4R. When . . . do you hope that she will call upon you?

5. Do you sometimes dream at night that you are in school and cannot answer the teacher's questions?
5R. Do you dream at night a lot of times that you are in school and can give the right answers to . . . ?

6. When the teacher says that she is going to find out how much you have learned, does your heart begin to beat faster?
6R. When . . . learned, do you feel relaxed and comfortable?

7. When the teacher is teaching you about arithmetic, do you feel that other children in the class understand her better than you?
7R. When . . . do you feel that you understand her better than other children in the class?

8. When you are in bed at night, do you sometimes worry about how you are going to do in class the next day?
8R. When . . . do you usually feel pleased about how good you are going to do . . . ?

9. When the teacher asks you to write on the blackboard in front of the class, does the hand you write with sometimes shake a little?
9R. When . . . do you write without your hand shaking?

10. When the teacher is teaching you about reading, do you feel that other children in the class understand her better than you?
10R. When . . . do you feel that you understand her better than other children in the class?

11. Do you think you worry more about school than other children?
11R. Do you think you worry less . . . ?

12. When you are at home and you are thinking about your arithmetic work for the next day, do you become afraid that you will get the answers wrong when the teacher calls upon you?
12R. When . . . do you feel sure that you will get the answers right . . . ?

13. If you are sick and miss school, do you worry that you will be far behind the other children when you return to school?
13R. If . . . do you think that it will be easy to catch up with the other children . . . ?

14. Do you sometimes dream at night that other boys and girls in your class can do things you cannot do?
14R. Do you dream at night a lot of times that you can do things that other boys and girls in your class cannot do?

15. When you are home and you are thinking about your reading group for the next day, do you worry that you will do poor work?
15R. When . . . do you feel that you will do good work?

16. When the teacher says that she is going to find out how much you have learned, do you get a funny feeling in your stomach?
16R. When . . . do you feel relaxed and comfortable?

TABLE 3 (*cont.*)

Question Content

17. If you did very poorly when the teacher called on you, would you probably feel like crying even though you would try not to cry?
17R. If . . . would you probably feel that it really didn't matter very much?

18. Do you sometimes dream at night that the teacher is angry because you do not know your work?
18R. Do you dream at night a lot of times that the teacher is pleased because you know your work?

19. Are you afraid of tests in school?
19R. Do you like tests in school?

20. Do you worry a lot *before* you take a test?
20R. Do you feel relaxed . . . ?

21. Do you worry a lot *while* you are taking a test?
21R. Do you feel relaxed . . . ?

22. *After* you have taken a test do you worry about how well you did on the test?
22R. *After* . . . do you soon forget about the test and think about other things?

23. Do you sometimes dream at night that you did poor work on a test you had in school that day?
23R. Do you dream at night a lot of times that you did good work . . . ?

24. When you are taking a test, does the hand you write with shake a little?
24R. When . . . do you write without your hand shaking?

25. When the teacher says that she is going to give the class a test, do you become afraid that you will do poor work?
25R. When . . . do you usually feel that you will do good work?

26. When you are taking a hard test, do you forget some things that you knew very well before you started taking the test?
26R. When . . . do you remember most things you knew very well before . . . ?

27. Do you wish a lot of times that you didn't worry so much about tests?

28. When the teacher says that she is going to give the class a test, do you get a nervous or funny feeling?
28R. When . . . do you feel relaxed and comfortable?

29. While you are taking a test do you usually think you are doing poor work?
29R. While . . . do you usually think you are doing good work?

30. While you are on your way to school, do you sometimes worry that the teacher may give the class a test?
30R. While . . . do you wish a lot of times that the teacher will give a test so you can show her how much you know?

31. When you are at home, do you think about your school work?

32. Do you sometimes dream at night about school?

Notes. An ellipsis indicates that the same words appeared in the reverse as in the original question.

Question 27, from the original TASC, did not have a reversed version for this study. Questions 31 and 32 were added for this study, but they were not designed to be reversals of any single original question.

Questions 5, 14, 18, and 23 concerning dreams, and questions 8, 12, 13, 15, and 30 concerning waking fantasies about school while at home, were not considered to be adequately reversed; replies of "Yes" to both versions of these questions did not appear to be necessarily psychologically inconsistent.

Questions 4, 12, 13, 15, 18, 19, 23, 25, 26, and 29 appear in slightly modified form from that used in the original TASC because the pretests indicated some difficulty in comprehension.

Because of time limitations in administering the tests, three parallel forms of the expanded Test Anxiety Scale for Children were developed. Each form included all thirty items from the Sarason scale,[15] the two neutral items about dreams and thoughts about school, and ten reversed questions. The reversed questions were randomly assigned to one of the three forms. The original questions from the Test Anxiety Scale for Children appeared in the same sequential order in all test forms; this order was the one used in previous studies. The new questions appeared at the same point in all forms; this sequential location was determined randomly, with the exception that no original item was immediately preceded or followed by its revised version. The Defensiveness Scale for Children[16] was revised in a similar fashion to yield two test forms.

Classroom Data Collection

Six test conditions resulted from all possible combinations of the three expanded forms of the Test Anxiety Scale for Children and the two expanded forms of the Defensiveness Scale for Children. Each 2nd grade class was assigned at random to one of the six test conditions.

All classroom data collection was done during a two-month period in the middle of the school year. The procedures were designed to test the children under normal classroom conditions. Testing was done in the regular classrooms, and women examiners were used since all of the teachers were women. At the time of the study, the remnants of a dual school system remained in evidence in the county; 89 per cent of the Negro 2nd graders were enrolled in fifteen all-Negro schools and had Negro teachers. Therefore, a Negro examiner was used in those schools. Because of staff limitations, a single Negro examiner did all the testing. This confounded race and examiner effects for most of the Negro subjects. In the remaining schools, eleven examiners were used, with the assignments made solely on the basis of convenience of scheduling.

The examiners were introduced to the children in a standard neutral manner by the teacher, who then left the room. The children each received three-page answer sheets. The middle page was blank; on the first and last pages were listed question numbers and alongside, the words "Yes" and "No." The examiner emphasized that she was the only one who would see the answers, that there were no right or wrong answers, and that different children thought and felt differently about the questions. The sub-

---

[15] Sarason *et al.*, *op. cit.*, Appendix B.
[16] S. B. Sarason, K. T. Hill, and P. G. Zimbardo, "A Longitudinal Study of the Relation of Test Anxiety to Performance on Intelligence and Achievement Tests," *Monographs of the Society for Research in Child Development,* 29 (1964), 7, Whole No. 98.

jects were told that their task was to listen to each question and then to circle either "Yes" or "No." The expanded Test Anxiety Scale for Children was administered first. Questions were repeated if the children so requested. Then, as a transition, the examiner led the children in a two- or three-minute series of stretching and bending exercises. The expanded Defensiveness Scale for Children was then administered. The testing sessions were scheduled for one hour and fifteen minutes. In most instances, this was ample time to complete the procedures.

School Record Data Collection Procedures

Information on family background, school tests, and school history was obtained from the cumulative folders maintained by the schools for each pupil. These transcribed data were then coded and punched on IBM cards.

The coding and punching procedures included checks for intercoder reliability. All checks indicated intercoder agreement above 97 per cent. There was no duplicate transcription of school-record data by the different clerks to provide reliability estimates. Any unreliability in the transcription procedures or in the information in the school records contributed unknown amounts of error to the data.

Data Analysis

Since several separate data analyses are reported, the statistical procedures are described separately.[17] Two general points should be noted. First, all probability values reported are for two-tailed tests. Second, most of the analyses are based on very large numbers of subjects and the null hypothesis is relatively easy to reject. Therefore, stringent significance levels were used, and the size of the relationships or extent of differences should be considered along with the probability values.

RESULTS

Symmetry of Reversals

Before the factor analyses are described, a report will be made of an attempt to assess the adequacy of the question reversals. This assessment followed the lead of Samelson,[18] who proposed a means of evaluating the equivalence of the extremity of item reversals using a scaling theory model.[19] This approach applies to any method of assessing a subject's posi-

---

[17] The Honeywell 800 and IBM 360 computers at the Computation and Data Processing Branch of the National Institutes of Health were utilized. The assistance of Gayle Hueston and Meyer Gordon is gratefully acknowledged.
[18] F. Samelson, "Agreement Set and Anticontent Attitudes in the F Scale: A Reinterpretation," Journal of Abnormal and Social Psychology, 68 (1964), 338–342.
[19] C. H. Coombs, "A Theory of Psychological Scaling," University of Michigan Engineering Research Institute Bulletin (1951), No. 34.

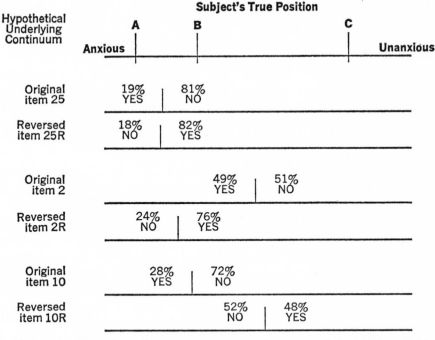

Figure 1. Hypothetical anxiety continuum placement of three subjects (A, B, and C) and three sets of original and reversed items differing in their reversal symmetry.

tion on some continuum by means of his agreement or disagreement with a stimulus question. Each item is assumed to be placed somewhere on an underlying attitude continuum. Each subject also has a position on the same continuum. The response of an individual subject is a function of both his position and the position of the item. In order for a pair of items to be considered adequate reversals, both items must scale at the same points on the underlying continuum—the reversal must be symmetrical. The scale position of an item is estimated by its level of acceptance or rejection in a sample, that is, by its marginal values. The assumption of symmetrical reversals therefore requires that the proportion of subjects accepting an original item equals the proportion of subjects rejecting its reversed version. Figure 1, adapted from Samelson, illustrates the implications of this theoretical position for the phenotypic responses of three subjects who differ in their true position on an anxiety continuum.

Consider items 25 and 25R in Figure 1, which are very close to being perfectly symmetrical. All three subjects could give phenotypically consistent replies to this pair of questions. Inconsistent replies ("Yes" to both, or "No" to both) could be considered a function of response set, unreliability in the subject's own position, or unreliability in the subject's judgment of the item's position.

Now consider what happens when there is not perfect agreement between the percentage of replies of "Yes" to the original item and "No" to the reversed item. For items 2 and 2R in Figure 1, rejection of the reversed item indicates more extreme anxiety than does acceptance of the original item. Subject A would again appear consistently anxious and Subject C consistently unanxious, but Subject B would appear to be inconsistently acquiescent by replying "Yes" to both items. For items 10 and 10R, where the original version is more extreme than the reversed version, Subject B would reply "No" to both questions, and appear inconsistently negativistic.

It does not seem parsimonious to conclude that Subjects A and C are consistently replying without either acquiescent or negativistic response set and that Subject B is alternately consistent, acquiescent, and negativistic. Samelson concludes that in order to use double agreement or disagreement as an indication of response set, it is first necessary to establish that reversals are symmetrical. If the reversals are not symmetrical, a more appropriate estimate of the extent of "true" response set may be obtained by comparing observed values of double agreement to "minimum" values that are determined by use of the marginals.

The adequacy of the symmetry of reversed test anxiety items was measured by this model. The data relevant to this are in Table 4. The percentage of subjects who replied "Yes" to an original item (Column 1) was compared with the percentage of subjects who replied "No" to the reversed form of that item (Column 2). The signed difference between these percentages was used as an index of extent and direction of asymmetry (Column 3). If the item had been symmetrically reversed, this difference would have been zero. The asymmetry index, in Column 3, shows considerable variation in the symmetry of the reversals. The predominant bias was toward less extreme scale placements for the reversed items; for eighteen of the thirty pairs of original and reversed items, the asymmetry index was negative: that is, the original item was *less* likely to be endorsed than the reversed item was to be rejected.

There was no precise way to estimate the degree of asymmetry that could be tolerated. It seemed necessary, however, to question the adequacy of reversals for those pairs of items where the asymmetry index was more than 20 per cent. This was true of six pairs of items; they are the top and bottom three pairs in Table 4. A majority of the item pairs (eighteen

167

TABLE 4   *Symmetry of Reversals and Double Agreement Patterns on the Expanded TASC*

Item # (Form)	1 % Yes Orig.	2 % No Rev.	3 % Yes − % No	4 % Yes, Yes Observed	5 % Yes, Yes > Min.	6 % Yes, Yes < Max.
2(3)	49.4	24.4	+25.0	37.1	+12.1	−12.3
8(2)	48.4	25.6	+22.8	35.9	+13.1	−12.5
4(2)	34.2	13.2	+21.0	25.8	+ 4.8	− 8.4
6(2)	50.4	38.1	+12.3	27.7	+15.4	−22.7
26(3)	41.8	31.7	+10.1	24.4	+14.3	−17.4
30(2)	27.9	19.1	+ 8.8	21.8	+13.0	− 6.1
22(3)	59.4	52.1	+ 7.3	27.5	+20.2	−20.4
16(3)	43.7	39.0	+ 4.7	23.4	+18.7	−20.3
29(1)	18.3	15.4	+ 2.9	12.5	+ 9.6	− 5.8
24(2)	39.0	37.7	+ 1.3	15.6	+14.3	−23.4
25(3)	20.2	18.3	+ 1.9	11.7	+ 9.8	− 8.5
25(1)	17.9	17.2	+ 0.7	11.5	+10.8	− 6.4
15(2)	14.6	15.0	− 0.4	9.4	+ 9.4	− 5.2
19(2)	12.3	15.0	− 2.7	6.3	+ 6.3	− 6.0
9(3)	42.6	45.6	− 3.0	21.7	+21.7	−20.9
28(3)	32.5	37.5	− 5.0	14.6	+14.6	−17.9
14(1)	32.8	39.4	− 6.6	20.3	+20.3	−12.5
18(1)	24.7	31.4	− 6.7	18.0	+18.0	− 6.7
3(3)	35.0	42.3	− 7.3	12.3	+12.3	−22.7
20(1)	26.2	34.0	− 7.8	13.2	+13.2	−13.0
13(2)	48.8	57.5	− 8.7	14.3	+14.3	−28.2
12(2)	26.6	35.6	− 9.0	12.7	+12.7	−13.9
23(1)	23.9	33.9	−10.0	15.6	+15.6	− 8.3
21(2)	24.0	35.2	−11.2	11.2	+11.2	−12.8
5(1)	26.4	41.9	−15.5	17.1	+17.1	− 9.3
1(1)	26.8	44.6	−17.8	12.3	+12.3	−14.5
7(1)	35.1	54.4	−19.3	14.9	+14.9	−20.2
10(1)	27.8	51.6	−23.8	13.7	+13.7	−14.1
11(3)	36.7	60.9	−24.2	15.8	+15.8	−20.9
17(3)	30.2	59.3	−29.1	13.0	+13.0	−17.2
Means						
All	(30)		− 2.97	17.71	+13.86	−14.28
+ Asymmetry (12)			+ 9.90	22.90	+13.00	−13.68
− Asymmetry (18)			+11.56	14.24	+14.24	−14.68

Notes. Cols. 1, 2, and 4 are reports of observed values.
Col. 3 = (Col. 1 − Col. 2) = asymmetry index.
Col. 5 = (Col. 4 − Col. 3) if Col. 3 is +; Col. 5 = Col. 4 if Col. 3 is −.
Col. 6 = (Col. 4 − Col. 1), except for items 22 and 13, where Col. 6 = Col. 4 − (1 − Col. 2).

of them) showed discrepancies of less than 10 per cent. These were judged to be relatively symmetrical reversals.

Estimates of Response Set in Individual Item Pairs

The asymmetry index also provides lower and upper bounds for the observed percentage of subjects replying "Yes" to both the original and reversed items, if the obtained marginals for any pair of items are assumed to be fixed. The assumption of fixed marginals is equivalent to assuming that the questions have stable scale values. This assumption is reasonable for

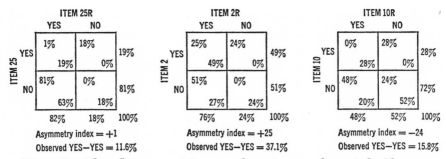

Figure 2. The effects on minimum and maximum values of double agreement and disagreement for three pairs of items that differ in their reversal symmetry. Marginal values are observed agreement and disagreement percentages. Cell entries in upper left are minimum values and those in lower right are maximum values, assuming fixed marginals.

these data. For the original items, the overall mean difference in the percentage of "Yes" replies to each question for the three random samples ($N \geqslant 2400$ each) that received the three forms of the expanded Test Anxiety Scale for Children was 2.7 per cent. Thus, these values were quite stable. The same type of comparison was not possible for the reversed items since they appeared on only one form of the expanded Test Anxiety Scale for Children. An indirect indication of the stability of the scale values for both the reversed and original items was available, however, since the asymmetry index was separately computed for the total samples of boys and girls. The correlation of .94 between the indexes for the two sexes on the thirty items can be taken to indicate that the reversals and originals had similar scale values in the two sexes.

Granting the assumption of fixed marginals, what is the relationship between the asymmetry index and the lower bound for the observed percentage of double agreement (replying "Yes" to both the original and reversed versions of an item)? This relationship is illustrated in Figure 2 for the same three sets of items previously discussed. The minimum possible value of double agreement equals the value of the asymmetry index if the index has a positive sign, and the minimum value equals zero if the asymmetry index is negative. For item 2, the marginal value of the "Yes" response was 49 per cent, and for item 2R, 76 per cent. The occurrence of these values indicates that a minimum of 25 per cent of the subjects must have replied "Yes" to both questions; this is equal to the asymmetry index. For items 10 and 10R, however, where the asymmetry index is negative, the minimum value for the double agreement cell was zero. If these minimum values for double agreement coincided with the observed values, it would support the hypothesis that the subjects were replying to the two items in terms of their content, and that the items were located at different positions on the underlying content dimension.

Table 4 also includes the data needed to compare the minimum and observed values of double agreement. Column 4 lists the percentage of subjects who replied "Yes" to both the original and reversed items in each pair; the mean was close to 18 per cent. The discrepancies between these observed values of double agreement and the minimum values are listed in Column 5; the mean excess above the minimum was 13.86 per cent for all items. These data imply that for any pair of matched items, approximately 14 per cent of the subjects were *inconsistently* acquiescent.

There is also a maximum figure for double agreement that is determined by the marginals, as can be seen by returning to Figure 2.[20] The maximum amount of double agreement possible is equal to the total percentage of subjects who said "Yes" to either the reversed or original item, whichever value is smaller. For items 2 and 2R (in Figure 2) this value was 49 per cent, and for items 10 and 10R it was 28 per cent. If these maximum values coincided with the observed values, they would support the hypothesis that the subjects were replying to the two items in a manner determined by acquiescent or negativistic response set. This comparison is given in Column 6 of Table 4. The maximum double agreement was never reached. The mean discrepancy below the maximum was 14.28 per cent, which was close to the mean discrepancy above the minimum.

Thus, the average observed percentage of double agreement could be described as falling midway between the theoretically expected minimum and maximum value. This indicated that neither the hypothesis of content nor of response style determinants was clearly supported by the data, when all items were considered. Certain item pairs did tend to have observed values of double agreement that were much closer to their minimum than to their maximum, which would support a content interpretation based on different scale values (e.g., items 4, 6, 3, 13). But other item pairs had values of double agreement that were much closer to their maximum values, which would support a response set interpretation (e.g., items 30, 18, 23, 5). In the report of the factor analyses it will be seen that these variations seemed to be related to the underlying dimension of anxiety that the items reflected.

---

[20] This consideration of minimum and maximum values is another aspect of the problem involved in using measures of association based on cross-classification of dichotomous variables with unequal marginals; measures based on such tables yield attenuated estimates because both diagonal cells cannot simultaneously attain zero values.

Factor Structure of the Original Test Anxiety Scale for Children

The first factor analyses to be reported concern the original Test Anxiety Scale for Children. This starting point is made here in order to provide a framework in which to view the factor analyses of the three forms of the expanded scale, which will be presented subsequently.

The thirty-two questions that were common to all three forms of the expanded scale were used in these analyses. These questions were the thirty items of the Sarason scale and the two affectively neutral items concerning dreams or thoughts about school while at home. Since these data have been reported elsewhere,[21] the results will be only briefly noted here.

For each sex ($N \geqslant 3600$), principal component factor analyses were computed from product-moment correlation matrices. The squared multiple correlation of each variable with all other variables was used as the estimate of communality. The first four principal components were rotated by use of Kaiser's normalized varimax solution for orthogonal rotation; independent rotations were performed for each sex.

Each rotation yielded four interpretable factors. By inspection, the same factor labels were assigned for both sexes. Relationships between the two factor matrices were then estimated by use of the coefficient of factor similarity.[22] This index is analogous to a correlation in that it varies between minus one and plus one. It is an estimate of the proportionality in the two sets of factor loadings.

In each instance the factors identified with common labels yielded indexes of factor similarity of .98 or .99. In contrast, the similarity coefficients for the remaining pairs of nonmatched factors were between .36 and .74. It was concluded that the four pairs of commonly-labeled factors for boys and girls were quite similar.

The Test Anxiety Factor accounted for the greatest common variance, about 40 per cent for both sexes. The items with the highest loadings included nearly all the items that mentioned the word *test*.

For example:

25. When the teacher says that she is going to give the class a test, do you become afraid that you will do poor work?

20. Do you worry a lot *before* you take a test?

The Remote School Concern Factor was the smallest one for both sexes (boys = 18 per cent, girls = 14 per cent). The highest loadings included all

[21] S. Feld and J. Lewis, "Further Evidence on the Stability of the Factor Structure of the Test Anxiety Scale for Children," *Journal of Consulting Psychology*, 31 (1967), 434.
[22] J. A. Barlow and C. Burt, "The Identification of Factors from Different Experiments," *British Journal of Statistical Psychology*, 7 (1954), 52–56.

the items describing dreams and most of the items dealing with thoughts about school while at home. The term *concern,* rather than anxiety, was chosen for its title because of the high loadings of the two affectively neutral items.

For example:

8. When you are in bed at night, do you sometimes worry about how you are going to do in class the next day?

31. When you are at home, do you think about your school work?

32. Do you sometimes dream at night about school?

18. Do you sometimes dream at night that the teacher is angry because you do not know your work?

The Comparative Poor Self-Evaluation Factor accounted for about 20 per cent of the common variance for each sex. Items with high loadings concerned expectations of failure, especially in comparisons with other children.

For example:

10. When the teacher is teaching you about reading, do you feel that other children in the class understand her better than you?

7. Do you sometimes dream at night that other boys and girls in your class can do things you cannot do?

The Somatic Signs of Anxiety Factor accounted for more common variance for girls than boys (26 per cent versus 20 per cent). All five items with somatic referents had the highest loadings on this factor, followed by items about expectations of poor work.

For example:

24. When you are taking a test, does the hand you write with shake a little?

9. When the teacher says that she is going to find out how much you have learned, do you get a funny feeling in your stomach?

These factor structures were compared with those reported by Dunn[23] for each sex at two older age levels—4th and 5th graders, and 7th and 9th graders. Dunn also interpreted four factors at each age level, and factors with labels similar to the ones used in the present research were always found. In addition, the coefficients of factor similarity calculated to compare the data from the two studies indicated marked stability across age and sex groupings. The Test Anxiety Factor was the largest one in each sample, and the most stable factor across all comparisons.

---

[23] "Stability of the Factor Structure."

Factor Structure of the Expanded Test Anxiety Scale for Children

The next issue concerned the effect that the inclusion of reversed questions in the item pool would have on the stable factor structure of the original Test Anxiety Scale for Children. For each of the three forms of the expanded scale, separate factor analyses were performed for each sex ($N \geqslant 1200$ each); all forty-two items were used, which included ten different reversed items for each form. Comparable procedures were used to those just reported. Depending on the sample, either five or six factors exhausted the originally estimated common variance. However, since it was desirable to compare the factor structures for the three forms of the expanded Test Anxiety Scale for Children, both five and six factors were rotated for all groups. The rotation solutions retained for interpretation were the ones yielding the highest coefficients of factor similarity across sex within a given form of the expanded Test Anxiety Scale for Children. Brief descriptions of each factor are provided in Table 5, along with the percentage of common variance accounted for by each factor, and the factor similarity coefficient for the two sexes on the same form.[24]

Three of the factors that had been identified in the total factor analyses (those based on the thirty-two questions asked of all subjects) also appeared in each of the six factor analyses based on the larger item pools and the three random subsets of the subjects. These factors were Test Anxiety, Poor Self-Evaluation, and Somatic Signs of Anxiety. Only one form of the expanded scale had a factor similar to Remote School Concern, which was the smallest factor in each of the total factor analyses.

Interestingly enough, the additional factors appearing in the expanded scales were not always primarily defined by the reversed items. (Only Factor *C* in Form 1, Factor *H* in Form 2, and Factors *K* and *L* in Form 3 were of that type.) For all three forms of the expanded Test Anxiety Scale for Children, at least one factor was interpreted that was primarily defined by items that had been in the total factor analyses but that had not defined a factor in those factor structures. (These were Factors *F* and *FF* in Forms 1 and 2 and Factor *J* in Forms 2 and 3.)

The patterns of factor loadings are briefly described below in terms of their support for a response set or content interpretation. The Test Anxiety Factor (Factor *A* in Table 5) always exhibited a pattern of factor loadings

---

[24] Tables with the complete pattern of factor loadings are available from the authors upon request for Working Paper #4 from Mental Health Study Center, Project 27, or, for a fee, from the National Auxiliary Publications Service. Order document NAPS–00217 from ASIS National Auxiliary Publications Service, c/o CCM Information Sciences, Inc., 22 West 34 Street, New York, New York, 10001, remitting $1 for microfiche or $3 for photocopies.

TABLE 5 *Comparisons of Factor Structures From Three Forms of the Expanded TASC*

	Form 1		Form 2		Form 3	
	Boys 6 Factors	**Girls 6 Factors**	**Boys 5 Factors**	**Girls 6 Factors**	**Boys 5 Factors**	**Girls 5 Factors**
A: Test Anxiety vs. Test Confidence	24.3% $(S = .98)$	25.6%	31.7% $(S = .96)$	21.8%	27.1% $(S = .92)$	31.5%
B: Remote School Interest	15.6% $(S = .94)$	14.9%				
C: Comparative Positive Self-Eval.	10.1% $(S = .94)$	11.4%				
D: Somatic Signs of Anxiety	19.5% $(S = .94)$	17.1%				
D: Somatic Signs of Anxiety vs. Somatic Relaxation			16.9% $(S = .94)$	15.7%		
DD: Somatic Signs of Anxiety and Worry or Dreams about School Failure					25.9% $(S = .91)$	
D: Somatic Signs of Anxiety (and fear of tests, worry or dreams about failure)						22.3% $(S = .92)$
E: Comparative Poor Self-Evaluation (and general expectations of failure)	14.6% $(S = .94)$	11.4%	16.6% $(S = .92)$	15.0%		
E: Comparative Poor Self-Eval. (and genl. expec. failure) vs. Limited Confidence					14.5%	
EE: Pervasive Expectations of Failure (including comparative) vs. Limited Confidence						21.7% $(S = .92)$

174

F: Pervasive Worries (especially about public evaluation) vs. Feels Relaxed

15.6%   (S = .92)   19.1%

F: Pervasive Worries about Failure vs. Limited School Confidence

22.4%   (S = .92)   18.3%

FF: Away from School Worries and Dreams about Failure vs. Limited School Confidence

H: Limited School Anxiety vs. General School Confidence and Interest

11.9%   (S = .88)   10.9%

J: Public Evaluation Anxiety vs. Public Eval. Confidence

17.9%

J: Public Evaluation Anxiety while at School vs. Public Eval. Confidence

20.7%   (S = .87)   16.5%

K: Limited Worries vs. Performance Confidence

11.3%

L: Expectations of Reading and Arith. Failure vs. Away from School Worries

7.6%

Notes. Letter designations were used to connote similarity in factors, with a double letter signifying that the factor was similar to, but not identical to, other factors with the same letter designation. The percentages reported are for common variance accounted for by each factor. The Index, S, is the coefficient of factor similarity across sex (Barlow & Burt, op. cit.).

175

that supported a content rather than a response set interpretation of the underlying dimension. It was always a bipolar factor, with original questions concerning test anxiety at the positive pole and reversed questions concerning test confidence at the negative pole. The matched original and reversed versions of the questions that defined the factor tended to have loadings of similar magnitude.[25]

None of the other factors that replicated in all three forms of the expanded scales showed such a clear pattern of bipolarity. The Somatic Signs of Anxiety Factor (Factors D and DD in Table 5) usually did not clearly support or refute the response set hypothesis. This ambiguity was probably related in part to the relatively small number of relevant items on the original scale (five). This meant that very few reversed items of this type appeared on any one form, and in fact, Form 1 did not have any reversed items with somatic content. Thus, the somatic factor could not show a clear bipolar pattern on Form 1. On the other two forms, two or three of the highest-loading items on the positive pole of the somatic factor had been reversed, and the loadings for the reversed items were generally negative, but of very low magnitude. On Form 2, two of the items concerning somatic signs of anxiety had reversals, but only one of these pairs had high defining loadings in both its original and reversed version. For the other pair, the reversed version, but not the original member, had a defining loading for boys, and the opposite pattern occurred for this pair for the girls. This pattern of oppositely-signed loadings on Form 2 was viewed as minimal support for a content interpretation of the factors. On Form 3 of the expanded scale, three of the items about somatic reactions to school were reversed. The original versions of these items had defining loadings on the Somatic Signs of Anxiety Factors; although all the reversed versions of these questions had negative factor loadings, they were of very small magnitude. A number of other matched original items besides those with somatic content had defining loadings, but none of their reversals did. The factors were essentially unipolar for both sexes and only original items had defining loadings. Two interpretations of this ambiguous pattern on Form 3 seemed plausible. The matched original and reversed items could be re-

---

[25] As rough rules of thumb, items with loadings of $\pm$ .20 were considered to contribute to the definition of a factor, and factor loadings of $\pm$ .30 or more were viewed as high loadings. The highest loading on any factor was usually between .50 and .60. These absolutely low levels of factor loadings are partially a result of using the lower-bound estimate for communality (the multiple squared correlation of each variable with all other variables), rather than factoring the total variance by placing unities in the diagonal of the correlation matrix.

flecting different dimensions, that is, the reversal process may have changed the meaning of the questions. Alternatively, response set could be operating to a sufficient extent to depress the appearance of a bipolar factor, but not sufficiently to produce a unipolar factor that included both versions of any item. The Somatic Signs of Anxiety Factors were, in general, not considered to offer clear support for either a content or response set interpretation.

A factor comparable to Comparative Poor Self-Evaluation also occurred in all three forms (Factors E and EE in Table 5). All these factors seemed to define a dimension of expectations of failure, with comparative self-other judgments most strongly reflecting this dimension. None of these factors had a clear bipolar pattern. An unusual pattern was found on Form 1, where three of the questions concerning self-other comparisons of adequacy of school performance were reversed. The matched original and reversed items of this type defined two factors, Comparative Poor Self-Evaluation (Factor E), and Comparative Positive Self-Evaluation (Factor C). This was taken to imply that these "reversals" were not polar opposites, but instead, were psychologically distinct from the original items; expectation of failure was an orthogonal dimension to expectation of success.

On the other two forms of the expanded scale, the patterns of factor loadings for the Poor Self-Evaluation Factor were usually equivocal in their support for the alternative hypotheses of response bias or content interpretation; the patterns were usually similar to those just described for the somatic factors. On Form 2, the Poor Self-Evaluation Factor was unipolar, with only original items having defining loadings. None of the original items with the highest loadings had reversed versions available on this form of the expanded Test Anxiety Scale for Children, so the opportunity for a bipolar pattern was limited. However, five of the original items with lower defining loadings for the boys and three of these items for the girls had matched reversals on this form of the expanded scale; none of the reversals of these items had defining loadings, although all but one of them had negative factor loadings. Similar ambiguity occurred for the comparable factor for the boys on Form 3 (Factor E) because only one of the items with a defining factor loading was a member of the ten reversed pairs on that form. This was a reversed item with a negative factor loading; its matched original version had a 0-order loading. For the girls who received Form 3, the pattern of factor loadings was somewhat different. One pair of matched items had positive loadings in *both* versions, which would be consistent with a response set interpretation. For three pairs of items, either the original form had a defining positive loading or the reversed form a defining *negative* loading, but the matched alternative versions had 0-order loadings. None of these items had very high loadings. There is, therefore, doubt about a content interpretation because of the positive loadings of both versions of one pair, but not enough clear evidence for an overall response set interpretation of this factor. In general, the Poor Self-Evaluation Factors raised more questions about a simple content interpretation than did the Test Anxiety or Somatic Signs of Anxiety Factors.

A factor comparable to Remote School Concern was identified only in Form 1 of the expanded scale (Factor B). It confirmed the authors' suggestion that the report or lack of report of dreams about school rather than the anxiety content of the dreams was the key element in these questions. All four questions concerning anxiety-laden dreams about school had reversed versions on Form 1. *Both* versions of these questions had positive factor loadings and most of them were of defining magnitude. The two neutral items concerning dreams or thoughts about school while at home also had high positive loadings on this factor. Since it had been recognized in advance that the reversals of the dream questions were not contradictory, this pattern was not viewed as supporting a response set interpretation.

None of the other factors that appeared only in the separate factor analyses by forms showed a pattern of factor loadings that was consistent with a response set interpretation (Factors F through L in Table 5); there were no instances where matched original and reversed items had defining factor loadings with the same sign. Most of the patterns were equivocal; the factors were bipolar with original items at the positive pole and reversed items at the negative pole, but, generally, only one matched pair of original and reversed items had high loadings with opposite signs. One of these factors did show fairly strong support for a content interpretation. The Public Evaluation Anxiety versus Public Evaluation Confidence Factor for the Form 2 Girls (Factor J) had three matched pairs of original and reversed items with appropriate bipolar defining loadings.

In summary, the six factor analyses each provided one large factor that clearly warranted a content interpretation. No factors were interpreted as clearly defining a response set dimension. Most of the factors did not provide an adequate test of these alternatives, but content interpretations were proposed because of apparent content similarities in the highly-loaded questions.

Factor Subscores

The stability of the factor structure of the Test Anxiety Scale for Children seemed to increase the likelihood that a multidimensional rescoring of the scale might prove useful, and a preliminary revised scoring system was devised. Subscales were developed based on the four factors from the total factor analyses. Items received a weight of 1 if they had comparatively high factor loadings for both sexes; all other items had 0 weights. The same weights were used for both sexes in order to facilitate sex comparisons. In most instances, the items chosen had factor loadings of at least .30, but in some cases items with a slightly lower loading in one sex were included. Weights were assigned on the basis of the loadings on each factor, without regard for loadings on any other factor. This resulted in some items being weighted on two subscales and other items not being included in any subscale. This simple scoring device was chosen because it might easily be applied to other data. A system of this type has been shown to yield fairly comparable results to that estimated by a least-squared regression of the actual factor scores onto the observable data.[26] The items included in each subscale are listed in Table 6, along with the means and standard deviations for the total sample.

The four subscale scores were positively intercorrelated (.32 to .65), as is typical when a simplified scoring technique is used to estimate factor scores. In part, these correlations represent item overlap, but this would not entirely account for the positive relationships. These correlations indicate that the subscales do not accurately reflect the orthogonal factors from which they were derived.

Sex and Race Differences

As one means of determining the usefulness of these subscales, sex and race differences were investigated. The entire sample of white subjects was compared with those Negro subjects attending all-Negro schools.[27] The raw scores on each subscale were converted to standard scores with a mean of 50 and a standard deviation of 10. This procedure eliminated mean differences in the four subscales that would result from the differing numbers of items in each index. It also equated the variances and therefore made the data more appropriate for Analysis of Variance techniques. Table 7 lists the means and standard deviations for each race and sex group.

---

[26] J. L. Horn, "An Empirical Comparison of Methods for Estimating Factor Scores," *Educational and Psychological Measurement*, 25 (1965), 313–322.

[27] There were two main reasons for deleting the few Negro subjects attending predominantly white schools from the present analyses ($N = 105$). First, the children attending racially mixed schools came from families with higher educational and occupational status than the remaining Negro children ($N = 826$). Second, they were a highly selective group, in that their attendance at a racially mixed school was the result of a parental request for change in their school attendance zone. While the school anxiety of these children is an important topic for investigation, it is beyond the scope of the present chapter.

TABLE 6 *Descriptive Information on Four Factorially Derived Subscales of the TASC*

Test Anxiety	Remote School Concern	Poor Self-Evaluation	Somatic Signs of Anxiety
25[a] When the teacher says that she is going to give the class a test, do you become afraid that you will do poor work?	8[a] When you are in bed at night, do you sometimes worry about how you are going to do in class the next day?	10[a] When the teacher is teaching you about reading, do you feel that other children in the class understand her better than you?	24[a] When you are taking a test, does the hand you write with shake a little?
20[a] Do you worry a lot before you take a test?	32[a] Do you sometimes dream at night about school?	7[a] When the teacher is teaching you about arithmetic, do you feel that other children in the class understand her better than you?	9[a] When the teacher asks you to write on the blackboard in front of the class, does the hand you write with sometimes shake a little?
19[a] Are you afraid of tests in school?	31[a] When you are at home, do you think about your school work?		
29[a] While you are taking a test do you usually think you are doing poor work?	18[a] Do you sometimes dream at night that the teacher is angry because you do not know your work?	14[a] Do you sometimes dream at night that other boys and girls in your class can do things you cannot do?	16[a] When the teacher says that she is going to find out how much you have learned, do you get a funny feeling in your stomach?
23 Do you sometimes dream at night that you did poor work on a test you had in school that day?	23 Do you sometimes dream at night that you did poor work on a test you had in school that day?	4[a] When the teacher says that she is going to call upon some boys and girls to answer arithmetic problems out loud, do you hope that she will call upon someone else and not on you?	28 When the teacher says that she is going to give the class a test, do you get a nervous or funny feeling?
28 When the teacher says that she is going to give the class a test, do you get a nervous or funny feeling?	22[a] After you have taken a test do you worry about how well you did on the test?		6[a] When the teacher says that she is going to find out how much you have learned, does your heart begin to beat faster?

21 Do you worry a lot while you are taking a test?

15 When you are home and you are thinking about your reading group for the next day, do you worry that you will do poor work?

12 When you are at home and you are thinking about your arithmetic work for the next day, do you become afraid that you will get the answers wrong when the teacher calls upon you?

30 While you are on your way to school, do you sometimes worry that the teacher may give the class a test?

$M = 2.253$
$SD = 2.427$
$Range = 0-10$

30 While you are on your way to school, do you sometimes worry that the teacher may give the class a test?

15 When you are home and you are thinking about your reading group for the next day, do you worry that you will do poor work?

12 When you are at home and you are thinking about your arithmetic work for the next day, do you become afraid that you will get the answers wrong when the teacher calls upon you?

$M = 3.241$
$SD = 1.715$
$Range = 0-7$

$M = 1.717$
$SD = 1.515$
$Range = 0-6$

17[a] If you did very poorly when the teacher called on you, would you probably feel like crying even though you would try not to cry?

21 Do you worry a lot while you are taking a test?

$M = 2.633$
$SD = 1.933$
$Range = 0-7$

Note. For the Sarason TASC (30 items), $M = 10.173$, $SD = 5.889$, Range = 0–30.
[a] Item appears on only one index.

| Sex and Race | N | Item | TASC Scores | | | |
			Test Anxiety	Remote School Concern	Poor Self-Eval.	Somatic Signs Anxiety
Boys, white	3357	M	48.949	48.255	49.333	48.886
		SD	9.604	9.915	9.681	9.634
Boys, Negro	411	M	53.505	55.301	53.742	51.734
		SD	9.816	9.386	10.474	9.886
Girls, white	3172	M	50.241	50.405	49.799	50.581
		SD	10.298	9.791	9.978	10.277
Girls, Negro	415	M	53.392	55.686	53.263	52.757
		SD	9.338	8.446	10.785	9.728

A 2×2 generalized Analysis of Variance factorial design was used, with the four subscales as the criteria variables.[28] This multivariate procedure tests the equality of the mean vectors (of the four criteria) for the race and sex groups. When the results of this test indicate a significant effect, it is appropriate to consider whether the effect is uniform across the four subscales, by means of a 2×2 univariate Analysis of Variance for each subscale. The results of these analyses are presented in Table 8, and the effects can be seen in Figure 3, where the standard score means on the four subscales are plotted for each of the race and sex groups.

The multivariate test for the main effect of sex was significant, indicating that the sexes differed in some way on the four subscales. (In this section all significant effects were beyond .001.) The univariate F tests for each subscale indicated that the sex effect was not uniform. The Poor Self-Evaluation Subscale did not show a significant main effect for sex. On the other three subscales, girls had significantly higher scores than boys. The relative importance of the subscales in contributing to the overall multivariate sex effect can be seen in the last column of Table 8. The standard-

---

[28] The scores for each subscale were skewed, with an excess of low scores. This violates the normality assumption for the analysis of variance, but the F test has been shown to be relatively robust in this regard (B. J. Winer, *Statistical Principles in Experimental Design* [New York: McGraw-Hill Book Company, 1962]).

Analogous to the homogeneity of variance assumption in a univariate test, the multivariate test includes an assumption of the homogeneity of the variance-covariance matrices. The present data did not meet this assumption when tested with the multivariate analogue of Barlett's test of homogeneity of variances (S. W. Greenhouse and S. Geisser, "On Methods in the Analysis of Profile Data, *Psychometrika*, 21 [1959], 95–112]; specifically, the covariance of Remote School Concern and Poor Self-Evaluation was smaller in both Negro samples than in the white samples. Since the test of the equality of the mean vectors, with which we were primarily concerned, is relatively insensitive to moderate departures from the assumption of homogeneity of dispersions (W. W. Cooley and P. R. Lohnes, *Multivariate Procedures for the Behavioral Sciences* [New York: John Wiley & Sons, 1962]), no further transformations of the data were attempted that might have equalized the dispersions. The general effect of failure to meet this assumption is to inflate the F values, and cases of borderline significance should therefore be discounted.

TABLE 8 *Multivariate and Univariate Analyses of Variance for Four Factorially Derived TASC Scores (by Sex and Race)*

Source	F	df	p<	Stand. Discrim. Func. Coeff.	Canon. Correl.
Sex (A)	23.926[a]	4/7348	.001		.113
Test Anxiety	24.069	1/7351	.001	−0.314	
Remote School Concern	73.494	1/7351	.001	0.847	
Poor Self-Evaluation	2.421	1/7351	.119	−0.135	
Somatic Signs Anxiety	48.802	1/7351	.001	0.612	
Race (B)	83.515[a]	4/7348	.001		.209
Test Anxiety	110.860	1/7351	.001	−0.188	
Remote School Concern	292.507	1/7351	.001	0.934	
Poor Self-Evaluation	115.381	1/7351	.001	0.426	
Somatic Signs Anxiety	46.833	1/7351	.001	−0.043	
Sex × Race (AB)	1.677[a]	4/7348	.152		.030
Test Anxiety	3.686	1/7351	.054	0.360	
Remote School Concern	5.996	1/7351	.014	0.800	
Poor Self-Evaluation	1.664	1/7351	.195	0.141	
Somatic Signs Anxiety	0.838	1/7351	.363	−0.262	
White Subjects					
Sex (A)	23.955[a]	4/6524	.001		.120
Test Anxiety	27.502	1/6527	.001	−0.258	
Remote School Concern	77.573	1/6527	.001	0.861	
Poor Self-Evaluation	3.672	1/6527	.055	−0.134	
Somatic Signs Anxiety	47.298	1/6527	.001	0.556	
Negro Subjects					
Sex (A)	1.192[a]	4/821	.313		.076
Test Anxiety	0.029	1/824	.865	0.858	
Remote School Concern	0.384	1/824	.536	−0.379	
Poor Self-Evaluation	0.419	1/824	.518	0.196	
Somatic Signs Anxiety	2.247	1/824	.134	−1.121	
Male Subjects					
Race (B)	52.835[a]	4/3763	.001		.231
Test Anxiety	81.982	1/3766	.001	− .055	
Remote School Concern	186.973	1/3766	.001	.886	
Poor Self-Evaluation	74.545	1/3766	.001	.386	
Somatic Signs Anxiety	31.802	1/3766	.001	− .071	
Female Subjects					
Race (B)	32.365[a]	4/3582	.001		.187
Test Anxiety	35.073	1/3585	.001	− .343	
Remote School Concern	110.006	1/3585	.001	.983	
Poor Self-Evaluation	43.369	1/3585	.001	.478	
Somatic Signs Anxiety	16.647	1/3585	.001	− .010	

[a] Multivariate analysis of variance evaluated with Wilk's lambda criterion and Rao's approximate F test, with an exact correction for unequal cell size (D. J. Clyde, E. M. Cramer, and R. J. Sherin, *Multivariate Statistical Programs* (1st ed.; Coral Gables, Fla.: Biometric laboratory, University of Miami, 1966).

ized discriminant function coefficients provide the weights that would best discriminate between the two sex groups, in a least squares sense, using a linear combination of scores on the four anxiety subscores. The Remote School Concern Subscale would be relatively most important in discriminating the sexes, and the Somatic Signs of Anxiety Subscale the next most important. Despite the significant univariate F associated with sex for the Test Anxiety Subscale, the low discriminant coefficient suggests that this subscale does not provide much independent contribution to the discrimination between the sexes. An explanation is probably found in the sizable positive within-group correlations between the Test Anxiety Subscale and both the Remote School Concern Subscale (.587) and the Somatic Signs of Anxiety Subscale (.646). Thus, the differences between the sexes in scores on Test Anxiety can be accounted for by Remote School Concern and Somatic Signs of Anxiety.

Although there were no significant interactive effects, inspection of the four sets of profiles in Figure 3 suggested that the significant main sex effects were primarily due to the white sample. To test this, one-way analyses of variance were computed for the simple main effect of sex, for each race group. These data are in the lower half of Table 8. The results for the white subjects duplicated those for the total sample, but there were no significant sex differences for the Negro sample. Thus, the overall main effect for sex was primarily due to the white sample.

The multivariate test of the main effect of race was also significant. Race had a more uniform effect than sex; Negro children had significantly higher anxiety scores than white children on all four subscales. The Remote School Concern Subscale was again most discriminating, but in contrast to the lack of a sex effect on Poor Self-Evaluation, that subscale was the next most important one in discriminating between the two race groups. Although Figure 3 indicates that the race effect appeared to be larger for males than females on each of the four subscales, the simple main effect of race was significant for each sex. Thus, both the males and females contributed significantly to the overall main effect for race.

The relatively greater importance of the race effect, as compared to the sex effect, also is apparent in Figure 3. The multivariate analysis of variance provided an estimate of the relative strength of the two main effects, in the related canonical correlation between each of the main effects and the four subscales. This correlation was .113 for the sex effect and .209 for the race effect. Thus, the trend of a stronger race than sex effect, apparent in Figure 3, was confirmed by the multivariate analysis.

The results derived from the subscale analysis were compared with those

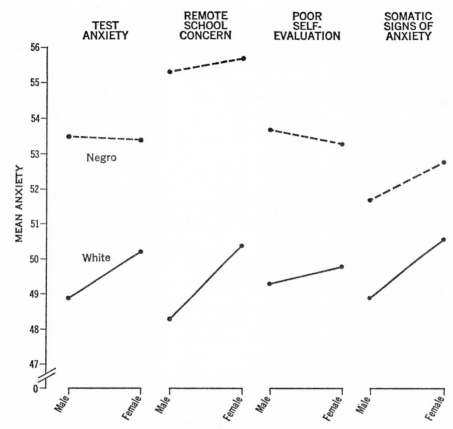

Figure 3. The effects of sex and race on four factorially derived TASC subscores.

obtained using the total score on the Test Anxiety Scale for Children.[29] The data for the total scores are presented in Table 9.[30] The main effects of

---

[29] The thirty-item Sarason scale.

[30] Raw scores are presented in Table 9 in order to facilitate comparisons with normative data from other studies. The following studies describe their subjects as middle-class, and presumably white. I. Sarnoff *et al.* ("A Cross-Cultural Study of Anxiety among American and English School Children," *Journal of Educational Psychology,* 49 [1958], 129–136) reported means for high and low "Liars." For the low Liars, the means for both boys and girls at Grades 1 and 2 were much lower than ours; they were between 6.3 and 8.7. K. T. Hill and S. B. Sarason ("The Relation of Test Anxiety and Defensiveness to Test and School Performance over the Elementary-School Years: A Further Longitudinal Study," *Monographs of the Society for Research in Child Development,* 31 [1966], 2, Whole No. 104) reported Grade 1 means of 7.5 for boys and 7.7 for girls, and Grade 3 means of 8.7 for boys and 10.6 for girls; only the 3rd grade girls in their study had as high scores as our sample.

Only one report of total score means for Negro children was found. (I. Katz, "The Socialization of Academic Motivation in Minority Group Children," in D. Levine [ed.], *Nebraska Symposium on Motivation* [Lincoln: University of Nebraska Press, 1967], 133–191). In

TABLE 9 *Means, Standard Deviations, and Analysis of Variance Summary for the Total TASC Scores (by Sex and Race)*

Sex and Race	N	Item	Total TASC Scores	
			Raw Score	Standard Score
Boys, white	3357	M	9.382	48.681
		SD	5.706	9.678
Boys, Negro	411	M	12.747	54.388
		SD	5.301	8.991
Girls, white	3172	M	10.280	50.206
		SD	6.033	10.233
Girls, Negro	415	M	12.978	54.780
		SD	5.209	8.834

Summary of Analysis of Variance

Source	F	df	p <
Sex (A)	37.038	1/7351	.001
Race (B)	199.970	1/7351	.001
Sex × Race	2.426	1/7351	.118

both sex and race were significant, but the interaction was not; girls and Negroes had higher total scores. The simple effects were also tested. White females had significantly higher total scores than white males ($t = 6.182$, $df = 6527$, $p < .001$), but the sex difference for Negroes, while in the same direction, was not significant ($t = 0.711$, $df = 824$). The simple race effect was significant for both sexes; Negro boys and girls had higher total anxiety scores than white boys and girls (for boys, $t = 12.027$, $df = 3766$, $p < .001$; for girls, $t = 9.791$, $df = 3587$, $p < .001$).

Thus, the general results using the total score were similar to those obtained with the multivariate test of the four subscales. Two important additional kinds of information were obtained by using the subscales. First, one component of the total scale did not contribute to the overall sex difference—the Poor Self-Evaluation Subscale. Second, even when significant sex or race effects were obtained, the several subscales were differentially useful in discriminating between the sexes or the races.

DISCUSSION AND CONCLUSIONS

The results presented in the previous section are now reviewed in terms of their relevance to three questions about the Test Anxiety Scale for Children:

that small and specially selected sample of 5th and 6th grade children in a Detroit school, the obtained means for both sexes were higher than those for the Negro children in the present study. In each sex, those subjects were chosen to equally represent children whom teachers rated as high and low achievers. For 10 girls, the mean was 18.7, and for 36 boys the mean was 13.6, with the sex difference significant at $p < .05$.

1. How important an influence is acquiescent response bias?

2. How does the nature of the multidimensional structure revise our conception of what the scale measures?

3. How useful is the simplified system for rescoring the scale in terms of its multidimensional structure?

Two kinds of estimates of the importance of response bias were presented. In the first analysis, each pair of original and reversed items was assumed to reflect the same underlying dimension of anxiety. The scale placements of the two forms of the items on the anxiety continuum were then used to determine the discrepancy between the observed percentage of double agreement for each item pair and a theoretical minimum or maximum value of double agreement. It was assumed that values close to the theoretical minimum would support a content interpretation of replies, while values close to the maximum would support a response set interpretation. The average observed percentage of double agreement fell midway between these two theoretical extremes. Thus, neither of the alternative hypotheses was clearly supported by the data when all items were considered. Certain item pairs clearly supported a content interpretation: The observed percentage of double agreement was much closer to the theoretical minimum than to the theoretical maximum. Other pairs elicited appreciable response bias: The observed percentage of double agreement was much closer to the theoretical maximum than to the minimum.

In the second estimate of response bias, the factor analyses based on the expanded scales were used to assess simultaneously the validity of the assumption that the reversals reflected the same dimensions as the original questions, and the influence of acquiescent or negativistic response set. The general assumption that the reversed and original questions always reflected the same dimensions could not be uniformly confirmed or rejected, as will be discussed shortly. The influence of response set could be partially determined. These analyses led to the conclusion that it is reasonable to eliminate the extreme argument that scores on the Test Anxiety Scale for Children are nothing but a reflection of acquiescent or negativistic response set. Furthermore, response bias is not the primary determinant of replies to the scale. The possibility of some minimal response set influence, however, cannot be excluded.

There were two main reasons for arriving at these conclusions about the influence of response set on the Test Anxiety Scale for Children. First, the largest single factor in each of the six factor analyses was clearly a content factor, the Test Anxiety versus Test Confidence Factor. Second, none of the factors in the six factor analyses clearly required a response set interpretation. For only one of the three forms of the expanded scale did a factor ever appear that could possibly be judged to be a response set factor: Both original and reversed versions of several pairs of items had positive loadings for Factor B on Form 1. Nevertheless, this relatively small factor, called Remote School Interest, was given a content rather than a response set interpretation because the questions concerned dreams and other fantasies about school. It had been assumed in advance of the data analysis that questions about these experiences would probably not be adequately reversed in the sense that replying "Yes" to the original and reversed versions of the same question were not necessarily contradictory. Consistent differences in the reporting and nonreporting of dreams have been found even under laboratory conditions.[31] On the other two forms, none of the factors showed a pattern of several matched original and reversed items defining the same pole, although there was one factor where a single matched pair of original and reversed items loaded on the positive pole (Factor EE for the girls on Form 3) along with many original items. The negative pole was defined by a single reversed item. This pattern did not seem to warrant the interpretation of a response set factor. At the same time, most of the factors could not definitely be interpreted as content factors because they did not show a clear pattern of bipolar loadings for several matched original and reversed items. Because of the similarity in the manifest content of the items, and the lack of any direct evidence for response set, these factors were not interpreted in terms of their content, although some minimal response set influence could not be discounted.

An important question to ask about this pattern of results is, why should one factor have a pattern of loadings that so clearly conforms to the ideal type for a content interpretation of its underlying dimension, while the other factors, which also appear to reflect content, do not? Two conjectures are offered. The first, already mentioned, is that the random division of the reversals into three sets resulted in the several types of content being represented on the three forms with differential frequency. In order to find bipolar factors in the factor analyses of each of the three forms of the expanded Test Anxiety Scale for Children, several reversed items representing each type of content would be required on each form. This condition was not always met since only ten reversed items (as compared with thirty original items) appeared on any one form of the expanded scale. According to this argument, the Test Anxiety versus Test Confidence Factor was always bipolar because several reversed items concerning tests appeared on each of the three forms. This frequency argument is only par-

[31] D. R. Goodenough *et al.*, "A Comparison of Dreamers and Nondreamers: Eye Movements, Electroencephalograms, and Recall of Dreams," *Journal of Abnormal and Social Psychology*, 59 (1959), 295–302.

tially satisfactory, however, since sufficient numbers of matched reversed and original items were available for other factors, at least on certain forms of the expanded scale. For example, on Form 1, the three highest-loading items on the Comparative Poor Self-Evaluation Factor did have reversed versions appearing on that form, but they defined another factor rather than the opposite pole. The limitation on the frequency of occurrence of different types of matched original and reversed items, therefore, does not appear to be the major reason for the absence of bipolarity. Instead, the *type* of content the factors reflect seems to be a more important influence on the occurrence of bipolarity.

It is proposed that factors defined by the *stimulus conditions* for anxiety are bipolar because the reversal technique does not change the occurrence of the stimulus in the questions. The Test Anxiety Factor was always bipolar because it defined a class of stimuli, tests; all the questions that mentioned the word *test* in their original version also did so in their reversed version. What changed in the reversed questions was the description of the type of reaction to that stimulus; these changes may not critically affect the loading of items on a stimulus factor so long as it is clearly possible for the subject to judge the reaction to the stimulus (e.g., tests) as being unpleasant, as compared with pleasant. On the other hand, the specific choices made for the reversals of the affective or cognitive reactions may be the critical determinant of the loadings of the reversed items on factors defined by anxiety *responses*. Somatic anxiety reactions were reversed by substituting the reaction of feeling relaxed and comfortable; self-derogation was changed to self-aggrandizement; worrying was changed to feeling confident or relaxed; expectations of success substituted for expectations of failure, and so forth. The factors that did not replicate as bipolar factors were defined by these various aspects of the anxiety *response*, and it is suggested that they were not always bipolar because of the methodological difficulty of finding appropriate reversals.

Furthermore, the assumption that there are polar opposites to these experiential states can be questioned. Tomkins,[32] for example, does not view the negative affects as simply the polar opposites of the positive affects. Instead, positive and negative affects are described as independent motivational aspects of the personality system. Several empirical studies of mood states in adults support this conclusion. Green and Nowlis[33] factor

---

[32] S. S. Tomkins, *Affect, Imagery, Consciousness* (*The Positive Affects*, Vol I [New York: Springer, 1962]); and *Affect, Imagery, Consciousness* (*The Negative Affects*, Vol. II [New York: Springer, 1963]).

[33] R. F. Green and V. Nowlis, "A Factor Analytic Study of the Domain of Mood with Independent Experiment Validation of the Factors," *American Psychologist*, 12 (1957), 438 (abstract).

analyzed self-ratings of college men on one hundred adjectives describing mood states and expected to find bipolar factors. Instead, they found unipolar factors that separated positive feelings from negative feelings, for example, elation from sadness, and surgency from fatigue. Bradburn and Caplovitz[34] obtained reports on several positive and negative feeling states occurring within the last week. They concluded that the items describing positive affects formed a separate cluster from those describing negative affects. In the present data the occurrence of separate factors for positive and negative self-evaluations and the lack of clear bipolar factors concerning somatic signs of anxiety, or worries, may also reflect the independence of positive and negative feeling states.

These considerations of the possible reasons for lack of bipolarity of certain factors raised several problems about the appropriate future directions for research. If bipolarity did not occur in the factor analyses because of inadequate reversals, one appropriate next step would be to develop other reversed questions. If bipolarity did not occur because the feeling states described by the original questions do not have polar opposites, then this reversal technique is an inappropriate way to separate the variance determined by content from that determined by response set, and further scale revisions may not be appropriate. The proper direction to take in assessing individual differences in acquiescence is also in doubt. Although it was concluded that response bias is not a primary determinant of scale scores, the possibility remains that certain individuals do show a consistent response set, and it would be interesting to isolate those persons. This may be difficult to do, since an overall index of acquiescence may not be appropriate if it is not contradictory to answer "Yes" to both items in certain reversed pairs.

In conclusion, it should be noted that the relatively minor role of acquiescence on the Test Anxiety Scale for Children is in agreement with the findings of two studies in which items from the Taylor Manifest Anxiety Scale[35] items were reversed.[36] Both investigations revealed high positive correlations between the true-keyed and false-keyed versions of that anxiety scale, thereby indicating the lack of acquiescent bias. Perhaps the evidence concerning acquiescence on attitude scales, where the subjects may not have strong opinions, led to an overconcern about the importance of this phe-

---

[34] N. M. Bradburn and D. Caplovitz, *Reports on Happiness: A Pilot Study of Behavior Related to Mental Health* (Chicago: Aldine Publishers, 1965).

[35] J. A. Taylor, "A Personality Scale of Manifest Anxiety," *Journal of Abnormal and Social Psychology*, 48 (1953), 285–290.

[36] H. E. Adams and A. C. Kirby, "Manifest Anxiety, Social Desirability, or Response Set," *Journal of Consulting Psychology*, 27 (1963), 59–61; L. J. Chapman and D. J. Campbell, "Absence of Acquiscence Response Set in the Taylor Manifest Anxiety Scale," *Journal of Consulting Psychology*, 23 (1959), 465–466.

nomena on other questionnaire devices. Anxiety scales do not seem to be seriously impaired by an acquiescent response set.

The second question under discussion concerns the ways in which the nature of the multidimensional structure of the Test Anxiety Scale for Children affects the theoretical conception of what it measures. As has been indicated, the dimensions revealed in the factor analyses are viewed as defining both the stimulus and response components of anxiety.[37] Since the development of the original scale was premised on the importance of limiting the stimulus for anxiety to academic evaluation situations, it is noteworthy that formal test situations define a separate factor from other school evaluation situations. Two other classes of school evaluation situations occurred with some frequency on the original scale—public evaluation or recitation situations, and direct mention of the teacher. In three of the factor analyses of the expanded scales, the stimulus of public evaluation did define one of the factors. Thus, this situation might also be a distinctive anxiety cue for some children. The explicit stimulus of the teacher never defined a factor. Nevertheless, it might be argued that the teacher was an implicit part of the stimulus condition in all the questions and that this was the reason this stimulus condition could not be distinguished.

The other factors differentiated among the various types of experiences that could be broadly classed as anxiety reactions. Factors concerning somatic reactions and self-derogatory feelings were found in all forms of the expanded scale. In some forms the experiences of dreams and fantasies about school, or worrying about school, also defined factors. It seems that a fuller specification and measurement of the several aspects of the achievement anxiety experience is an important area for future research. If the ways in which school performance can be affected by "anxiety" are to be understood, one must distinguish among children who have different types of unpleasant reactions. The child who perceives that he is having unpleasant physiological reactions should react differently to a learning task than the child who expects failure. These two response patterns might also elicit different reactions from a teacher. If a child who believes that his hand is shaking overtly manifests this symptom, his anxiety might be more easily recognized by a teacher than the anxiety of a child who privately expects failure.

Two different conceptions of what is being measured by the Test Anxiety Scale for Children have been prominent in the literature and the multidimensional structure of the scale has implications for these con-

---

[37] N. S. Endler, J. McV. Hunt, and A. J. Rosenstein, "An S–R Inventory of Anxiousness," *Psychological Monographs*, 76 (1962), 17, Whole No. 536.

ceptualizations. The original developers of the scale[38] viewed it as reflecting anxiety that had its roots in the parent-child relationship and that was manifested during evaluation by a significant adult figure, the teacher. Recently, Sarason[39] has questioned whether the child who describes himself as highly anxious on the Test Anxiety Scale for Children frequently manifests overt signs of a severe anxiety reaction. He has suggested, instead, that the child is reporting the private experience of thoughts and feelings that may be a form of defense against the experience of severe anxiety. The responses differentiated by the factors provide a way to begin to specify the types of reactions that so-called anxious children may experience in lieu of a severe anxiety attack. Viewing oneself as less competent than one's peers may be a defense against a severe anxiety attack. It would be interesting to compare the developmental histories and achievement performance of persons with this response pattern with that of persons who ruminate or dream about school, or those who react with physiological symptoms.

Atkinson and Feather,[40] on the other hand, have used the Test Anxiety Scale for Children as an indirect measure of the motive to avoid failure. According to their formulation, the motive to avoid failure is defined as ". . . a disposition to avoid failure and/or a capacity for experiencing shame and humiliation as a consequence of failure."[41] In schools or other settings where achievement-oriented situations cannot be avoided, anxiety is experienced in proportion to the strength of a person's tendency to avoid failure. The person who is dominated by a motive to avoid failure, rather than a motive to achieve success, will, whenever possible, act so as to minimize his anxiety about failure. The multidimensional structure of the scale raises the question of whether the kinds of "pain" experienced in potential failure situations have different implications for inferences about the strength of the tendency to avoid failure. It would be interesting to see whether predictions based on this theory of achievement motivation would more clearly be supported by subscales measuring one or another of the components of the scale. For example, the Test Anxiety Factor seems to come closest to the formulation of anxiety as an indicator of the tendency to avoid failure: It defines anxiety experienced in response to a constrained situation where achievement evaluation, and possibly failure,

[38] Sarason *et al.*, *op. cit.*
[39] S. B. Sarason, "The Measurement of Anxiety in Children: Some Questions and Problems," in C. D. Spielberger (ed.), *Anxiety and Behavior* (New York: Academic Press, 1966), 63–79.
[40] J. W. Atkinson and N. T. Feather (eds.), *A Theory of Achievement Motivation* (New York: John Wiley & Sons, 1966), Chap. 20.
[41] *Ibid.*, 13.

will occur. In contrast, it is more difficult to conceive of the Remote School Concern Factor as indicative of a tendency to inhibit encounters with situations that might lead to failure. This factor describes a tendency to think about possible school failure even when not directly confronted by that situation. A person with a high score on this factor engages in rumination and fantasy about possible school failure when he is at home, a behavior pattern which does not appear to minimize anxiety about failure.

The third question under discussion is the usefulness of the simple re-scoring of the Test Anxiety Scale for Children in terms of its factor structure. If the above speculations about the interpretation of these factors are appropriate, factor scores should differentiate several types of children corresponding to the several anxiety response patterns and stimulus conditions for anxiety. This proposition was considered by testing sex and race differences on the four subscales used as indexes of the factors. This attempt rested on the assumption that these subscales were good representations of the factors. The fairly strong correlations among these four subscales suggested that they were not good indexes of the orthogonal dimensions underlying the factors, but even so, the race and sex effects were not uniform across the four subscales.

Girls are often found to have higher scores on the Test Anxiety Scale for Children than boys, and the difference seems to increase with increased time at school or increased age.[42] For the present 2nd grade subjects, this significant overall sex difference was found only for the white sample. The subscale analysis indicated that the strongest sex differences occurred on the two factors that seemed to be most clearly describing emotional types of responses, Remote School Concern and Somatic Signs of Anxiety. There are some other indications in the literature of similar sex differences concerning somatic reactions. For example, adult women report a greater frequency of psychophysiological or hypochondriacal symptomatology,[43] and L'Abate[44] found grade-school girls reported more daydreams than boys. However, sex differences in the frequency of night dreams or daydreams reported have not usually been obtained.[45] The

[42] R. D. Bloom, *Some Correlates of Test Anxiety* (Doctoral dissertation, University of Michigan [Ann Arbor: University Microfilms, 1963]), No. 63–4939; F. N. Cox and P. M. Leaper, "General and Test Anxiety Scales for Children," *Australian Journal of Psychology,* 11 (1959), 70–80; Dunn, "School Approach-Avoidance Values"; Hill and Sarason, *op. cit.;* Sarnoff *et al., op. cit.*

[43] D. C. Leighton, "The Distribution of Psychiatric Symptoms in a Small Town," *American Journal of Psychiatry,* 112 (1956), 716–723; G. S. Welsh and W. C. Dahlstrom (eds.), *Basic Readings on the MMPI in Psychology and Medicine* (Minneapolis: University of Minnesota Press, 1956).

[44] L. L'Abate, "Personality Correlates of Manifest Anxiety in Children," *Journal of Consulting Psychology,* 24 (1960), 342–348.

[45] J. L. Singer, *Daydreaming: An Introduction to the Experimental Study of Inner Experience* (New York: Random House, 1966).

present findings can also be viewed as consistent with some of the exciting recent work on neonatal differences in responsiveness to auditory, tactile, or oral stimulation. Silverman[46] recently reviewed some of this work on neonatal response patterns, where there have been suggestions that female infants are more sensitive to external stimulation than male infants.[47] He proposes that there are two unique cognitive styles or experience types, for males and for females, and that these have a constitutional basis. The feminine style is typified by intuitive perceptions of feeling situations, openness to images from the unconscious, and openness to the external environment. The masculine style involves discrimination and analysis, observing and inquiring. Thus, he speculates that the characteristics usually ascribed to appropriate sex role behavior may be rooted in constitutional differences. Whatever their origin, it seems likely that the feminine style—sensitivity to external stimuli, responsiveness, and fantasy —characterizes the factors represented by the three subscales on which the sexes differed (Test Anxiety, Somatic Signs of Anxiety, and Remote School Concerns).

In contrast to the aforementioned subscales, the Poor Self-Evaluation Subcale did not differentiate the white boys and girls. More clearly than any of the other factors, it defined an analytic type of cognitive response, in which one's own competence was compared to that of other people. It is also possible that the Poor Self-Evaluation Factor reflects realistic self-appraisal. Since young girls generally perform better in school than boys, it would be unrealistic for girls to compare themselves more unfavorably to other children, even if they have stronger emotional responses to school evaluation. There is some evidence that the Poor Self-Evaluation Subscale shows stronger relationships to past performance in school than do the other subcales. Several family background and three achievement-related measures were used in multiple correlation predictions of each of the four subscores, within each race and sex subgroup. For the white boys, the 1st grade IQ scores and the 1st grade reading readiness scores, as well as prior retention in grade, independently entered into the prediction of Poor Self-Evaluation. For the other subscales, either the IQ or reading readiness scores entered into the prediction, but not both, and retention was never a significant predictor.[48]

[46] J. Silverman, "Temperament, Sex, and Cognitive Styles" (Unpublished manuscript, National Institute of Mental Health, 1966).

[47] M. Lewis et al., "Attention to Visual Patterns in Infants" (Paper presented at the meeting of the American Psychological Association, Philadelphia, September, 1963); R. Q. Bell and J. F. Darling, "The Prone Head Reaction in the Human Neonate: Relation with Sex and Tactile Sensitivity," Child Development, 36 (1965), 943–949.

[48] The authors also view the results of Silverstein and Mohan's (op. cit.) factor analysis of the Test Anxiety Scale for Children for mentally retarded children as consistent with this

Race differences were obtained for the total score on the Test Anxiety Scale for Children as well as for all subscales, with the Negro children having higher scores. The strength of the race effect was not uniform across the subscales. The Remote School Concern and Poor Self-Evaluation Subscales, in that order, contributed the most toward discriminating the race groups. Differences on the latter scale seem readily interpreted as consistent with other research showing stronger expectations of failure and self-derogation in Negro than in white children.[49] For example, Epps[50] recently reported that Negro elementary school children are higher in fear of failure than white children in the same school system; Phillips[51] found that non-Anglo (Mexican and Negro) children were higher than Anglo children on a measure of school anxiety that included most of the items from the Test Anxiety Scale for Children. No reason can be offered why dreams and fantasies about school should be especially high among Negro children, but this is seen as an important question raised by the subscale analysis. Other data suggest that the race results are not fully explainable in terms of social class differences. In multiple correlation predictions of each of the four subscores for the entire sample, race and sex, as well as a variety of family background and school achievement measures, were used as predictor variables. For all four subscores, race made a significant independent contribution to the multiple correlations over and above contributions from ability measures and measures of social status of the parents.

To sum up this discussion, the following tentative answers to the three questions posed earlier are proposed:

1. Acquiescent response set does not appear to be a major source of variance in the Test Anxiety Scale for Children, but the extent of individual differences in this response tendency warrants assessment.

2. The multidimensional structure of the scale directs attention away from the distinction between anxious and non-anxious children. Instead, interest is focused on children for whom different types of school situa-

---

view of the realistic element in the Poor Self-Evaluation Factor. The largest factor in their study was not Test Anxiety; it was a factor they labeled Generalized School Anxiety, but which Feld proposed (S. Feld, "Generalized School Anxiety or Negative Self-Image: Letter to the Editor," *American Journal of Mental Deficiency*, 70 [1966], 930–931) could more appropriately be labeled Negative School Self-Image. That factor was very similar to the Poor Self-Evaluation Factor; all the questions about negative self-other comparisons had very high loadings.

[49] See I. Katz, "Review of Evidence Relating to Effects of Desegregation on the Intellectual Performance of Negroes," *American Psychologist*, 19 (1964), 381–399.

[50] E. G. Epps, "Social Background and Motivation" (Unpublished manuscript, Survey Research Center, University of Michigan, April, 1966).

[51] B. N. Phillips, *An Analysis of Causes of Anxiety Among Children in School* (Austin: The University of Texas, 1966). The Final Report to the Office of Education, U.S. Department of Health, Education, and Welfare: Project No. 2616, Contract No. OE–5–10–012.

tions elicit anxiety responses and on children who experience different types of anxiety reactions to school evaluation situations.

3. The lack of independence of the four subscales indicate that they do not accurately reflect the orthogonal multidimensional structure of the Test Anxiety Scale for Children, and this may be a serious problem in future efforts to differentiate the correlates of the dimensions using these subscales. Despite this problem, these measures of the factors yield certain interesting results that are not simple duplications of the results using the total score.

SUMMARY

This chapter reports on a project that was the first stage of a long-term program of research concerning positive (achievement motivation) and negative (achievement anxiety) achievement strivings in children and those aspects of the social environment in the home and school that are related to their development and manifestations. There were three general purposes for this project, which was designed to deal with general methodological and normative problems in the measurement of achievement anxiety: (1) consideration of the methodological issues of response set and multidimensionality, which might lead to refinement of the Test Anxiety Scale for Children; (2) investigation of social background and school achievement correlates of test anxiety and defensiveness in a more heterogeneous sample of children than had previously been done; and (3) establishment of a pool of subjects with measured levels of test anxiety and defensiveness, from which subjects could be selected for further studies that required certain levels of these variables.

Factor analyses designed to investigate the importance of response set, as well as the multidimensional structure of the Test Anxiety Scale for Children (TASC) were presented. As an illustration of the usefulness of a simplified procedure for rescoring the original scale in a multidimensional fashion, race and sex differences on the total scale and the subscales were analyzed.

Expanded forms of the TASC that included original and reversed questions were devised. The results presented in this chapter were based on 7,551 2nd grade Ss who were orally administered the scale in the classroom. Data concerning family background, school tests, and school history were obtained from school files.

Factor analyses of the original TASC were performed for each sex. Four factors appeared in both sexes, and were labeled: Test Anxiety, Somatic Signs of Anxiety, Poor Self-Evaluation, and Remote School Concern. For each of three forms of the expanded TASC, separate factor analyses were also performed for each sex. Five or six factors were interpreted. Three of the factors identified in the original TASC replicated in each of the six factor analyses based on the expanded versions of the scale, which included reversed items. In each form of the expanded scale, the largest factor was the bipolar Test Anxiety Factor, which was a content factor that included original and reversed items. Most of the other factors did not provide an adequate test of the alternative interpretations of underlying content or response set dimensions, but content interpretations were proposed because of apparent content similarities in the highly-loaded questions. None of the factors were interpreted as clearly defining a response set dimension. The content of the factors were interpreted as defining both the stimulus conditions that elicit anxiety and the types of reactions that are components of anxiety.

Subscales were developed based on the four factors found in the original TASC. Items received a weight of one if they had comparatively high factor loadings for both sexes; all other items had zero weights. Although the subscales were intended to represent four independent factors, there were, nevertheless, small but significant positive correlations among them.

A two-way multivariate analysis of variance was performed to test the race and sex effects on the four subscales. The main effects of sex and race were significant. The overall sex effect indicated higher anxiety scores for girls, and girls also had significantly higher scores on the Remote School Concern, Somatic Signs of Anxiety, and Test Anxiety Subscales. However, only the first two subscales showed sizable independent contributions to a significant discriminant between the sexes. The overall sex effect was due to the white sample only. All four subscales showed a significant race effect, indicating higher anxiety scores for Negroes than whites. The Remote School Concern and Poor Self-Evaluation Subscales, in that order of importance, made sizable independent contributions to a race discriminant. These results were compared with those obtained using the total score on the TASC. The main effects of sex and race were once again significant. Thus, the general results using the total score were similar to those obtained with the multivariate test of the four subscales. Two important additional kinds of information were obtained by using the subscales. First, one component of the total scale did not contribute to the overall sex difference—the Poor Self-Evaluation Subscale. Second, even when significant sex or race effects were obtained, the several subscales were differentially useful in discriminating between the sexes or the races.

The following conclusions and directions for future research were proposed: (1) Acquiescent response set does not appear to be a major source of variance in the TASC, but the extent of individual differences in this response tendency warrants assessment. (2) The multidimensional structure of the scale directs attention away from the distinction between anxious and non-anxious children. Instead, the focus shifts to children who experience anxiety in response to different types of school situations and to children who experience different types of anxiety reactions to school evaluation situations. (3) The lack of independence of the four subscales indicates that they do not accurately reflect the orthogonal multidimensional structure of the TASC, and this may be a serious problem in future efforts to differentiate the correlates of the dimensions using these subscales. Despite this problem, these measures of the factors yield certain interesting sex and race results that are not simple duplications of the results using the total score.

APPENDIX MATERIALS

The instructions that each examiner read to the children in administering the expanded Test Anxiety Scale for Children are presented below in their entirety. Since all questions included in the expanded scales appeared in Table 3, they are not reproduced here. Instead, the questions that appeared on each form are listed in their order of appearance. The children's answer sheet was numbered from 1 to 42 with "Yes" and "No" next to each number.

Instructions
My name is ———. I'm going to be asking you some questions. These are different from the usual school questions for these are about how you feel and so have no right or wrong answers. First I'll hand out the answer sheets and then I'll tell you more about the questions. . . .

Before we begin, I want to make sure that each boy and girl has a pencil with an eraser. Does everyone have a pencil and an eraser? (Hand out pencils to those who don't have them.) Write *both your first and your last* names at the top of the first page.

Now I am going to ask you some questions. No one but myself will see your answers to these questions, not your teacher or your principal or your parents. These questions are different from other questions that you are asked in school. These questions are different because there are no right or wrong answers. You are to listen to each question and then put a circle around either "Yes" or "No." These questions are about how *you* think and feel. Children think and feel differently. The person sitting next to you might put a circle around "Yes" and you may put a circle around "No." For example, if I asked you this question: "Do you like to play ball?" some of you would put a circle around "Yes" because you like to play ball, and some of you would put it around "No" because you don't like playing ball. Your answer depends on how *you* think and feel. These questions are about how you think and feel about school, and about a lot of other things. Remember, listen carefully to each question and answer it "Yes" or "No" by deciding how you think and feel. If you don't understand a question, hold up your hand. Be sure to answer every question.

QUESTIONS IN EXPANDED TASC SCALES

Sequence #	Question # Form 1	Form 2	Form 3
1	1	1	1
2	5R	12R	3R
3	2	2	2
4	1R	4R	17R
5	3	3	3
6	4	4	4
7	32	32	32
8	5	5	5
9	14R	13R	9R
10	6	6	6
11	7	7	7
12	8	8	8
13	9	9	9
14	10	10	10
15	11	11	11
16	18R	6R	2R
17	12	12	12
18	13	13	13
19	10R	8R	16R
20	14	14	14
21	31	31	31
22	15	15	15
23	16	16	16
24	7R	15R	11R
25	17	17	17
26	18	18	18
27	25R	21R	22R
28	19	19	19
29	29R	30R	25R
30	20	20	20
31	21	21	21
32	22	22	22
33	20R	19R	26R
34	23	23	23
35	24	24	24
36	25	25	25
37	23R	24R	28R
38	26	26	26
39	27	27	27
40	28	28	28
41	29	29	29
42	30	30	30

CHAPTER SIX

Comments on Papers
by Crandall and Veroff

JOHN W. ATKINSON

SOME of us outside the developmental psychology of achievement motivation, viewing this work from the perspective of typical research on the college sophomore, must be impressed with certain features of it. Particularly encouraging is the much more elaborate analysis of the development of achievement motivation which guides current work. For those initially excited by McClelland and Friedman[1] and Marian Winterbottom's[2] exploration of the origins of the achievement motive in parental training practices, who perhaps mistakenly came away thinking that achievement motivation had to be pounded into the head of a youngster by parental demands followed by affectionate rewards, the Veroff three-stage theory is an enlightening elaboration and a nice synthesis of concepts drawn from a number of sources.

My own oversimplified notion that acquisition of a motive to achieve was probably to be considered merely a subparagraph under the general topic of secondary reward and/or social reinforcement seemed credible until we had our own children and began to observe them. I remember when my faith in this oversimplified conception collapsed. One night our first boy, sometime in his first year, woke my wife and me in the middle

---

[1] D. C. McClelland and G. A. Friedman, "A Cross-Cultural Study of the Relationship Between Child-Training Practices and Achievement Motivation Appearing in Folk-Tales," in G. E. Swanson, T. M. Newcomb, and E. L. Hartley (eds.), *Readings in Social Psychology* (New York: Henry Holt & Co., 1952).

[2] Marian R. Winterbottom, "The Relation of Childhood Training in Independence to Achievement Motivation" (Unpublished doctoral dissertation, University of Michigan, 1953); and "The Relation of Need for Achievement to Learning Experiences in Independence and Mastery," in J. W. Atkinson (ed.), *Motives in Fantasy, Action, and Society* (Princeton: D. Van Nostrand Co., 1958), 453–478.

of the night. We heard a thumping sound followed by an explosive laugh, then a pause, then a repetition. This is the sort of thing my colleague David McClelland would have then called *affective arousal,* one of the essential ingredients in the formation of motives.[3] After a number of thumps, followed by a number of laughs, we surreptitiously tiptoed into the nursery and by flashlight observed our son practicing a skill he had never before exhibited, the act of standing up in bed and then letting himself fall. I wasn't then, nor am I now, certain about the source of his enjoyment— the display of skill in standing up or the surprise in falling down. But needless to say I was then, and have been ever since, sensitized to the kind of thing White[4] has called competence and the need for the more elaborate kind of conception that Joseph Veroff has enunciated.

It is also obvious to an observer outside the developmental psychology of achievement motivation that the empirical work being done with children is solid. It makes for invidious comparisons when we consider the size of the samples in the typical experimental study of the college sophomore in relation to the immense numbers here.

It is also plain to see that there are many common issues in the current work with children and the traditional experimental studies with college students. Not all of the work being done with children is essentially developmental. A good part of it represents the same kind of conceptual and experimental analysis of the effects of motivation on direction, vigor, and persistence of achievement-oriented behavior that preoccupies the specialist in the field of motivation. And since the issues are common, and the data obtained from children and college sophomores look comparable, I am led to wonder: What is the appropriate relationship between the two funds of information?

Engaging in a little social comparison myself, I come to the view that the disciplined and systematic empirical work, the tracking of a problem with emphasis on solid evidence and replication, coupled with innovation in method of study, that is, the empirical side of the work with children, is more sound than much of the earlier work and contemporary work with college students. But on the whole, it seems less sophisticated in its conceptual analysis. I kept asking myself: Why don't the researchers now studying children profit by the hard-won gains in conceptual analysis of the determinants of achievement-oriented behavior? Why do they dart in and out of the conceptual scheme evolved studying older subjects but

---

[3] See, for example, D. C. McClelland *et al., The Achievement Motive* (New York: Appleton-Century-Crofts, 1953), Chap. 2.
[4] R. W. White, "Motivation Reconsidered: The Concept of Competence," *Psychological Review,* 66 (1959), 297–333.

never seem to make full and systematic use of it in their analysis of their problems?

Now, as devil's advocate, I will try to illustrate what I mean. Here is an example from Virginia Crandall's paper. She has argued that successful academic work has positive valence for all children. Since this is true, one can assume that in the study of effects of variations in strength of expectancy of successful academic work it can be inferred that there will be a stronger tendency to undertake this kind of activity the stronger the expectancy, and this will be expressed in greater vigor and persistence in pursuit of academic work with the logical outcome of greater accomplishment. The line of inference is clear enough. But what about the rest of it? If one is to use an expectancy × value principle to account for the strength of a behavioral tendency, why not take seriously the full implication of the decision model? What decision theorists call the subjective expected utility (SEU) of an activity (corresponding to what in common language we might refer to as the strength of the urge to do something) is attributable to the sum of expectancy × value of the outcome *across all possible consequences or outcomes of an activity.*[5] What, then, about the expectancy of failure and the negative valence of failure? What about the fact that individuals are known to differ in valence of success and valence of failure in achievement-oriented settings?[6] Sometimes, following this more complete conceptual analysis of the problem, the summation of the products of expectancy × value over all anticipated outcomes will not be an approach tendency, as Crandall has assumed, but an avoidance tendency, a tendency *not* to undertake the activity, that is, resistance to achievement-oriented activity.

Does a more complete conceptual analysis of the determinants of motivation for academic performance have an implication that might be useful in reference to Virginia Crandall's results? I think so. There is some evidence that expectancies are influenced by, or at least related to, differences in motivation. Even in the disciplined empirical work associated with decision models,[7] there is evidence that the utility of an outcome may influence the subjective probability of its occurrence. If there is anything to this hypothesis, it is suggested that the magnitude of valence of failure may be greater among girls. It has been found among college men that those for whom the negative valence of failure is presumably very large

---

[5] W. Edwards, "The Theory of Decision Making," *Psychological Bulletin,* 51 (1954), 380–417.

[6] J. W. Atkinson and N. T. Feather (eds.), *A Theory of Achievement Motivation* (New York: John Wiley & Sons, 1966).

[7] E.g., P. Slovic, "Value as a Determiner of Subjective Probability" (Unpublished doctoral dissertation, University of Michigan, 1964).

(viz., those who score high in Test Anxiety) are the ones who report weaker expectation of success.[8] So the question naturally comes to mind: Isn't this a possible link between the work with older subjects and the sex difference among children? The only fact that is needed to complete the argument is evidence that girls are more anxious than boys.

Virginia Crandall has contended that the cause-effect relationship goes the other way.[9] The issue is debatable, I would not deny. But—and this is the point of my comment—when one focuses on measurement of expectancy, the conceptual analysis of the problem has to be complete. We already know quite a bit about the complications in determination of behavior that involves motives to achieve and to avoid failure, expectancies of success and failure, incentive values of success and failure, as well as extrinsic motives and incentives. And *all* of what we think we already know from the study of older subjects should be given full consideration in dealing with the analogous problem in children.

A similar point concerning the appropriate relationship between work with older subjects and children can be made in reference to Joseph Veroff's paper. The tests he has developed to measure *autonomous* achievement motivation and *social* achievement motivation in children are ingenious. A parallel step should be taken for the study of older subjects. I tend to view both measures as sound because he has used the logic of a theory of achievement motivation to arrive at the conclusion that if a child prefers a moderately difficult task in terms of his own standards, he must have a strong positive motive to achieve. The logic of this conclusion is the logic of a theory that asserts that the strength of a tendency to undertake a task with interest and the intention of performing well (T_s) is a multiplicative function of motive to achieve (M_s), strength of expectancy of success (P_s), and incentive value of success in that particular activity (I_s), where it is generally assumed that incentive value of success is greater the more difficult the task (i.e., $I_s = 1 - P_s$). These two assumptions provide a useful memory aid, one capable of recovering a substantial number of empirical facts concerning achievement-oriented activity.[10]

When Dr. Veroff then applied the same logic to the social comparisons problem, it seemed that he was arguing that if a child had learned to take pride in accomplishment of difficult tasks *as defined by the social group* then again he will prefer the moderately difficult task with reference to

---

[8] E.g., N. T. Feather, "The Relationship of Expectation of Success to *n* Achievement and Test Anxiety," *Journal of Personality and Social Psychology*, 1 (1965), 118–126.
[9] Virginia Crandall's position was elaborated in a discussion following the presentation of her paper at the Research Conference on the Development of Achievement-Related Motives and Self-Esteem in Children, October 19, 1967. [Editor's note.]
[10] Atkinson and Feather, *op. cit.*

social comparison. This again seemed to me to be a sound application of the conceptual scheme evolved with older subjects where difficulty has been defined both ways. But then, as he proceeded with his discussion, it seemed that at some point he loosened his commitment to the logic of the theory that provided a foundation for his instruments. I could no longer be sure whether or not he was continuing to think of the current theory of achievement motivation as a tenable theory of the actions observed in his research or whether once he had established the tools for measurement of the motives he loosened the tie with the logic of that kind of theory. I say this because of the kinds of statements made to describe some of the developmental changes that occur.

For example, Dr. Veroff's data show very clearly that among boys in kindergarten given a choice among easy, moderately difficult, and very difficult box tasks defined in terms of the social comparisons process, 77 per cent will pick the easy task. By 4th grade, 50 per cent of them are picking the moderately difficult task. It is an obvious change from choice of easy task to choice of moderately difficult task. Now why didn't he say that what the children had learned is that the incentive value of success is related to difficulty as defined by the social group? Originally the children behaved as if the incentive value of success was constant for all of the activities because the definition of difficulty based on social comparisons meant nothing to them; they had to learn that people react more approvingly and whatnot when you have done something that is difficult. Why, instead of describing the change in the language of the theory employed to develop his measures, did he slip into a commonsensical, phenomenological language to describe the results? Why in the study of children's motivation should we depart from the conceptual analysis already won in the study of older subjects?

In order to make an argument, I shall state a position. Developmental psychologists should look to current theory of motivation to define their problem. The conceptual analysis of the problem of motivation, that is, the contemporaneous determinants of action, is logically prior to developmental psychology and logically prior to the study of learning. Why? Because change in behavior from occasion 1 to occasion 2 provides the researcher with two instances of behavior: two instances of choice, vigor, or persistence of activity. And if we do not already know how to think coherently about the several determinants of the behavior on one occasion, how can we describe coherently the nature of the change that has occurred to account for the observed change in behavior on the second occasion? I would thus argue that the psychology of achievement motivation, the current conceptual analysis—in all its complexity—of the determinants of achievement-oriented activity, has a kind of logical priority in the study and analysis of developmental problems. The theory of achievement motivation defines what the developmental psychologist ought to be interested in studying the development of: motives (conceived as relatively general dispositions), expectations (conceived as the link between the cognitive structure of the individual and action), and incentive values, that is, preferences among outcomes that belong to the same general class. The conceptual analysis in developmental studies of achievement motivation should begin with the kind of analysis that is currently useful in reference to the behavior of older subjects and then point out *explicitly* where and why that kind of theory is inadequate. Because neither Crandall nor Veroff has done this clearly and completely, there is, as I have tried to say, more ambiguity than necessary concerning the relationship of this new fund of empirical information to the already existent fund of knowledge about college students. Dr. Veroff made use of the current conceptual scheme to get clues as to what to use as his diagnostic tests. But then he slipped out of the logic of the scheme so that it is not quite clear to me now whether he is implying (a) that there are two separate achievement motives, a capacity for pride in the accomplishment of meeting one's own standards, and a second one, a capacity for pride in the accomplishment of meeting the standards defined by one's social group; or (b) that there is one achievement motive but two different ways in which difficulty is defined—in terms of own standards and in terms of some measure of frequency of success within a social group.

There is one other general comment. Virginia Crandall's discussion of expectancy points up two things about that concept—both its general utility to many social scientists and some of the ambiguities in its use. I would like to suggest that we ought to achieve some consensus that expectancies when employed in a functional sense (in the kind of theory that takes us from the cognitive structure of an individual to his behavior) have two referents or subscripts. An expectancy refers to an act and to an anticipated outcome or consequence of that act. In a given stimulus situation an individual expects that a certain act will produce a certain consequence. The content of an expectation is a given act and a given kind of consequence. The strength of expectation is the subjective probability of the consequence given the act.

There are several other terminological problems. I wondered whether or not Veroff's distinction between *autonomous* achievement motivation and *social* achievement motivation corresponds to the distinction between motivation to achieve versus motivation for social approval contingent on achievement that is sometimes made in work with older subjects.[11]

We can enhance the prospect of conceptual integration of work up and down the age ladder by striving for commensurate language and distinctions. Conversation is a two-way street. Those of us primarily immersed in the task of trying to develop the theory of motivation can see the firm empirical basis being established in research with children. Hopefully those involved in studying children will not isolate themselves from others also involved in systematic analysis of the process of achievement motivation. And hopefully they will not feel the need to start again from scratch. Considerable progress has been made toward integration of the study of individual differences and the process of motivation. We have come to realize that the full theory of behavior is on the line in every particular study, so as complete a conceptual analysis as possible must be made in every instance.

---

[11] E.g., J. W. Atkinson and Patricia O'Connor, "Neglected Factors in Studies of Achievement-Oriented Performance: Social Approval as an Incentive and Performance Decrement," in Atkinson and Feather, *op. cit.*, 299–326.

CHAPTER SEVEN

Comments on Papers by Smith and by Feld and Lewis

SEYMOUR B. SARASON

THESE are not simple papers; these are not short papers; these are very important papers. In the last article I wrote in the anxiety area,[1] which I considered a kind of swan song, I made the point that anxiety research, and I daresay achievement research, was a quite fashionable thing and that they may be very much the victims of success. That is to say, you develop a scale which, like the Binet, seems to work, and you do study after study, and you get the findings you expect, or some of the findings that you expect, and on and on you go. You don't give any thought to whether this is the way it's always going to be. My point in that article was that anxiety research in particular had gotten to the point where, unless there were developments insofar as the measuring instruments were concerned, and also on a conceptual level, we were not likely to see much more progress.

I think the two papers by Charles Smith and by Sheila Feld and Judith Lewis are good examples of what needed to be done. Now, let me, before making some general points, go to some specifics, starting with Smith's paper. He reported that the correlation between test anxiety and reading grades was, as he expected, higher than the correlation between test anxiety and the SRA reading materials. His correlation for test anxiety and reading is somewhat lower than ours.[2] I just want to point out that

---

[1] S. B. Sarason, "The Measurement of Anxiety in Children: Some Questions and Problems," in C. D. Spielberger (ed.), *Anxiety and Behavior* (New York: Academic Press, 1966), 63–79.

[2] S. B. Sarason, K. T. Hill, and P. G. Zimbardo, "A Longitudinal Study of the Relation of Test Anxiety to Performance on Intelligence and Achievement Tests," *Monographs of the Society for Research in Child Development,* Serial No. 98, Vol. 29 (1964), No. 7.

from what Smith has said I gather that he had a relatively restricted range of intelligence among his subjects compared to our correlations which were based on all children in two grades in a relatively large suburban school system.

I would like to focus on some of Smith's findings in relation to test anxiety scores and maternal values. He reported that the more parents value independence, assertiveness, or pride in accomplishment, the higher the test anxiety. The general question that I want to raise here is the possibility that we are oversimplifying, to our peril, what we know about parents. When a parent states a value for a child, it does not follow that it is a value that the parents themselves have satisfactorily experienced in their own lives. It seems to me it could make a big difference if one parent valued independence in the child because in her own life this was experienced as a satisfaction and a basis for growth, as compared to the instance where a parent wants for the child what the parent herself or himself did not experience. I am suggesting that the problem of parental value has to be viewed in terms of whether it is a compensation for the parent or whether it has in the parent's life been an ego-syntonic thing. An area of conflict for the parent can make for a kind of overreaction of the parent in this area in relation to the child. Smith's paper is entitled "The Origin and Expression of Achievement-Related Motives." The simple point that I am trying to make is that this cannot be viewed independent of the history of that motivation in the parent. We must not forget that we are dealing here with findings, and this is true of the research of most of us, where the correlations are relatively low, however significant they may be statistically. And we must ask ourselves, "What are some of the considerations that may be keeping these factors this low?" Some of them undoubtedly are methodological; others I feel reflect the scope of our conceptual framework.

On one other point I would like to quote what Smith says and then comment. He says,

Both mothers and fathers report that they frequently respond to the successful behavior of the high test anxiety child by telling him how much they love him. Bartlett and Smith[3] introduced this item into a list of maternal reactions to success in their study with the specific prediction that high test anxiety would be related to love contingent upon success. In their study this item was checked significantly more often by mothers of sons with low Need for Achievement than by mothers of sons with high Need for Achievement, but it was not significantly related to test anxiety. The possibility that "conditional love" fosters the develop-

---

[3] E. W. Bartlett and C. P. Smith, "Childrearing Practices, Birth Order and the Development of Achievement-Related Motives," *Psychological Reports*, 19 (1966), 1207–1216.

ment of high test anxiety and/or low Need for Achievement warrants further investigation.

Now, I am going to use that as a basis for making a more general point. It is my opinion that if one were to look at the natural history of achievement motivation—by which I mean developmentally over time—he would find at least one variable that is fateful for achievement motivation as we measure it and see it in older children, a variable that we considered extremely important in our own formulations,[4] but a variable that we never studied. I am referring here to the hostility variable, the aggression variable, the assertiveness variable. The idea of conditional love being contingent merely on the love aspect (rewarding the child in the way Smith indicated) I feel is insufficient. I would suggest that the conceptualization of achievement motivation should in some way differentiate aggressiveness from assertiveness. It is interesting that Smith started his paper by giving two responses of children to a Thematic Apperceptive Measure. One of them said, "Boy, this is the World Series, and he hits a home run at the end and the game is over." And the other subject gives a story filled with aggression, hostility, and blame assignment. Now if you score achievement in a certain way, as indeed one should, then it rules out the possibility of scoring other kinds of things, particularly if your conceptual framework does not include these variables. The point that I am making here, and I think it is a semi-speculative one, is that there is a developmental relationship between what we consider achievement motivation, on the one hand, and assertiveness and aggression on the other hand.

I feel that our micro-theories about anxiety, our micro-theories about achievement motivation, have taken us up to a certain point. When we developed these micro-theories, they could be justified at the time because the overall theory did not seem to give us any clear handle as to where to start, so we started in a relatively narrow kind of way. I feel there reaches a point where one has to come back to the larger conceptualization in order to understand better the complexity of what it is one is dealing with. If there is anything that these papers have demonstrated, it is that the situation is undoubtedly far more complex than we imagined. I am puzzled why in so much of the anxiety literature (and our own theoretical formulations intimately tie anxiety and hostility) hostility has not been focused upon as a very important variable.

There is a question about the significance of IQ. It is a "chicken and egg" kind of question. Smith speculates that parents may respond to the

[4] Sarason *et al., Anxiety in Elementary School Children* (New York: John Wiley & Sons, 1960).

bright kid in a certain kind of way because that is the way he is. Well, this would raise certain problems for the finding that the correlation between brightness (however that is measured) in very, very young children and what they are later on is awfully low. Smith's argument would suggest that these kids are bright and the parent responsive in that way, and on and on they go. But the correlation between intellectual evaluation in the very young child and, let us say, the school-age child, is nothing to do gyrations of enthusiasm about.

Now, I would like to shift to the paper by Sheila Feld and Judith Lewis which I thought was the kind of study that was long overdue precisely because it gives promise of introducing changes into our measuring devices. This is an heroic effort. There are relatively few people, unfortunately, who are willing to devote themselves to the tooling-up job and to the retooling-up job, and I think that the Feld and Lewis approach gives every promise of providing us with a greater variety of instruments to deal with the problem of individual differences.

They say,

It seems that a fuller specification and measurement of the several aspects of the achievement anxiety experience is an important area for future research. If the ways in which school performance can be affected by "anxiety" are to be understood, one must distinguish among children who have different types of unpleasant reactions. The child who perceives that he is having unpleasant physiological reactions should react differently to a learning task than the child who expects failure. These two response patterns might also elicit different reactions from a teacher. If a child who believes that his hand is shaking overtly manifests this symptom, his anxiety might be more easily recognized by a teacher than the anxiety of a child who privately expects failure.

I want to suggest something that is not done as frequently as I think it should be, and that is to try direct observations of children. For example, I think it is time (and this I am not directing at Feld and Lewis, since we have been as guilty of this as anybody) that we ask the question of the relation of self-report to the behavior of the individual in the situation about which he is giving a self-report. I am not at all convinced that the self-reports of children will manifest themselves in situations in the way that the self-report would lead one to expect. I am sure all of us have known instances of individuals who were quite convinced that their hands were shaking and yet nobody else seemed to recognize this.

Now Feld and Lewis identify four different factors. One of them that intrigues me (and one which, as was pointed out, a couple of other studies have come up with) is what they have called the "remote concern." I suppose it intrigues me because I am intrigued with the problem of time perspective, and this seemed to be a remote concern not only in a geographical sense but in a time sense. These are items in which the child is thinking about events that are not immediate in the here and now, but things that are going to take place tomorrow or next week. And I think that children, and people in general, differ tremendously in time perspective and how time perspective becomes a mode of coping with problems.

That leads me to another overall point which is relevant in my mind both to Smith's paper and to the paper by Feld and Lewis. I think the time has come when we have to decide how we are using the term "defense." Just as some of us have to make a decision as to what it is we are going to call "anxiety" or "achievement motivation," I feel that this word "defense" is the biggest obstacle confronting us in this area. When the writers interpret their results they utilize this idea of the concept of defense. It is by no means a clear one, and I think we have to eat or leave the table insofar as the concept is concerned. For example, one can look at remote concerns as a defense symptom, shall we say, a behavior which is ego-syntonic (i.e., although the individual worries, it is not in a basic sense upsetting). In other words, the person needs to worry, and if he didn't worry, he would have to develop something else in order to cope with the situation. Defenses differ remarkably in the extent to which they are ego-syntonic or ego-conflicting, and it is never clear to me how we are using the term "defense." For example, poor self-evaluation can be a defense, but it can be an ego-syntonic defense. If you engage in sustained psychotherapy with individuals with poor self-evaluation, you quickly learn that that symptom is a treasured one, very much a part of the individual's ego, because to give it up would confront him with far more difficulties than he is now experiencing. So, it makes a difference whether a defense is successful or whether, in fact, it is unsuccessful.

Another aspect of this problem of defense is whether it is facilitated by reality or in a sense prevented by reality. What I am saying is that there are constellations of parental relationships and parental behaviors which make certain kinds of defensive maneuvers far more likely than others. For example, I think somatic concerns are far more ego-syntonic in girls than they are in boys, and that they are so responded to by parents. The question that everybody is so interested in is what is the relation between parental factors and the child's behavior and development? Now we think that in some way the defensive maneuvers of children are related to parental behavior. I don't think that is sufficient. I think we can assume that to be the case. The question is how choice of maneuver, how choice of defense, how the options about defense are determined, in part, by parental behavior.

Finally, I take a relatively dim view of the tendency to dichotomize the human race into males and females on a biological basis. I think Freud never said a more wise thing in all his life when he said that everybody, male or female, is confronted with the problem of activity or passivity, and that to equate psychological with biological sex differentiation is to oversimplify the problem. In all of us the activity-passivity continuum is one we always wrestle with. It has to be true for children, if it is true for us, and I think that we have to start conceptualizing the problem in psychological terms and less in biological terms. For example, who are the girls in Crandall's group who consistently expect the way boys expect, and who are the boys who consistently expect the way girls expect? This is the same kind of possibility that is raised by the findings of Feld and Lewis.

CHAPTER EIGHT

Comments on All Papers

HOWARD A. MOSS

THE task given to me, to synthesize the presentations collected here, represents quite a formidable undertaking. The papers presented by Crandall, Veroff, Feld and Lewis, and Smith cover such a broad range of concepts and issues and include so much interesting data that one would do well to assimilate all this material, let alone synthesize it. However, I do have a few general comments that perhaps will provide some integration for a number of the papers presented.

Most of the research reported here gives special attention to a mediating variable (associated with achievement behavior) that deals with the individual's evaluation of his own skill. This mediating variable has been conceptualized variously in the respective presentations as expectancy for success, fear of failure, achievement anxiety, and self-esteem. Although these concepts bear similarity to one another, in that they all pertain to self-evaluation in some area of competence, they also differ in certain significant respects, and it would seem useful to consider some of the major implications of these differences.

One way that these concepts differ from one another is in terms of the number of dimensions that each subsumes. In this respect anxiety and self-esteem appear to be multidimensional whereas expectancy tends to be unidimensional. For example, test anxiety involves such factors as how well a person believes he will do, how important success in that activity is for him, as well as the individual's general reactivity to stress. On the other hand, expectancy deals quite specifically with a single dimension involving a probability statement of success or failure. Thus, anxiety and self-esteem are much more complex variables than is expectancy. The former two may have some usefulness in simplifying informal communication by summarizing many aspects of psychological functioning, but are inefficient, loose, and imprecise in specifying aspects of behavior that can be translated into meaningfully predictive research operations. It seems desirable first to understand the role of a unitary variable and once this is accomplished, build toward more complex configurations of variables such as anxiety or self-esteem.

A few of the obvious advantages for the use of expectancy are that you can regulate the level of generality in requested expectancy statements and you can determine expectancies for various classes of behaviors. An example of the specificity that can be obtained in expectancy statements and the usefulness of such explicit denotations was nicely demonstrated in Virginia Crandall's paper. In this regard she showed that the correlations between expectancy and grades decreased as a function of the dissimilarity between the type of expectancy statements made and the particular area of achievement for which the grades were given.

I felt some confusion concerning the way the concept of achievement motivation has been used throughout the papers. To begin with, there seems to be general agreement among the contributors that achievement motivation involves striving to attain high standards of excellence. Yet it seems dubious, or at least undetermined, that these strivings for excellence actually underlie many of the behaviors that are labeled as representing achievement motivation. One source of difficulty seems to be that certain situations, such as the school classroom, are classified as achievement situations so that any behavior that occurs in those settings is interpreted as reflecting achievement motivation. There are alternative interpretations, however, concerning the motivation leading to achievement-type activities in these situations. For instance, many individuals may be compliant to the demands or social expectations associated with a given situation and therefore engage in achievement-like behavior without having any intrinsic motivation to excel at the task at hand. Thus, inferring the motivation for behavior from the phenotypic characteristics of a situation may incorrectly represent what is actually occurring. There are other instances where being guided by phenotypes can misrepresent the underlying motivation. Preparation for the Ph.D. foreign language exam, as a rule, has little to do with striving for standards of excellence. The language exam is typically seen as a form of harassment from the academic establishment and once the Ph.D. candidate has successfully passed this hurdle there is usually little inclination to retain or improve upon his language competence. Yet, if one relied strictly on the phenotypic behavior, preparations for the language exam would be viewed as reflecting achievement motivation. There are many aspects of life where one strives for certain minimal levels of competence simply because of societal requirements or because acquisition of a skill has functional utility for the individual. Interest in learning to read is traditionally regarded as one evidence of achievement motivation. In this respect, I am reminded of an anecdote that a friend related to me concerning her six-year-old daughter. One day her daughter surprised her with a comment, "Mommy, I don't want to learn how to read." While the mother was attempting to assimilate this disconcerting bit of news her daughter added, "I want to know how to read." I think this child was making an important distinction here between mastery and achievement motivation. There are many instances throughout the life span where people strive to attain a certain level of success at an activity because they find it useful to master a particular skill. Once certain minimal levels of competence are acquired they are satisfied. There is little effort or interest in improving these skills beyond a level where they serve the desired functional purpose. A common example of this would be learning to drive an automobile, but the same reasoning may apply equally to such things as reading. The main goal is to acquire a skill because it is useful and not because of the wish to excel. Again, in such instances as these, it is important to avoid equating the phenotype with a particular motivational construct.

I felt that Joseph Veroff made a noteworthy contribution in attempting to relate the developmental accomplishments of infancy and early childhood (such as walking, talking, grasping, etc.) to later achievement behavior. An understanding of the early antecedents of achievement behavior can facilitate sorting out the factors that determine an achievement orientation and help plot the developmental course of this behavior. If one does accept the general definition of achievement behavior as strivings for particular standards of excellence, however, it is tenuous to regard many of these earlier developmental attainments as reflections of achievement behavior per se. Children acquire many skills over the early years of life—they learn to use their hands, they learn to walk, they learn to grasp objects. What basically seems to be involved in these behaviors is becoming competent in mastering particular functions. I feel that it is necessary here to make this distinction.

One could look at early mastery behavior as having a bearing on later achievement in two respects: (1) the individual first has to master certain fundamental skills before he can consider excelling in an area where those skills are involved, (2) individual differences in mastery and coping behavior, in regard to such factors as persistence, efficiency, and intensity of effort, might represent antecedent characteristics or dispositions of the individual that become manifest in later achievement behavior.

In his paper, Veroff made reference to the concept of competence facilitation. The illustration used was of the mother giving her child ample opportunity to explore his environment by being nonrestrictive. In a study we conducted recently at the Child Research Branch of NIMH we observed a pattern of maternal behavior toward 18-month-old children which supports and extends the relevance of the idea of competence facilitation. The phenomenon we observed was of the mother, whether she was free or busy with household activities, matching the verbalizations of the child. That is, when a child would utter some word, the mother would automatically repeat the word but refine it, thus reinforcing the child's verbal behavior and at the same time providing instruction in articulation. This verbal matching and corrective feedback[1] was evident among the majority of mothers and often seemed to occur as an unselfconscious response in which the mother was compelled to react. I am sure many of us recall similar incidents where we were unable to resist making corrective semimatching responses to the early verbal behavior of children. This phenomenon seems similar to observations from ethological studies where the parent is stimulated by the offspring to make responses that in turn facilitate the offspring's development.

There were some crucial methodological issues and problems associated with some of the research presented in this conference that I think need comment. It has been a fairly widespread practice in child development research to rely on parental reports in order to obtain information on child behavior and parental practices. Indeed this source of data was used in some of the research presented here. However, it is a weak and poorly supported assumption that parents are reliable informants of their own and their child's behavior. In a recent report bearing on this point, Yarrow, Campbell, and Burton[2] obtained data concerning the reliability of parental reports. They coded data available on mother-child relations from the records of a research nursery school. They also interviewed the mothers from the sample when their children were between the preschool years and young adulthood and made codings from these interviews on the same dimensions coded from the nursery school records. These investigators found a median correlation of .37 between initial and recall data for variables dealing with infant personality characteristics, relations with peers, early traumatic experiences, and parent-child interaction. Such a median correlation is not very satisfactory when one considers using parental recall

---

[1] The concepts of matching and corrective feedback were coined by Gertrude Wyatt to describe procedures she uses for treating children with speech problems. This information is based on a lecture she gave at NIMH.

[2] M. R. Yarrow, J. D. Campbell, and R. V. Burton, "Reliability of Maternal Retrospection: A Preliminary Report," *Family Process*, 3 (1964), 207–218.

data as a substitute for direct observation. In terms of the nature of the shifts that occurred, the mothers saw themselves as more nurturant, warmer, closer to the child, and recalled the father as being absent from the home more than was indicated from the earlier evidence. Also, during the interview the child was seen as happier, easier to manage, and as having walked earlier than was reported in the nursery school record. Generally, the mothers distorted more when they were asked about abstract classes of behavior and where value-laden behaviors were involved. Thus it would seem that retrospective parental reports represent a source of data in which one has to exercise extreme care in terms of how it is obtained and how it is interpreted.

Another questionable assumption evident in some of the research presented here is that when a correlation is found (or sought) between a parental treatment variable and a child behavior it necessarily reflects the outcome of the parental treatment. That is, the cause-effect sequence generally is assumed to work in terms of the parent influencing the child behavior and not the other way around. Nevertheless, one could in many instances argue convincingly that certain parental behaviors could just as easily be products of characteristics present in the child. Bell[3] has systematically reviewed and analyzed this dilemma in developmental research. He refers to this issue as "the problem of direction of effects" and contends that because of certain biases we tend to interpret correlations between parent-child behaviors as being a function of parental treatment when, in fact, a correlation does not indicate direction of effects. He maintains that much of the research conducted on early development has been influenced by the prevailing social philosophy which states that the individual is largely a product of his environment, and that what an individual becomes is determined by his experience and the treatment he receives. Bell contends that this value orientation has resulted in overlooking requirements for scientific evidence in many of the studies and theories of child development. As a result, investigations of mother-infant relations have focused mainly on the ways that the mother affects the child with little attention given to the effects the child (through his congenital makeup) may have on the mother. Yet, many of the findings reported in the literature can just as easily be interpreted either way. For example, the finding that aggression in children is associated with a greater incidence of physical punishment by parents tends to be taken as evidence that parental punishment has led to the aggressive behavior. Nevertheless,

---

[3] R. Q. Bell, "A Reinterpretation of the Direction of Effects in Studies of Socialization," *Psychological Review*, 75 (1968), 81–95.

one could easily conjecture that it operated the other way around: It was the existing aggressive tendency in the children that elicited the observed parental behavior. In reference to achievement behavior, a parent setting high standards for his child and encouraging interest in academic activities certainly could be influenced by his having a bright child. A study by Yarrow[4] is quite illuminating in regard to the importance of the notion of "direction of effects." He studied mother-infant interaction among a group of infants placed in foster and adoptive homes. Since the same foster mother cared for various infants over a period of time he was able to demonstrate the extent to which maternal behavior can be influenced by characteristics of the infant. The following excerpt illustrates one foster mother's respective behaviors toward two infants in her care.

The first infant, a girl, was given much physical contact and handled with great warmth. The mother showed a high degree of sensitivity to the child's individual characteristics and needs. She had a basically positive attitude toward this child's idiosyncratic attributes. The infant was valued as a child who knew what she wanted and insisted on getting it. The foster mother was very protective toward the infant and attempted to shield her as much as possible from normal frustrations in the environment. The second child, a month-old boy, was placed in the same home a few months after the girl had left for an adoptive home. He was a tense, irritable, demanding infant. The foster mother consistently expressed negative feelings about him. In contrast to her flexibility in scheduling the first infant, she arranged the child's feeding on the basis of her own convenience. The child's crying was often ignored; long delays in responding to him were characteristic. He was held very little and high levels of tension were allowed to build up. In this environment the infant continued to become more irritable and demanding. The basis for a very disturbing mother-infant relationship had been established.

One final point concerns the use of the statistical test of significance for determining the psychological significance of results. There are certain clear advantages for having large-size samples. In computing correlations where large samples are involved, however, one may of course obtain statistically significant results with correlations of relatively low magnitude, which was the case for some of the findings presented here. Under such circumstances very little of the variance is accounted for. It is necessary to be cautious and qualify such results even though they may be clearly significant from a statistical standpoint. There are not any conventionally agreed upon guidelines concerning the amount of variance that should be accounted for before one can be assured of the psychological significance of a finding. Certainly the purpose for which the results are

---

[4] L. J. Yarrow, "Research in Dimensions of Early Maternal Care," *Merrill-Palmer Quarterly*, 9 (1963), 101–114.

used will affect the importance associated with a finding of a given magnitude, irrespective of the statistical significance level of that result. Nevertheless, if correlations are much below .30 I feel it is the responsibility of the investigator to bring forth some additional reasoning for insisting that others in the field accept these relations as facts worth considering, or as evidence relevant to any theoretical position. Baldwin,[5] in reviewing a report of a major study on socialization where many of the significant correlations were below .20, concluded that results of this magnitude were not convincing by themselves.

---

[5] A. L. Baldwin, "The Theory and Practice of Bringing Up Johnny," *Contemporary Psychology*, 2 (1957), 305–307.

CHAPTER NINE

Conclusion[1]

CHARLES P. SMITH

WHEN different investigators explore the same area of behavior independently, their results can be reminiscent of the blind man and the elephant—with each researcher believing that his idiosyncratic description is the correct one. When the achievement-related behavior of children of different sexes, ages, socioeconomic and ethnic groups is studied by different methods and from different theoretical points of view, such an outcome would not be unexpected. It is perhaps surprising and encouraging, therefore, that there is as much agreement about the subject as is found in the present volume, for the findings reported here are often similar, or at least complementary, and they are rarely, if ever, contradictory.

This concluding chapter reviews the major findings reported in the foregoing research papers and calls attention to common themes and ways in which the findings can be integrated. Methodological innovations are discussed as well as some of the implications of the findings for child-rearing and education. A number of provocative new issues are also noted which point the way for future research.

First, it may be helpful to consider why these reports have been brought together in a single volume, and to ask what such topics as expectancies of academic attainment, sensitivity to the evaluations of others, independence training, and apprehensiveness about failure have in common. The answer, of course, is that these things are all relevant to how a child will behave in a situation in which his performance or skill at a task will be evaluated. In such a situation his behavior will be influenced by his motives to succeed and to avoid failure, his estimate of his chances of attaining various levels of accomplishment, and his value for the possible outcomes of his per-

---

[1] I am indebted to Harold Freeman, Jr., and Ian McMahan for their comments and suggestions concerning the contents of this chapter.

formance. It is hoped that the studies reported here will provide a better understanding of the way in which achievement-related personality characteristics develop and function in evaluative or competitive situations.

Since test anxiety has been dealt with in some of the preceding chapters as an index of the motive to avoid failure, it should be made explicit that test anxiety is defined as a *specific* form of anxiety, namely, anxiety about intellectual and academic evaluation.[2] Statements about test anxiety are not intended to apply to "general" anxiety as measured, for example, by the Taylor Manifest Anxiety Scale, or to specific fears such as fear of pain or fear of the dark. Such specific fears may be related only minimally to the kind of anxiety a person experiences when he knows that he is responsible for the unpleasant consequences of poor performance. A person waiting apprehensively for a shock over which he has no control will not have to berate himself or alter his conception of his abilities because of the painful outcome he experiences. Anxiety associated with failure is tied up with one's skill, one's feeling of competence, and the knowledge that the outcome is contingent on one's performance—in short, it is associated with the specific characteristics of evaluative situations and can be conceived as indicative of a motive to avoid the painful consequences of poor performance.[3]

Developmental Trends in Achievement-Related Motivation and Behavior

To date there has been a dearth of descriptive information about how motives and expectancies change with age. Although achievement motivation has been studied in both children and adults, prior to the research presented by Veroff in Chapter 3 there have been no norms for the achievement motive scores of children of different ages. Veroff presents three relevant sets of findings: first, the achievement motive scores comparable to those obtained in other studies are those obtained with his fantasy measure (i.e., coding of achievement imagery in stories told about pictures of males). These scores reveal a gradual increase in achievement motivation for both boys and girls from grades 1 through 6. The next two Veroff tests are intended to measure *resultant* achievement-related motivation rather than the achievement motive alone. That is, the greater the score on the autonomous achievement motivation measure and on the normative achievement motivation measure, the greater the achievement motive is *in relation to* the motive to avoid failure. Veroff's data reveal that auton-

---

[2] See S. B. Sarason *et al.*, *Anxiety in Elementary School Children* (New York: John Wiley & Sons, 1960).

[3] Cf. J. W. Atkinson and N. T. Feather, A *Theory of Achievement Motivation* (New York: John Wiley & Sons, 1966).

omous achievement scores (i.e., frequency of choosing to repeat a challenging task of intermediate difficulty) increase for boys up to the 3rd grade and then decline somewhat. A similar pattern is found for girls with the decline coming after the 4th grade. The age trends for the normative measure of social achievement motivation show a consistent decrease for both boys and girls in preference for the easiest task (defined in terms of the number of other children who can do it) from kindergarten to the 6th grade, and an increasing preference for tasks of intermediate difficulty.

Test anxiety scores also increase from the 1st to the 5th grade,[4] and test anxiety scores become more strongly (negatively) related over time to indexes of intellectual and academic performance.[5] These trends may indicate that stress on evaluation increases during the school years and that making good grades becomes more important as the child grows older. Alternatively, it is possible that these trends are the result of measurement error due to the inability of the youngest children to report their inner experiences accurately. Counteracting this interpretation, however, is the evidence presented by Feld and Lewis in Chapter 5 which indicates that test anxiety is already well formed as early as the 2nd grade. In a related study Feld and Lewis[6] point out that the four factors they find in their analysis of the test anxiety scores of 2nd graders are similar to those reported in factor analytic studies of the test anxiety scores of children in grades 4 through 9.

No systematic data on changes in expectancies with age are known to the present writer, though it is probably safe to assume that for a given task a child's expectation of performing at a certain level would typically increase with age. The interesting fact so decisively demonstrated by Virginia Crandall in Chapter 2 is that despite whatever changes in level of exceptancy that may occur with age, girls have consistently lower expectancies of success for intellectual and academic activities than boys from elementary school to college. Possible reasons for this finding will be discussed later in a review of findings on sex differences.

The developmental generalizations relevant to achievement-related motivation which have been described may be summarized as follows:

1. Fantasy Need for Achievement scores and scores on the Test Anxiety

---

[4] K. T. Hill and S. B. Sarason, "The Relation of Test Anxiety and Defensiveness to Test and School Performance over the Elementary-School Years: A Further Longitudinal Study," *Monographs of the Society for Research in Child Development,* Serial No. 104, Vol. 31 (1966), No. 2.

[5] S. B. Sarason, K. T. Hill, and P. G. Zimbardo, "A Longitudinal Study of the Relation of Test Anxiety to Performance on Intelligence and Achievement Tests," *Monographs of the Society for Research in Child Development,* Serial No. 98, Vol. 29 (1964), No. 7.

[6] S. Feld and J. Lewis, "Further Evidence on the Stability of the Factor Structure of the Test Anxiety Scale for Children," *Journal of Consulting Psychology,* 31 (1967), 434.

Scale for Children increase gradually throughout the elementary school years.

2. The debilitating effects of test anxiety on intellectual and academic performance become gradually stronger throughout the elementary school years.

3. The components of test anxiety present in 2nd grade children remain essentially the same as the children grow older.

4. Despite whatever changes in level of expectancy which may occur with age, girls from elementary school to college consistently state lower expectancies than boys for academic and intellectual tasks.

5. When given a choice among tasks to repeat, children tend to choose the easiest tasks in kindergarten and gradually shift to preference for tasks of intermediate difficulty by the 3rd and 4th grades.

6. When difficulty is defined in terms of the number of peers who can do a task, both boys and girls show a gradually decreasing preference for easy tasks and an increasing preference for tasks of intermediate and extreme difficulty.

Regarding the last finding, Atkinson raises an interesting question in Chapter 6. Is the change away from an easy task due to the fact that children learn that the incentive value of success is related to difficulty as defined by the social group—that other people react with greater approval for success at a difficult task? Atkinson's question points to the need for more information about the way in which a child's value for success develops, and how and when the child learns that greater pride in accomplishment is usually associated with the successful completion of difficult rather than easy tasks.

The possibility of an age trend in the role of defensiveness is suggested by a finding concerning goal setting reported by Smith in Chapter 4. Although defensiveness scores tend to decrease with age,[7] Smith reports that defensiveness is more strongly related to unrealistic goal setting in 5th graders than in 4th graders. This finding is consistent with the observation of Sarason, Hill and Zimbardo[8] that changes in anxiety level during the elementary school years are related to strong reciprocal changes in defensiveness. That is, some subjects with high test anxiety apparently become less willing to admit their anxiety as they grow older and/or they develop defenses which make them unaware of their anxiety. In any event, as their anxiety scores decrease, their defensiveness scores increase. The goal setting of such subjects would be expected to be consistently unrealistic over time, but it should be initially related most strongly to test

---

[7] Hill and Sarason, *op. cit.*
[8] Sarason, Hill, and Zimbardo, *op. cit.*

anxiety scores and later to defensiveness scores or to some combination of the two types of scores.

Smith's results also indicate that the variability of goal-setting scores decreases markedly from the 4th to the 5th grade, suggesting that as subjects grow older they learn to estimate more accurately both their abilities and the difficulty of tasks. There appears to be a great need for more descriptive information about such important determinants of behavior in achievement situations as age changes in expectancies, incentive values, and accuracy of estimating task difficulty.

Social Comparison

One of the contributions of the research papers collected here is to call attention to the importance of social comparison in achievement activities. In different ways each of these reports has illustrated the importance of this process. Veroff proposes that social comparison does not typically become an important aspect of achievement activities until the elementary school years. The present writer is inclined to set the beginnings of social comparison between 4½ and 5 years of age, but as Veroff points out, the specific age at which this kind of concern arises may be influenced by such factors as the number of siblings a child has and whether or not he attends nursery school.

In any event, at about the time he enters kindergarten the child becomes competitive and shows an interest in how well he is doing in relation to others, and, as Feld and Lewis have reported in Chapter 5, he also manifests concern about the possibility of doing less well than other children. Feld and Lewis find anxiety about "comparative poor self-evaluation" in their 2nd grade boys and girls. Along these lines, Mandler[9] reports that college students with high test anxiety are more preoccupied than those with low test anxiety with worries about how well other students might perform. So we see the importance for both achievement motivation and fear of failure, of concern with social comparison as the child enters school and as the source of sanctions and standards comes to include peers and teachers as well as parents and siblings.

Within the school the strength of the influence of the social environment on a child's expectations of success in academic endeavors is pointed up in Crandall's discussion of ability grouping in Chapter 2. She shows that the child's frame of reference is not simply his own class (i.e., the classmates in the same ability level) but the whole ability group structure. That is, the child apparently compares himself with pupils in higher and lower ability

---

[9] G. Mandler and D. L. Watson, "Anxiety and the Interruption of Behavior," in C. D. Spielberger (ed.), *Anxiety and Behavior* (New York: Academic Press, 1966), 263–290.

levels as well as with his classmates. In her results, it is this total framework for social comparison rather than his standing within his own class which is most strongly associated with the child's expectations about his academic performance.

Allport[10] and others have previously called attention to the age at which competitiveness first appears, and Piaget[11] has noted that the child first thinks that everybody wins when playing a game and later learns that only one person can come out on top. Taking a lead from Piaget, one can develop this idea and note that a child goes from (1) a stage in which there is no concept of winning (ca. birth to 2½ years) to (2) a stage in which everybody is seen as winning (ca. 2½ years to 4½ years) to (3) a stage in which the child wants to be the only winner and wants to win all the time. This orientation seems to persist throughout life in some persons, but (4) it typically undergoes gradual modification by the recognition that other persons have to win some of the time. Wanting to win all the time at around the age of 5 is not a kind of motivation limited to achievement per se. It is part of a general social comparison process in which the child wants to be older than another child, wants to think that his toys are better, his daddy is stronger, and so forth. A competitive tendency at this age seems to be part of an overall tendency toward self-aggrandizement. It is essentially self-centered; only later does the child come to take the point of view of his competitor as well as that of himself.

In his factor analysis of parental childrearing values in Chapter 4, Smith reports that parents typically distinguish between (a) competitive achievement (which appears to be associated with general social assertiveness and social competence in the minds of the parents) and (b) standards for individual achievement such as "doing his best at things" which do not involve competition with other people. A parent can place a high value on neither, both, or one or the other of these kinds of achievement orientation. These parental attitudes may have some influence on the extent to which the child progresses through the sequence described by Veroff in which the child first develops an autonomous achievement motive, then a social achievement motive, and finally an integrated achievement motive that enables him effectively to achieve both individually and in competition with others.

It is not entirely clear, however, how to conceptualize these two kinds of achievement motivation, as Atkinson points out in Chapter 6. He asks whether there are two different achievement motives (autonomous and

---

[10] G. W. Allport, *Pattern and Growth in Personality* (New York: Holt, Rinehart and Winston, 1961).
[11] J. Piaget, *The Moral Judgment of the Child* (Glencoe, Ill.: Free Press, 1948).

social) or whether there is one achievement motive and two different ways of defining the difficulty of a task (individual standards and group standards). Or is it possible that what is being called social achievement motivation is an altogether different kind of motivation such as motivation for social approval? It appears to the present writer that Veroff may have combined two different kinds of dispositions under the rubric of social comparison by utilizing as measures of social achievement motivation a normative measure of level of aspiration (choice among tasks which differ in terms of how many peers can succeed at them) and field dependence (as measured by an embedded figures test). The first measure may indeed assess a motive to achieve, that is, to gain satisfaction from successful competition with (socially defined) standards of excellence. The second measure may assess something more akin to a need for approval, which, though it is an important motive involving social comparison, would not be expected to operate in the same way as a motive to achieve. These are some theoretical questions that will have to be dealt with in future research.

Measurement of Achievement-Related Motives

A brief comment on the problems and progress in the measurement of children's achievement motivation and achievement anxiety seems appropriate at this point. Veroff presents two new methods of measuring achievement motivation in children: a measure of autonomous achievement motivation which involves choosing to repeat one of several tasks which vary in difficulty, and a measure of normative or social achievement motivation which involves choosing one of several tasks which differ in socially defined difficulty. Both of these tasks directly assess preference for tasks of intermediate difficulty, and this in turn is regarded as an indirect measure of *resultant* achievement tendencies. That is, it is a way of inferring the resultant strength of motivation to achieve success (approach) and motivation to avoid failure (avoidance). The assumption is made, following Atkinson's[12] theory of risk-taking behavior, that a person in whom motivation to achieve is stronger than motivation to avoid failure will set goals of intermediate difficulty, while a person with the opposite motivational pattern will tend to avoid tasks of intermediate difficulty and prefer instead more easy or more difficult tasks.

Veroff also employs a more traditional projective measure of achievement motivation, namely the analysis of the achievement-related content of thematic apperceptive stories. Because he uses pictures of males, Veroff's stimuli may not be equally appropriate for both sexes, and be-

---

[12] J. W. Atkinson, "Motivational Determinants of Risk-Taking Behavior," *Psychological Review*, 64 (1957), 359–372.

cause he obtains stories from children as young as 1st graders, he has to employ a revised version of the original McClelland *et al.*[13] Need for Achievement scoring system in order to enable the stories to be coded reliably. Even then the coding reliability, while respectable, is not as high as it is with older children.

The Veroff measures of autonomous and normative achievement motivation are particularly important contributions because of these problems involved in obtaining a fantasy measure of Need for Achievement in very young children. Smith, using verbal cues, elicited satisfactory stories from 4th and 5th graders in individual interviews, and these stories permitted reliable scoring with the original McClelland *et al.*[14] scoring system. A major advantage of the verbal cues is the ease of equating the masculine or feminine properties of the cues. For example, the cue for boys "Tell me a story about a boy who is in school" is presented to girls as "Tell me a story about a girl who is in school."

In view of the differing parental emphasis on individual versus competitive achievement, and in view of the stages of development from autonomous to social to integrated achievement motivation proposed by Veroff, it may be helpful in future research to revise the procedures that have been used to arouse achievement motivation experimentally—to place differing emphasis as needed on individual or competitive achievement—and to revise the content analysis system for scoring projective stories for achievement imagery. The original scoring system does not distinguish between a boy wanting to win a race and a boy wanting to discover a new chemical formula. Both kinds of achievement imagery contribute equally to a single overall score. Possibly separate pictures should be used to elicit individual and social achievement imagery, and separate scoring criteria should be devised to assess autonomous achievement imagery and social comparison achievement imagery.

Although thematic apperceptive procedures elicit satisfactory stories from nearly all 4th graders and from many 3rd graders, both the collection and the scoring of the stories are unusually time consuming, and new behavioral measures such as those devised by Veroff have many advantages if their reliability and validity can be satisfactorily demonstrated in further research.

Results concerning the measurement of achievement anxiety in young children are encouraging. Feld and Lewis in Chapter 5 show that acquiescence response set is not a major problem in measuring test anxiety in 2nd

---

[13] D. C. McClelland *et al.*, *The Achievement Motive* (New York: Appleton-Century-Crofts, 1953).
[14] *Ibid.*

graders, and that subscales of the total Test Anxiety Scale for Children can be devised to assess different components of achievement anxiety more accurately. Further work on the influence of defensiveness on test anxiety scores is needed, however, and research on the measurement of anxiety about other kinds of achievement situations than academic situations will also help to round out our understanding of how motivation to avoid achievement activities develops and operates.

Childrearing Practices and the Development of Achievement-Related Motivation

The chapters by Veroff and Smith deal with some of the issues involved in the relationship between childrearing and the development of achievement motivation and test anxiety. Parental practices related to the development of achievement motivation will be considered first, and those pertaining to the development of test anxiety second.

Achievement motivation. The early theory of the development of achievement motivation put forth by McClelland and his colleagues is summarized in the following statement: "If a family does not set high standards of excellence, or if it does not permit the child to compete or strive to meet them on his own, then he could not be expected to have had the affective experiences connected with meeting or failing to meet achievement standards which cumulatively produce an achievement motive."[15] In other words, the prerequisites of achievement motivation were considered to be: high standards, independent accomplishment (i.e., doing a job on one's own), and a positive affective experience in connection with success. Many such experiences in many different areas of activity were expected to produce a generalized expectation of positive affect contingent on successful performance.

Early studies by McClelland and Friedman[16] and by Winterbottom[17] produced results consistent with this theory. Later studies reviewed by Smith in Chapter 4 suggested some modifications, and the research presented in this volume suggests some additional changes. To begin with, McClelland's early theory implied that the positive affective reward associated with accomplishment came from parental reactions to the child's successes, and consistent with this, Winterbottom[18] found that mothers

---

[15] *Ibid.*, 275–276.
[16] D. C. McClelland and G. A. Friedman, "A Cross-Cultural Study of the Relationship Between Child-Training Practices and Achievement Motivation Appearing in Folk Tales," in G. E. Swanson, T. M. Newcomb, and E. L. Hartley (eds.), *Readings in Social Psychology* (Rev. ed.; New York: Henry Holt, 1952), 243–249.
[17] M. R. Winterbottom, "The Relation of Need for Achievement to Learning Experiences in Independence and Mastery," in J. W. Atkinson (ed.), *Motives in Fantasy, Action and Society* (Princeton: D. Van Nostrand Co., 1958), 453–478.
[18] *Ibid.*

of 8- to 10-year-old boys with high Need for Achievement reported using more intense affective rewards (e.g., physical affection) in response to their sons' achievements than mothers of boys with low Need for Achievement.

Nevertheless, prior to the age at which parental approval is a major source of reinforcement the child experiences pleasure in developing his skills which stems directly from the activities themselves and not from external sources of reward.[19] The present writer has noted elsewhere that

As early as the second year of life the child reveals a budding sense of accomplishment and goal direction in his delight over such things as climbing all the way up the stairs for the first time or building a tower of blocks. In the third year he becomes interested in his parent's approval of what he is doing and he develops language which facilitates his understanding of standards by which performances are judged. At the age of four he begins to develop a sense of shame over incompetence.[20]

In Chapter 3, Veroff proposes that autonomous achievement motivation is developed in the first four years or so more or less independently from social approval or parental approval. He believes the child must have a reasonable amount of success in mastering his environment in order for such motivation to develop. Veroff suggests that it is the child's *evaluation* of his competence which makes an experience an "achievement." Veroff states: "A child has to be aware of what he has done and act evaluatively toward it. In order to be evaluative toward his behavior the child must have a sense of personal agency in accomplishment, some notion that *he* did it. The joy an infant may experience from the exercise of muscles or vision even when oriented to complex stimuli is, no doubt, inspired by competence, but it is *not* the result of autonomous achievement. No evaluation, however primitive, has presumably taken place."

In Smith's study, reported in Chapter 4, there are no strong relationships between reported parental reactions to success and children's achievement-related motives. In fact, there is a tendency ($p < .10$) for parents of children with high Need for Achievement to react *less* often with physical affection to the child's success than parents of children with low Need for Achievement. This finding is the opposite of that reported by Winterbottom, but her children were, on the average, two years younger. The results may simply indicate that by the time boys reach the 4th grade, their mothers have given up hugging them for their accomplishments. If Veroff's analysis of the development of motivation is correct, the 4th and

[19] Cf. R. W. White, "Motivation Reconsidered: The Concept of Competence," *Psychological Review*, 66 (1959), 297–333.
[20] C. P. Smith, *Child Development* (Dubuque, Iowa: Wm. C. Brown, 1966), 31.

5th grade children may be more concerned with social comparison than with parental reward for their achievements, and it may be that the reactions of peers rather than parents is more closely related to achievement motivation at that age.

Earliness of reported independence training is not related to the strength of boys' achievement motivation in the data described by either Veroff or Smith. This could be due to errors in retrospective recall of childrearing practices, but it may also indicate that independence training per se is not a major aspect of the early experience of the child who develops high Need for Achievement.

On the other hand, Veroff has theorized that the child needs to experience autonomous mastery in order to develop strong motivation to achieve. In addition to implying some degree of independence from external supervision, the concept of autonomy may also imply a feeling of self-control and a sense of responsibility for one's actions. The concept of internal control appears to be relevant here, that is, the feeling that one is personally responsible for one's successes and failures rather than outside forces or events. In their research on internal-external control of reinforcements, Katkovsky, Crandall and Good[21] found that in general warm, praising, protective and supportive parent behaviors were positively associated with belief in internal control on the part of 6- to 10-year-old children, while dominance, rejection, and criticism on the part of parents were negatively associated with belief in internal control. These authors state: "It seems likely that the more a parent initiates and encourages his child's achievement behavior and the development of his skills, the more the child will learn that it is his own behavior, and not external factors, which will determine the reinforcements he receives."[22] From these results it appears reasonable to expect that in general the same kinds of parental behaviors which lead to a feeling of internal control will also be consistent with the development of strong achievement motivation, while those which lead to external control will also contribute to high test anxiety. Although there is some evidence indicating an association between external control and high anxiety, no consistent relationship has been found between Need for Achievement and internal-external control.[23] Feather[24] cautions against

---

[21] W. Katkovsky, V. C. Crandall, and S. Good, "Parental Antecedents of Children's Beliefs in Internal-External Control of Reinforcements in Intellectual Achievement Situations," *Child Development*, 38 (1967), 765–776.
[22] *Ibid.*, 766.
[23] Cf. N. T. Feather, "Some Personality Correlates of External Control," *Australian Journal of Psychology*, 19 (1967), 253–260; D. Watson, "Relationship Between Locus of Control and Anxiety," *Journal of Personality and Social Psychology*, 6 (1967), 91–92.
[24] N. T. Feather, "Valence of Outcome and Expectation of Success in Relation to Task Difficulty and Perceived Locus of Control," *Journal of Personality and Social Psychology*, 7 (1967), 372–386.

equating internal control with success orientation and external control with failure orientation, since these variables, while related, are not the same in all respects.

In contrast to the ambiguous relationship between *independence* training and Need for Achievement, *achievement* training has generally been more clearly and consistently related to the development of Need for Achievement.[25] A finding reported by Smith in Chapter 4 brings some new information to bear on the nature of achievement training. The parents in his sample who made earlier demands of their children to dress themselves, put their clothes away, and do some regular tasks around the house had children with high Need for Achievement. This relationship was especially clear when only Protestant families were considered. McClelland,[26] however, had found the opposite relationship between these so-called "caretaking" items and children's achievement motivation. It may be that the same demand (e.g., "to dress himself") means something very different for parents of different socioeconomic status or different family size. For example, to a lower-class Catholic mother with many children the demand for a child to dress himself may mean that she needs to shift some of the caretaking chores onto the child, and it may indicate that she has little time or relatively little concern for the child's developing personality. For a middle-class Protestant mother with a small family, urging a child to learn to dress himself may represent early achievement training, with the intent being not so much to lessen the mother's work as to increase the child's sense of mastery and responsibility. In short, these demands may be indicative for middle-class Protestant mothers of a general emphasis on responsibility and/or mastery training which may in turn foster the development of achievement motivation in their children.

In addition to parental reactions to success and failure, and parental demands for independence and achievement, parental attitudes and values are also related to the achievement motivation of their children. In Chapter 4, Smith reports that parents of children with high Need for Achievement have a more favorable view of their children's competence than parents of children with low Need for Achievement, a finding which is consistent with earlier research.[27] Smith's data on parental childrearing

---

[25] Cf. M. Argyle and P. Robinson, "Two Origins of Achievement Motivation," *British Journal of Social and Clinical Psychology*, 1 (1962), 107–120; I. L. Child, T. Storm, and J. Veroff, "Achievement Themes in Folk Tales Related to Socialization Practice," in J. W. Atkinson (ed.), *Motives in Fantasy, Action and Society* (Princeton: D. Van Nostrand Co., 1958), Chap. 34; J. Kagan and H. A. Moss, *Birth to Maturity* (New York: John Wiley & Sons, 1962); B. Rosen and R. D'Andrade, "The Psychosocial Origins of Achievement Motivation," *Sociometry*, 22 (1959), 185–218.

[26] D. C. McClelland, *The Achieving Society* (Princeton: D. Van Nostrand Co., 1961).

[27] Cf. Rosen and D'Andrade, *op. cit.*; Winterbottom, *op cit.*

values indicate that parents distinguish between assertive and competitive achievement on the one hand and individual achievement on the other hand. It is possible for a parent to regard both kinds of achievement characteristics as important for his child, neither as important, or one and not the other. A similar distinction between two types of parental values for achievement is reported by Stoltz.[28] This distinction suggests that achievement motivation may not be as general across situations as has been implicitly assumed in much research on achievement motivation, and it lends support to Veroff's contention that a child can develop relatively separate orientations to individual achievement and to competitive achievement.

Achievement anxiety. Theory and research[29] suggest that high test anxiety results from parental criticism of the preschool child's achievement efforts, from delayed independence training and the encouragement of dependence, and from the giving or withholding of love as a way of insuring conformity to achievement demands. In the data reported by Smith in Chapter 4, teacher ratings provided clear evidence that the high test anxiety children were in fact less independent in the classroom than the low test anxiety children. The parents of children with high test anxiety tended ($p < .10$) to react to their son's success by telling him they loved him, and by showing him how he could have done better. Although the evidence is slim, it seems worth pursuing the notion that the highly anxious child may get the impression that parental love is contingent on his doing well, and he may become apprehensive about losing that love in the event of failure. There is also a suggestion of a difference between the parental orientations that produce achievement motivation and achievement anxiety. It may be that parents of children with high achievement motivation react to *partial* success with encouragement so that the child may feel essentially positive toward himself and his level of performance. The parent of the highly anxious child may react to the same performance by indicating how it falls short, thus giving the child an essentially negative feeling about his work and his abilities.

Smith's results also indicate that parents of highly test anxious children hold a lower view of their children's competence, and that they more often urge their children to perform well or to improve their performance than parents of boys with low test anxiety. These findings suggest that the par-

[28] L. M. Stoltz, *Influences on Parent Behavior* (Stanford, Calif.: Stanford University Press, 1967), 52.

[29] E. W. Bartlett and C. P. Smith, "Childrearing Practices, Birth Order and the Development of Achievement-Related Motives," *Psychological Reports*, 19 (1966), 1207–1216; S. C. Feld, "Longitudinal Study of the Origins of Achievement Strivings," *Journal of Personality and Social Psychology*, 7 (1967), 408–414; Sarason *et al., op. cit.*

ent of the highly anxious child places a high value on achievement, but that he has a low expectancy that his child will achieve.

Research by Feld[30] suggests that parental demands for independence and achievement on the child with high test anxiety may not be made at an early age, but the parent may then find that at a later age the child has become dependent and nonassertive and in reaction, the parent may express disapproval of these traits and exert pressure for greater independence and achievement. If this kind of process does occur, the data reported by Smith suggest that the parental reaction has already begun by the time the child is 10 or 11 years old.

Sarason, in his comments in Chapter 7, has suggested still another perspective on the finding that parents of boys with high test anxiety are dissatisfied with their sons. He points out that these parents may have conflicts about achievement themselves and that their attitudes toward their children may reflect their own unresolved problems in these areas. If this is true it may help to account for a general impression that derives from research on these problems, namely, that the parental actions that lead to high achievement motivation tend to be actions that are taken with the good of the child in mind. That is, the parent is concerned to see the child develop in his own right. Parental behaviors that have been hypothesized to lead to anxiety, on the other hand, seem to emanate from a self-centered parental point of view which tends to ignore the child's interests.

As Moss and others have noted in this volume, there is a tendency to assume that childrearing practices cause personality characteristics to develop, but the opposite might be the case. For example, the parents of a timid and fearful child might delay demands for independence because the child does not seem capable of fulfilling them, or alternatively, demands for achievement may be made relatively early because another child shows earlier promise of being able to fulfill such demands. Since we know that there are constitutional differences in such factors as activity level, assertiveness, fearfulness, and intelligence, we should begin to look for the interaction of these factors with childrearing in future studies of the development of achievement motivation. If one could hold constitutional differences equal, then it would be possible to contrast the effects of different childrearing pressure for independence and achievement. Since it is difficult to equate for constitutional differences, it may be possible to measure them and to relate the kinds of childrearing behaviors associated with them to the various outcomes which are detected in longitudinal research.

---

[30] *Op. cit.*

Implications for childrearing. Along with the high regard for excellence in contemporary America, come parental requests for information about how to raise a child who will want to achieve, make good grades in school, be a success in a prestigious occupation, make a contribution to knowledge or technology or art, or break a record. Some behaviorists have been so confident of their control of human behavior that they have unhesitatingly proffered advice about how to tailor-make children into whatever kinds of adults are desired.[31] Although these psychologists had studied child development, their primary research efforts were invested in the study of simpler organisms such as rats or pigeons, and they tended to believe that a few simple principles of conditioning and reinforcement were all that were required to shape the course of human development. Although their ideas are not necessarily incorrect, they are almost surely insufficiently complex and misleading in emphasis.

The hubris of these behaviorists raises two important questions: First, do psychologists know enough to be able to tell parents how to transform a child into a particular kind of adult personality, and second, should the psychologist be a party to so value-laden an activity? In the first place, both the behavioristic approach and McClelland's view that all motives are learned place insufficient emphasis on the role of constitutional differences. Presumably such differences place restrictions on the degree to which behavior can be shaped by environmental influences, and they also complicate attempts to prescribe training procedures since demands which are appropriate for a child who is constitutionally predisposed to be active and intelligent may not be appropriate for a child who is innately less active and intelligent. In the second place it is highly unlikely that all parents could follow advice effectively even if the advice were valid, since, as has been pointed out, the parent's behavior is not necessarily directed by rational considerations but may reflect unresolved personal problems. Third, constitutional predispositions aside, the experiences necessary for producing a child who is eager to achieve and who is not fearful of failure are more complex than had been previously imagined, and it appears that many additional factors may be important which are just beginning to be seen as relevant.

Although the primary orientation of the research reported here has been the understanding of behavior without regard for its positive or negative value, it is also true that it is hard not to regard persons with high Need for Achievement and low test anxiety as more fortunate than those with

---

[31] B. F. Skinner, *Walden Two* (New York: The Macmillan Company, 1948); J. B. Watson, *Psychological Care of Infant and Child* (New York: W. W. Norton Co., 1928).

low Need for Achievement and high test anxiety. While it is not possible, therefore, to give definitive information on how a parent can influence a child's achievement tendencies, it may be desirable to discuss the issues and to adumbrate a general pattern of influences which will require the verification of future research.

At the outset it should be noted that achievement motivation and fear of failure are only two aspects of personality that develop concomitantly with other motivational dispositions and cognitive structures. It seems highly likely that the training methods which influence the development of these motives occur within a configuration of parental behaviors, and that those behaviors influence various aspects of the child's personality in addition to his achievement-related motives. For example, high achievement motivation may typically be associated with self-confidence, field independence, ability to postpone gratification, and a future-oriented time perspective. Persons who have high anxiety about failure are more likely to be lacking in self-confidence, field dependent, and to believe in external control of reinforcement.

Parental practices that have been theoretically, and to a modest extent empirically, associated with the presence of high achievement motivation in children involve: (1) providing opportunities for the development of skill, (2) making achievement activities rewarding (through their intrinsic interest and the positive response of the parents rather than by means of extrinsic rewards such as money or privileges, and through minimizing criticism and oversupervision), (3) setting goals which are challenging rather than too easy or too difficult, (4) conveying a sense of confidence in the child's chances for success and a high regard for his abilities, and (5) generally having the interest of the child at heart in the sense of providing him skills and attitudes which will stand him in good stead, rather than using the child to enhance the parent's sense of self-esteem or to satisfy the parent's need to dominate or be loved.

On the other hand, the parent who restricts opportunities for independent accomplishment, who criticizes performance, downgrades the child's ability, and makes love conditional upon success is likely to produce a fearful child who finds achievement activities unpleasant and who has a low opinion of his own competence.

Sex Differences in Achievement-Related Motivation

Students of human behavior have almost come to expect that if data obtained from boys show one thing, then data obtained from girls will show something else. The findings reported in this volume are no exception; they reveal significant sex differences for each of the major motivational variables under consideration: Need for Achievement, test anxiety, and expectations of success.

Need for achievement. Veroff reports in Chapter 3 that boys are significantly higher than girls with respect to scores obtained from a fantasy measure of achievement motivation. In every grade from the 1st to the 6th boys have higher mean fantasy Need for Achievement scores. Veroff obtained stories in response to two pictures (a man at a desk, two men at a machine) and employed a modified version of the original McClelland *et al.*[32] scoring system in order to insure satisfactory coding reliability. (No attempt will be made here to discuss the complex findings concerning the amount of imagery elicited from girls by pictures of males versus pictures of females.)

These results are surprising since several studies by Veroff and others[33] have shown that high school and college girls write a *greater* amount of achievement imagery in response to pictures of men than high school or college males. If Veroff's fantasy measure as used with children is comparable to the procedure employed with adults, then at some point during the years from 12 to 16 girls must surpass boys in the amount of achievement imagery they write in response to pictures of men. Modest support for this inference is provided by the data of Kagan and Moss[34] who compared the responses of boys and girls of different ages to cards from the Thematic Apperception Test. At the age of 8, more boys produced achievement themes than girls. At 11, the difference was in the same direction but smaller, and by 14, slightly more girls produced achievement themes than boys. In future research a systematic study comparing the amount and kind of achievement imagery produced by males and females at regular intervals from elementary school to college would afford valuable descriptive information for the understanding of sex differences in achievement motivation.

Veroff's measure of normative achievement motivation shows that boys choose the most difficult task more often than girls. The proportion of girls who choose tasks of intermediate difficulty tends to be slightly lower than the proportion of boys through the 3rd grade and slightly higher thereafter. And on Veroff's measure of autonomous achievement motivation girls make higher scores than boys in each grade from the 1st to the 6th. Veroff conjectures that girls are more concerned about social approval than boys and that the achievement motivation of girls tends to be aroused

---

[32] *Op. cit.*

[33] McClelland *et al., op. cit.*

[34] J. Kagan and H. A. Moss, "Stability and Validity of Achievement Fantasy," *Journal of Abnormal and Social Psychology*, 58 (1959), 357–364.

most completely in situations in which approval is dependent on achievement. He suggests that the imagery in thematic apperceptive stories be separated into autonomous imagery and social comparison imagery to see if female Need for Achievement scores are primarily the result of social comparison or social approval imagery.

In summary the results concerning sex differences in Need for Achievement as reported by Veroff are not consistent. In grades 1 through 6, girls are significantly (though not substantially) lower in fantasy Need for Achievement and significantly (though not substantially) higher in autonomous achievement motivation, and in normative achievement motivation girls tend to be lower in the first three grades and higher in the last three. The results do not permit the conclusion that girls, on the average, are either especially low or high in Need for Achievement during childhood as compared with boys. The difference between the sexes is more clear-cut with respect to anxiety, however.

Test anxiety. Feld and Lewis in Chapter 5 report that white 2nd grade girls have significantly higher test anxiety than white 2nd grade boys, but they find no difference between the test anxiety scores of Negro girls and boys. Hill and Sarason[35] report that the difference in test anxiety scores between boys and girls increases through elementary school. In the 1st grade girls are slightly but not significantly higher, by the 3rd grade the difference is significant, and by the 5th grade it is highly significant. Veroff also reports that girls are substantially higher in general anxiety than boys in grades 3 through 6. As Sarason *et al.*[36] suggest, girls may simply be more willing to admit anxiety than boys because boys are not supposed to be fearful. Consistent with this hypothesis are data presented by Hill and Sarason[37] showing that boys have higher scores than girls on defensiveness and lie scales. The alternative interpretation would be that girls are genuinely more anxious either because of a constitutional predisposition or differential experience, or some combination of constitution and experience. One indirect line of reasoning may provide support for the notion that girls are genuinely more anxious than boys, especially in the later grades in school. Anxiety is negatively related to intellectual performance (especially under stressful conditions), but more than this, those children whose test anxiety decreases during the elementary school years tend to increase in intelligence, whereas those whose test anxiety increases tend to decrease in intelligence.[38] Girls' test anxiety scores increase more

---

[35] *Op. cit.*
[36] *Op. cit.*
[37] *Op. cit.*
[38] Hill and Sarason, *op. cit.*

than boys' during elementary school,[39] and girls' IQ's less often increase and more often decrease during elementary school than boys'.[40] It seems possible, therefore, that the greater increase in anxiety in girls accounts for, or is related to, their relatively less favorable intellectual development during the elementary school years.

One other indirect source of evidence may indicate that girls genuinely have higher anxiety than boys. Dependency is a correlate of anxiety, and girls are more dependent[41] and are lower in field independence than boys.[42]

Expectations of success. Virginia Crandall in Chapter 2 shows that girls from elementary school to college have lower expectations of accomplishment in intellectual and academic activities than boys. A possibly related finding is the greater preference for difficult tasks demonstrated by boys in Veroff's normative level of aspiration data. A task that is defined as difficult should, according to the previously mentioned differences in expectancy, be perceived as more difficult by girls than by boys. In fact it is possible that the same task would be seen as too difficult by girls and just right by boys. In other words, sex differences in expectancy could help to account for the differences in preference for difficult tasks reported by Veroff.

A finding similar to that described by Crandall is reported by Brim *et al.*,[43] who studied a nationwide sample of 10th to 12th graders in public and private schools. These authors compared measures of verbal intelligence with self-estimates of intelligence and found that boys have higher estimates of their ability relative to their actual ability than girls. Brim suggests that the obtained sex differences in expectancy may be due to differential treatment of boys and girls by their parents.[44] He hypothesizes that parents value intellectual achievement more highly for boys than for girls and reward boys more for intellectual achievement. If this is true, then differences in expectancy should be more pronounced in lower-class subjects because there is greater sex differentiation in child-

---

[39] *Ibid.*
[40] L. W. Sontag, C. T. Baker, and V. L. Nelson, "Mental Growth and Personality Development: A Longitudinal Study," *Monographs of the Society for Research in Child Development*, 23 (1958), Serial 68.
[41] A. Haeberle, "Interactions of Sex, Birth Order and Dependency with Behavior Problems and Symptoms in Emotionally Disturbed Pre-School Children" (Paper read at Eastern Psychological Association, Philadelphia, 1958).
[42] H. A. Witkin *et al.*, *Psychological Differentiation* (New York: John Wiley & Sons, 1962).
[43] O. G. Brim, Jr., *et al.*, *American Beliefs and Attitudes About Intelligence* (New York: Russell Sage Foundation, in press).
[44] This point was made during a discussion session at the Research Conference on The Development of Achievement-Related Motives and Self-Esteem in Children at the City University of New York, October, 1967.

rearing in the lower class than in the middle class.[45] Brim reports that there are indeed greater sex differences in expectancy among his lower-class subjects which supports the hypothesis that differences in expectancy are a function of differential childrearing values and rewards.

An alternative explanation for the sex difference in expectancy is provided from research on achievement-related motivation. There is a tendency for the probability of success at a particular task to be judged as higher by a person with high Need for Achievement than by a person with low Need for Achievement, and as lower by a person with high test anxiety than by a person with low test anxiety.[46] Feather suggests that these relationships may be due to the influence of the subjective attractiveness of success and the subjective repulsiveness of failure on a person's probability statements:

. . . subjects high in the motive to achieve success (M_S) may tend to perceive success as more attractive than do subjects low in the motive to achieve success. This relatively higher perceived attractiveness may tend to dominate the judgments of probability of success made by subjects who are high in M_S such that these judgments are more "wishful" than reality-oriented . . . subjects high in the motive to avoid failure (M_{AF}) may tend to perceive failure as more repulsive than do subjects low in the motive to avoid failure. This relatively higher perceived repulsiveness may determine lower judgments of probability of success among subjects who are high in M_{AF}. . . . Subjects high in M_{AF} may, as it were, react defensively by stating low probability estimates, since failure would not be so repulsive if the task were accepted as fairly difficult.[47]

Since there is reason to believe that girls have higher test anxiety than boys, it would follow that girls would tend to have lower expectations of success than boys. Even if girls, on the average, tend to be high in both Need for Achievement and test anxiety, their estimates would tend to be lower than the estimates of subjects who tend to be high in Need for Achievement and relatively low in test anxiety. In further research along the lines begun by Crandall, it should be possible to classify males and females according to their Need for Achievement and test anxiety scores and to compare their expectancies. Girls with high Need for Achievement and low test anxiety should have expectancies similar to the expectancies of boys with high Need for Achievement and low test anxiety, but a greater

---

[45] J. Kagan, "Acquisition and Significance of Sex Typing and Sex Role Identity," in M. L. Hoffman and L. W. Hoffman (eds.), *Review of Child Development Research* (New York: Russell Sage Foundation, 1964), I, 137–168.

[46] N. T. Feather, "The Relationship of Expectation of Success to Need Achievement and Test Anxiety," *Journal of Personality and Social Psychology*, 1 (1965), 118–126.

[47] *Ibid.*, 273–274.

proportion of boys should fall into this category if the proposed explanation is correct.

Educational Implications of the Research

Current theory on achievement-related motivation[48] has implications for three kinds of behavior in educational settings: performance level, persistence, and goal setting. The theory states that the motive to achieve success (M_S), and the motive to avoid failure (M_{AF}) are aroused in achievement situations, and that these motives, in combination with expectancies of success and failure, and the incentive values of success and failure produce approach and avoidance tendencies which yield a *resultant* motivational tendency either to approach or to avoid an achievement activity, depending on which component tendency is stronger. For persons in whom M_S is greater than M_{AF} the resultant tendency is to approach success, and for persons in whom M_{AF} is greater than M_S the resultant tendency is to avoid the possibility of failure.

The classroom tends to be an achievement-oriented setting in which children are urged to do well—to meet high standards of performance. Their performance is evaluated; they are told when they have done well or poorly. With respect to performance level in such an achievement setting, the theory implies that persons with $M_S > M_{AF}$ should work harder than persons with $M_{AF} > M_S$, especially when the task to be done is of *intermediate* difficulty.[49]

As Weiner[50] has pointed out, this suggests the advisability of giving persons in whom $M_S > M_{AF}$ challenging work (e.g., honors classes) while giving persons in whom $M_{AF} > M_S$ work at which success is fairly certain. This principle applies to a situation in which some parents find themselves faced with a choice between putting a child in a more or less advanced grade. Sometimes a child is on the borderline between two grades because of his age or because his family has moved to a new community. It would appear that one factor of relevance to a decision is the child's motivational makeup. Holding ability constant, if his resultant motivation is to achieve success, then he may benefit from being placed in the higher grade where he will encounter more challenging work. If his resultant motivation is to avoid failure, then the lower grade may be more appropriate.

Although it is obvious, it should be noted explicitly that achievement

---

[48] Cf. Atkinson, *op. cit.*; Atkinson and Feather, *op. cit.*
[49] Atkinson and Feather, *op. cit.*, Chap. 20.
[50] B. Weiner, "Implications of the Current Theory of Achievement Motivation for Research and Performance in the Classroom," *Psychology in the Schools*, 4 (1967), 164–171.

motivation and achievement anxiety are not the only motives influencing academic performance. Other motives operate in academic situations which may insure, for example, that the student who is low in achievement motivation may nevertheless get good grades. For example, some such students may be motivated for the approval of the teacher or by "extrinsic" incentives such as a monetary prize or special privileges offered by parents. Unless the influence of these factors is controlled, in addition to the degree of challenge of the academic work, it is not possible to demonstrate strong relationships between achievement-related motives and academic performance.

It should also be noted that the effect of test anxiety on academic performance is complex. Test anxiety is typically accompanied by a relatively low expectation of success, dependent behavior, and low self-esteem. The syndrome of apprehensiveness about evaluation, and doubts about one's ability and one's chances of success is detrimental to academic performance for a variety of reasons. The anxious child prefers to avoid achievement activities because they are potentially unpleasant; when he does find himself in such a situation, he can't work effectively under testlike conditions because he is preoccupied with thoughts of how well or how poorly he will do, and how well others will do.[51] A vicious circle is established in which anxiety leads to poor performance which makes achievement activities all the more unpleasant the next time around.

Feld and Lewis in Chapter 5 note that their 2nd grade Negro pupils have higher test anxiety than their white students, and Epps[52] has reported a similar finding comparing Negro and white high school students. The anxiety of Negro children, as Feld and Lewis point out, includes worrying and dreaming about school even when the children are away from school.

It seems understandable that many Negro children would develop high test anxiety. The importance of school is frequently stressed at home since Negro parents view education as the best means of improving the lives of their children. However, some of the children may find that they lack language skills and middle-class values that contribute to successful academic performance. An activity which is highly important but where the chances of success are low is likely to engender low self-esteem, avoidance, and resentment. Negro children who are not deficient in basic skills may nevertheless find the classroom to be a place in which they are explicitly devalued and expected to perform poorly. A high degree of anxiety

---

[51] Mandler and Watson, *op. cit.*
[52] E. G. Epps, "Social Background and Motivation" (Unpublished manuscript, Survey Research Center, University of Michigan, April, 1966).

about school matters would appear to be a natural response to such a threatening situation.

As Veroff notes, one effect of desegregation may be to introduce Negro pupils into a more challenging social comparison situation. He cautions that: "Desegregation can positively affect children with sufficiently strong feelings of competence, but could have drastic consequences for those who do not or who are in the throes of unmastered social comparison."

Another aspect of academic behavior which is affected by achievement-related motives is a student's reaction to success and failure. If a student "plays it safe" after success by repeating the same task over and over again, he does not increase his mastery of new activities. According to Veroff this reaction to success is most typical of children with low autonomous achievement motivation and low field independence. In contrast, children with high autonomous achievement motivation and high field independence are more likely to go on to a different task following success, thus extending their range of experience and mastery. From the point of view of Atkinson's theory,[53] these persons turn to something more challenging, while those with lower achievement motivation prefer easier tasks.

Following failure most children avoid the failed task when given a choice among alternatives ranging in similarity from the same task to dissimilar tasks. Veroff finds that children with high autonomous achievement motivation and high field independence again react constructively by choosing, not the same, but moderately similar tasks to try the second time, thereby having further practice in the general area in which lack of success was experienced. Children with low autonomous achievement motivation and high field independence turned to the most dissimilar tasks the second time around, thus losing an opportunity for mastery of the failed activity. Willingness to move on to new things following success and to try again following failure are important personality tendencies affecting academic performance. If a child's proclivities are observed and understood to follow from his motivational makeup, the teacher may be able to guide his selection of activities more effectively.

What educational practices can be devised to take advantage of positive motivation for achievement and to reduce the problems caused by low motivation to achieve and high anxiety about achievement? Veroff suggests identifying children who are not ready for social comparison in kindergarten and 1st grade and giving them special training in autonomy to build their sense of effectiveness. The child should first feel "I can do it

---

[53] *Op. cit.*

myself" before he is ready to ask "How do I compare with others?" After the child has a satisfactory degree of competence and autonomy, he must then experience a reasonable amount of success in social comparison. One way to insure this kind of experience which has been suggested is ability grouping.

Ability grouping appears on first thought to be a good solution for children with low expectations of success. In Veroff's terms, placing a child with low ability with other children of similar aptitude should give the child a feeling of success in competition with others, and a favorable experience with social comparison is presumably necessary for the development of social achievement motivation. Crandall's results, however, reported in Chapter 2, indicate some problems with this approach. They show that the child is highly aware of his standing in the entire ability group structure, and that his expectations of success are influenced more by the total structure than by the other students in his particular class. Thus, the low ability child reports a low expectation of success despite the ability grouping. However, it is possible that these low ability children would have given *even lower* expectations of success had they not had the experience of ability grouping. Crandall's study does not include a control group which might provide evidence on this point.

Possibly some combination of ability grouping and motivation grouping is theoretically most appropriate. The results of one study illustrate the possibilities inherent in such a procedure. The findings show that "students who are relatively high in n Achievement show greater interest and enhancement in learning when they are grouped by ability than when they are not. Ability grouping does not, however, produce the expected decrement in performance among students who are relatively high in Test Anxiety, although there is evidence of a significant decline of interest in schoolwork when these students are placed in ability-grouped classes."[54]

Desegregation may, in some instances, have the opposite effect of ability grouping: It can create a situation in which Negro children who, in segregated schools, feel comparable in ability to their classmates, find themselves to be ranked among the lowest members of the class in a desegregated school. For these children it may be possible to emphasize success at particular individual skills in which they excel, or it may be even more effective to introduce an ungraded curriculum and to rely on teaching materials which minimize social comparison and enable each child to proceed at his own pace.

Programed instruction holds out the possibility of providing highly

---

[54] Atkinson and Feather, *op. cit.,* 347.

individualized education. The materials used are intended to engender a high level of interest, and to enable pupils with different levels of ability to progress to the same criterion at different paces. In Chapter 4 Smith reports on the relationship of achievement-related motives to performance on semi-programed reading materials. The self-tests for these materials were so easy that few mistakes were made, presumably minimizing feelings of failure. Each child corrected his own answers and assigned himself a grade. Hence, teacher criticism and evaluation were virtually eliminated. Smith finds no relationship between performance on these materials and either Need for Achievement or test anxiety. The latter finding may be important, however, since there is a nonsignificant but suggestive tendency for anxiety to impair reading performance to a lesser degree with programed reading materials than with the standard classroom reading curriculum. An apparently related finding is reported by Grimes and Allinsmith,[55] namely, that anxiety makes no difference in performance under structured learning conditions, but it impairs performance in unstructured conditions. Kight and Sassenrath[56] find that highly anxious students using programed materials actually outperform students with low test anxiety on two out of three criterion measures. They also report a positive relationship between Need for Achievement and performance on programed materials.

Smith conjectures that the programed materials he used may have conflicting properties with respect to the arousal of anxiety. The easy questions and absence of competition and teacher evaluation should have minimized anxiety, but the necessity for self-reliance may have aroused anxiety, since anxious persons tend to be dependent. It may be of value in future research to vary the motivationally relevant characteristics of programed materials such as difficulty level, source of evaluation, amount of competition and social comparison, and the degree of self-reliance required. It may be possible to adapt such materials for children with different motivational patterns. For example, the difficulty of the material could be varied to provide either easy or challenging steps. Easy material would eliminate the experience of failure so painful for the anxious child; moderately difficult material would provide a genuine sense of accomplishment for children with strong achievement motivation when they perform well.

---

[55] J. W. Grimes and W. Allinsmith, "Compulsivity, Anxiety and School Achievement," in J. F. Rosenblith and W. Allinsmith (eds.), *The Causes of Behavior* (Boston: Allyn and Bacon, 1962), 420–433.
[56] H. R. Kight and J. M. Sassenrath, "Relation of Achievement Motivation and Test Anxiety to Performance in Programed Instruction," *Journal of Educational Psychology,* 57 (1966), 14–17.

Persistence in academic settings can be manifested in a variety of ways. Smith[57] provides evidence that students with relatively strong Motive to Achieve Success leave an exam more quickly than students with relatively strong Motive to Avoid Failure when the questions are perceived as easy, but the opposite is true when the questions are perceived as more difficult. Employing a somewhat different theoretical approach, Crandall, in Chapter 2, reviews studies showing that, on the average, children with higher expectancies of success persist longer in attempts to solve problems than children with low expectancies. Clearly, academic persistence is influenced by achievement-related motives.

It is not necessarily desirable under all conditions to persist for a long time at a task. If the task is so difficult that it is beyond a person's ability or so easy that it provides no challenge, then it is not useful to persist, yet these are the conditions under which subjects who are high in test anxiety and low in Need for Achievement do tend to persist, whereas they are likely to give up quickly in the face of a moderately difficult task.[58]

A teacher who understands that anxiety may cause a child to give up at some tasks too soon because they threaten failure or spend too long at others because they insure success is in a position to deal with these behaviors constructively. In such instances neither censure nor pressure to behave differently is likely to have a beneficial effect. To get the child to persist in a more adaptive manner the teacher may need to make special efforts to reduce the threat of failure associated with a task and to provide extra sources of positive gratification for certain activities.

Goal setting or level of aspiration is a third aspect of academic behavior which is influenced by achievement-related motives. A student may select a course or an activity partly on the basis of its level of difficulty; he may try to earn a particular grade in a course; he may elect to prepare for an occupation which is more or less demanding. All these choices involve the selection of a single goal from among alternatives with varying likelihoods of success. How close does a person usually come to attaining the goals he sets for himself? Are his goals commensurate with his abilities? Does he tend to overaspire or underaspire? These are questions that have a bearing on learning and academic performance, but that are not often dealt with explicitly by teachers.

The current theory of achievement-related motivation[59] leads to the

[57] C. P. Smith, "Relationships Between Achievement-Related Motives and Intelligence, Performance Level, and Persistence," *Journal of Abnormal and Social Psychology*, 68 (1964), 523–532.
[58] R. J. Mixson, "Motivational Determinants of Persistence in and Attrition from an Engineering Program" (Unpublished doctoral dissertation, Princeton University, 1966); N. T. Feather, "The Study of Persistence," *Psychological Bulletin*, 59 (1962), 94–115.
[59] Cf. Atkinson and Feather, *op. cit.*

expectation that in situations conducive to achievement the motivational pattern of motive to achieve success greater than motive to avoid failure will normally augment the level of performance, increase persistence at moderately difficult tasks, and produce realistic goal setting. In contrast, the motivational pattern of motive to avoid failure greater than the motive to achieve success will impair performance level, and produce maladaptive persistence and unrealistic goal setting. A number of studies have shown that subjects with $M_S > M_{AF}$ are more likely to set goals of intermediate difficulty than subjects with $M_{AF} > M_S$.[60] Smith, in Chapter 4, has demonstrated this relationship with 4th and 5th grade boys, and Veroff, in Chapter 3, has shown that Negro boys with low autonomous achievement motivation and high test anxiety tend to overaspire. Setting extremely high goals may be a way of insuring social approval for one's aspirations, and since they are difficult to attain, the person may feel little humiliation when he fails to reach them. However, such a strategy almost guarantees a constant record of failure, and it may not direct the individual's efforts and short-term plans along the lines which will eventually be the most constructive.

Apart from the fact that it is probably helpful for a teacher to understand the dynamics of goal setting, it is difficult to prescribe an educational procedure for dealing with disorders of goal setting. It should be possible to give explicit training in how to set goals. Such training might involve giving the child practice in assessing his own abilities and the difficulty of various tasks. He could be given the experience of setting a level of aspiration, receiving feedback, and then adjusting his new level of aspiration up or down in response to the information about his past performance. There may also be a tendency for a person with high fear of failure to avoid information relevant to a choice (e.g., ignoring opportunities to find out about an occupation the person says he wants to enter). It should be possible to teach the person the general rule of investigating a variety of alternatives as fully as possible before making a choice. It should be recognized, however, that the influence of motivation on goal setting tends to be greatest when the situation is most ambiguous, that is, when there is least information available for estimating the level of future performance, and it is difficult to train a person in advance how to handle such ambiguous situations. In cases of extremely disordered goal setting the need for counseling and consultation with the parents is indicated in order to try to get at the basic source of anxiety rather than simply to teach the child ways of coping with his anxiety.

---

[60] *Ibid.;* C. H. Mahone, "Fear of Failure and Unrealistic Vocational Aspiration," *Journal of Abnormal and Social Psychology,* 60 (1960), 253–261.

In conclusion, it appears that increased knowledge of achievement-related motives and expectancies has important implications for education as well as for childrearing, desegregation, and the overall personality development of the child. Many instances of child behavior that the teacher or parent may regard as isolated incidents can now be seen as attributable to the pervasive and general influence of patterns of motivational personality characteristics.

It is clear that knowledge of achievement-related motivation is in its early stages. There is much room for improved measurement techniques, additional descriptive information, and more adequate theory, and there is a need for integration of knowledge in this area with information about cognitive development and personality development in general. The complexity of the problems is revealed here, but also the potential for obtaining information in future research which will lead to a more effective and enlightened approach to some major human problems.

Bibliography

Abelson, W. D. "Differential Performance and Personality Patterns Among Anxious Children." Unpublished doctoral dissertation, Harvard University, 1961.

Adams, E. B., and Sarason, I. G. "Relation Between Anxiety in Children and Their Parents," *Child Development,* 34 (1963), 237–246.

Adams, H. E., and Kirby, A. C. "Manifest Anxiety, Social Desirability, or Response Set," *Journal of Consulting Psychology,* 27 (1963), 59–61.

Allport, G. W. *Pattern and Growth in Personality.* New York: Holt, Rinehart and Winston, 1961.

Argyle, M., and Robinson, P. "Two Origins of Achievement Motivation," *British Journal of Social and Clinical Psychology,* 1 (1962), 107–120.

Atkinson, J .W. "Motivational Determinants of Risk-Taking Behavior," *Psychological Review,* 64 (1957), 359–372.

———. *An Introduction to Motivation.* Princeton: D. Van Nostrand Co., 1964.

Atkinson, J. W. (ed.) *Motives in Fantasy, Action, and Society.* Princeton: D. Van Nostrand Co., 1958.

Atkinson, J. W., Bastian, J. R., Earl, R. W., and Litwin, G. H. "The Achievement Motive, Goal Setting, and Probability Preferences," *Journal of Abnormal and Social Psychology,* 60 (1960), 27–36.

Atkinson, J. W., and Feather, N. T. (eds.). *A Theory of Achievement Motivation.* New York: John Wiley & Sons, 1966.

Atkinson, J. W., and O'Connor, Patricia. "Neglected Factors in Studies of Achievement-Oriented Performance: Social Approval as an Incentive and Performance Decrement." In J. W. Atkinson and N. T. Feather (eds.), *A Theory of Achievement Motivation.* New York: John Wiley & Sons, 1966, 299–326.

Baldwin, A. L. "The Theory and Practice of Bringing Up Johnny," *Contemporary Psychology,* 2 (1957), 305–307.

Barlow, J. A., and Burt, C. "The Identification of Factors from Different Experiments," *British Journal of Statistical Psychology,* 7 (1954), 52–56.

Barnard, J. W., Zimbardo, P. G., and Sarason, S. B. "Bias in Teacher's Ratings of Student Personality Traits Due to I.Q. and Social Desirability." Unpublished study, 1965.

Barry, H., Bacon, Margaret K., and Child, I. L. "A Cross-Cultural Survey of Some Sex Differences in Socialization," *Journal of Abnormal and Social Psychology,* 55 (1957), 327–332.

Bartlett, E. W., and Smith, C. P. "Childrearing Practices, Birth Order and the Development of Achievement-Related Motives," *Psychological Reports*, 19 (1966), 1207–1216.

Battle, E. "Motivational Determinants of Academic Task Persistence," *Journal of Personality and Social Psychology*, 2 (1965), 209–218.

———. "Motivational Determinants of Academic Competence," *Journal of Personality and Social Psychology*, 4 (1966), 634–642.

Baumrind, Diana, and Black, A. E. "Socialization Practices Associated with Dimensions of Competence in Preschool Boys and Girls," *Child Development*, 38 (1967), 291–328.

Bell, R. Q. "A Reinterpretation of the Direction of Effects in Studies of Socialization," *Psychological Review*, 75 (1968), 81–95.

Bell, R. Q., and Darling, J. F. "The Prone Head Reaction in the Human Neonate: Relation with Sex and Tactile Sensitivity," *Child Development*, 36 (1965), 943–949.

Birney, R. C. "The Effect of Threat on Thematic Apperception." Unpublished Honors thesis, Wesleyan University, 1950.

Birney, R. C., Burdick, H., and Teevan, R. *Fear of Failure*. Princeton: D. Van Nostrand Co., in press.

Bloom, R. D. *Some Correlates of Test Anxiety*. Doctoral dissertation, University of Michigan. Ann Arbor: University Microfilms, 1963, No. 63–4939.

Bradburn, N. M., and Caplovitz, D. *Reports on Happiness: A Pilot Study of Behavior Related to Mental Health*. Chicago: Aldine Publishers, 1965.

Brim, O. G. Jr., Goslin, D. A., Glass, D. C., and Goldberg, I. *American Beliefs and Attitudes About Intelligence*. New York: Russell Sage Foundation, in press.

Burdick, H. *The Effect of Value of Success upon the Expectation of Success.* (Technical Report #14, Contract Nonr 3591 (01) Office of Naval Research, NR 171–803.) Lewisburg, Pa.: Bucknell University, 1965.

Burdick, H., and Stoddard, N. *The Relationship Between Incentive and Expectations of Success.* (Technical Report #7, Contract Nonr 3591 (01) Office of Naval Research, NR 171–803.) Lewisburg, Pa.: Bucknell University, 1964.

Callard, E. "Achievement Motive in the Four Year Old and Its Relationship to Achievement Expectancies of the Mother." Unpublished doctoral dissertation, University of Michigan, 1964.

Chapman, L. J., and Campbell, D. J. "Absence of Acquiescence Response Set in the Taylor Manifest Anxiety Scale," *Journal of Consulting Psychology*, 23 (1959), 465–466.

Child, I. L., Storm, T., and Veroff, J. "Achievement Themes in Folk Tales Related to Socialization Practice." In J. W. Atkinson (ed.), *Motives in Fantasy, Action and Society*. Princeton: D. Van Nostrand Co., 1958, Chap. 34.

Cronbach, L. J. "Response Set and Test Validity," *Educational and Psychological Measurement*, 6 (1946), 475–494.

Clyde, D. J., Cramer, E. M., and Sherin, R. J. *Multivariate Statistical Programs* (1st ed.). Coral Gables, Fla.: Biometric laboratory, University of Miami, 1966.

Coleman, J. *The Adolescent Society*. New York: Free Press, 1961.

Coleman, J. S., Campbell, E. Q., Hobson, C. J., McPartland, J., Mood, A. M.,

Weinfeld, F. D., and York, R. L. *Equality of Educational Opportunity.* Superintendent of Documents, Catalog No. FS 5: 238: 38001. Washington, D.C.: Government Printing Office, 1966.

Cooley, W. W., and Lohnes, P. R. *Multivariate Procedures for the Behavioral Sciences.* New York: John Wiley & Sons, 1962.

Coombs, C. H. "A Theory of Psychological Scaling," *University of Michigan Engineering Research Institute Bulletin* (1951), No. 34.

Coopersmith, S. "Self-Esteem and Need for Achievement as Determinants of Selective Recall and Repetition," *Journal of Abnormal and Social Psychology,* 60 (1960), 310–317.

Cox, F. N., and Leaper, P. M. "General and Test Anxiety Scales for Children," *Australian Journal of Psychology,* 11 (1959), 70–80.

Crandall, V. C. "Reinforcement Effects of Adult Reactions and Non-Reactions on Children's Achievement Expectations," *Child Development,* 34 (1963), 335–354.

––––––. "Achievement Behavior in Young Children," *Young Children,* 20 (1964), 77–90.

––––––. "Personality Characteristics, and Social and Achievement Behaviors Associated with Children's Social Desirability Response Tendencies," *Journal of Personality and Social Psychology,* 4 (1966), 477–486.

Crandall, V. C., Crandall, V. J., and Katkovsky, W. "A Children's Social Desirability Questionnaire," *Journal of Consulting Psychology,* 29 (1965), 27–36.

Crandall, V. C., Good, S., and Crandall, V. J. "Reinforcement Effects of Adult Reactions and Nonreactions on Children's Achievement Expectations: A Replication Study," *Child Development,* 35 (1964), 485–497.

Crandall, V. C., Katkovsky, W., and Crandall, V. J. "Children's Beliefs in Their Own Control of Reinforcements in Intellectual-Academic Achievement Situations," *Child Development,* 36 (1965), 91–109.

Crandall, V. J. "Achievement." In H. W. Stevenson (ed.), *Child Psychology.* The 62nd Yearbook of the National Society for the Study of Education Part 1. Chicago: University of Chicago Press, 1963, 416–459.

Crandall, V. J., Dewey, R., Katkovsky, W., and Preston, A. "Parents' Attitudes and Behaviors and Grade School Children's Academic Achievements," *Journal of Genetic Psychology,* 104 (1964), 53–66.

Crandall, V. J., Katkovsky, W., and Preston, Anne. "A Conceptual Formulation for Some Research on Children's Achievement Development," *Child Development,* 31 (1960), 787–797.

––––––. "Motivational and Ability Determinants of Young Children's Intellectual Achievement Behaviors," *Child Development,* 33 (1962), 643–661.

Crandall, V. J., Preston, Anne, and Rabson, A. "Maternal Reactions and the Development of Independence and Achievement Behavior in Young Children," *Child Development,* 31 (1960), 243–251.

Crandall, V. J., and Rabson, Alice. "Children's Repetition Choices in an Intellectual Achievement Situation Following Success and Failure," *Journal of Genetic Psychology,* 97 (1960), 161–168.

Crandall, V. J., Solomon, D., and Kellaway, R. "Expectancy Statements and Decision Times as Functions of Objective Probabilities and Reinforcement Values," *Journal of Personality,* 24 (1955), 192–203.

250

———. "The Value of Anticipated Events as a Determinant of Probability Learning and Extinction," *Journal of Genetic Psychology*, 58 (1958), 3–10.

Crowne, D. P., and Marlowe, D. *The Approval Motive*. New York: John Wiley & Sons, 1964.

De Pree, Suzanne. "The Influence of Parental Achievement Expectations and Role Definitions on Achievement Motive Development in Girls." Unpublished honors thesis, University of Michigan, 1962.

Dunn, J. A. "Factor Structure of the Test Anxiety Scale for Children," *Journal of Consulting Psychology*, 28 (1964), 92.

———. "School Approach-Avoidance Values: A Differential Study of Children's Affect and Value Patterns for the Academic as Contrasted to the Social Aspects of School." Paper presented at the meeting of the American Psychological Association, New York, September, 1966.

———. "Stability of the Factor Structure of the Test Anxiety Scale for Children Across Age and Sex Groups," *Journal of Consulting Psychology*, 29 (1965), 187.

Edwards, W. "The Theory of Decision Making," *Psychological Bulletin*, 51 (1954), 380–417.

Endler, N. S., Hunt, J. McV., and Rosenstein, A. J. "An S-R Inventory of Anxiousness," *Psychological Monographs*, 76 (1962), 17, Whole No. 536.

Epps, E. G. "Social Background and Motivation." Unpublished manuscript, Survey Research Center, University of Michigan, April, 1966.

Escalona, S. K. "The Effect of Success and Failure upon the Level of Aspiration and Behavior in Manic-Depressive Psychoses," *University of Iowa Study of Child Welfare*, 16 (1940), 199–302.

Feather, N. T. "Effects of Prior Success and Failure on Expectations of Success and Subsequent Performance," *Journal of Personality and Social Psychology*, 3 (1966), 287–298.

———. "Persistence at a Difficult Task with Alternative Task of Intermediate Difficulty," *Journal of Abnormal and Social Psychology*, 66 (1963), 604–609.

———. "The Relationship of Expectation of Success to Need Achievement and Test Anxiety," *Journal of Personality and Social Psychology*, 1 (1965), 118–126.

———. "The Relationship of Persistence at a task to Expectation of Success and Achievement Related Motives," *Journal of Abnormal and Social Psychology*, 63 (1961), 552–561.

———. "Some Personality Correlates of External Control," *Australian Journal of Psychology*, 19 (1967), 253–260.

———. "The Study of Persistence," *Psychological Bulletin*, 59, (1962), 94–115.

———. "Valence of Outcome and Expectation of Success in Relation to Task Difficulty and Perceived Locus of Control," *Journal of Personality and Social Psychology*, 7 (1967), 372–386.

Feher, B. "Children's Reactions to Social Comparison." Unpublished master's paper, University of Michigan, 1967.

Feld, Sheila C. "Longitudinal Study of the Origins of Achievement Strivings," *Journal of Personality and Social Psychology*, 7 (1967), 408–414.

———. *Studies in the Origins of Achievement Strivings*. Doctoral dissertation,

251

University of Michigan. Ann Arbor: University Microfilms, 1960, No. 60–1759.

———. "Generalized School Anxiety or Negative Self-Image: Letter to the Editor," *American Journal of Mental Deficiency,* 70 (1966), 930–931.

Feld, S., and Lewis, J. "Further Evidence on the Stability of the Factor Structure of the Test Anxiety Scale for Children," *Journal of Consulting Psychology,* 31 (1967), 434.

Feld, S., Owen, W., and Sarason, S. B. "Interviews with Parents of Anxious and Defensive Young Boys." Unpublished manuscript, National Institute of Mental Health, 1963.

Festinger, L. "A Theory of Social Comparison Processes," *Human Relations,* 7 (1954), 117–140.

Gerwitz, Hava B. "Generalization of Children's Preferences as a Function of Reinforcement," *Journal of Abnormal and Social Psychology,* 58 (1959), 111–118.

Glanzer, M., Huttenlocher, J., and Clark, W. H. "Systematic Operations in Solving Concept Problems," *Psychological Monographs,* 77 (1963), 1, Whole No. 564.

Goldsmith, H. F., and Stockwell, E. G. "Socio-Demographic Characteristics of Rapid Growth Counties in the United States: Some preliminary Considerations." Laboratory paper #12, Mental Health Study Center, National Institute of Mental Health, August, 1965.

Goodenough, D. R., Shapiro, A., Holden, M., and Steinschriber, L. "A Comparison of Dreamers and Nondreamers: Eye Movements, Electroencephalograms, and Recall of Dreams," *Journal of Abnormal and Social Psychology,* 59 (1959), 295–302.

Gough, H. G. *The California Psychological Inventory.* Palo Alto, Calif.: Consulting Psychologists Press, 1957.

Green, R. F., and Nowlis, V. "A Factor Analytic Study of the Domain of Mood with Independent Experimental Validation of the Factors," *American Psychologist,* 12 (1957), 438. (Abstract)

Greenhouse, S. W., and Geisser, S. "On Methods in the Analysis of Profile Data," *Psychometrika,* 21 (1959), 95–112.

Grimes, J. W., and Allinsmith, W. "Compulsivity, Anxiety, and School Achievement." In J. F. Rosenblith and W. Allinsmith (eds.), *The Causes of Behavior.* Boston: Allyn and Bacon, 1962, 420–433.

Haeberle, A. "Interactions of Sex, Birth Order and Dependency with Behavior Problems and Symptoms in Emotionally Disturbed Pre-School Children." Paper read at Eastern Psychological Association, Philadelphia, 1958.

Hartup, W. W. "Dependence and Independence." In H. W. Stevenson (ed.), *Child Psychology.* The 62nd Yearbook of the National Society for the Study of Education Part I. Chicago: University of Chicago Press, 1963, 333–363.

Harvey, O. J., Hunt, D., and Schroder, H. *Conceptual Systems and Personality Organization.* New York: John Wiley & Sons, 1961.

Hess, H., and Jessor, R. "The Influence of Reinforcement Value on Rate of Learning and Asymptotic Level of Expectancies," *Journal of General Psychology,* 63 (1960), 89–102.

Hess, R., and Shipman, V. "Early Experience and the Socialization of Cognitive Modes in Children," *Child Development,* 36 (1965), 869–886.

———. "Cognitive Elements in Maternal Behavior." *Minnesota Symposia on Child Psychology*, Vol. 1. Minneapolis–St. Paul: University of Minnesota Press, 1967.

Hill, K. T., and Sarason, S. B. "The Relation of Test Anxiety and Defensiveness to Test and School Performance over the Elementary-School Years: A Further Longitudinal Study," *Monographs of the Society for Research in Child Development*, 31 (1966), 2, Whole No. 104.

Horn, J. L. "An Empirical Comparison of Methods for Estimating Factor Scores," *Educational and Psychological Measurement*, 25 (1965), 313–322.

Horner, Tina. "The Motive to Avoid Success: A Thesis Proposal." Unpublished, University of Michigan, 1965.

Hunt, J. McV. *Intelligence and Experience*. New York: Ronald Press, 1961.

Irwin, F. W. "Stated Expectations as Functions of Probability and Desirability of Outcomes," *Journal of Personality*, 21 (1953), 329–335.

Jessor, R., and Readio, J. "The Influence of the Value of an Event upon the Expectancy for Its Occurrence," *Journal of General Psychology*, 56 (1957), 219–228.

Kagan, J. "Acquisition and Significance of Sex Typing and Sex Role Identity." In M. L. Hoffman, and L. W. Hoffman (eds.), *Review of Child Development Research*. New York: Russell Sage Foundation, 1964, I, 137–168.

———. "Thematic Apperceptive Techniques with Children." In *Projective Techniques with Children*. New York and London: Grune and Stratton, 1960.

Kagan, J., and Moss, H. A. *Birth to Maturity*. New York: John Wiley & Sons, 1962.

———. "Stability and Validity of Achievement Fantasy," *Journal of Abnormal and Social Psychology*, 58 (1959), 357–364.

Katkovsky, W., Crandall, V. C., and Good, S. "Parental Antecedents of Children's Beliefs in Internal-External Control of Reinforcements in Intellectual Achievement Situations," *Child Development*, 38 (1967), 765–776.

Katz I. "Review of Evidence Relating to Effects of Desegregation on the Intellectual Performance of Negroes," *American Psychologist*, 19 (1964), 381–399.

———. "The Socialization of Academic Motivation in Minority Group Children." In D. Levine (ed.), *Nebraska Symposium on Motivation*. Lincoln: University of Nebraska Press, 1967, 133–191.

Kight, H. R. and Sassenrath, J. M. "Relation of Achievement Motivation and Test Anxiety to Performance in Programed Instruction," *Journal of Educational Psychology*, 57 (1966), 14–17.

Koenig, K. "Social Psychological Correlates of Self-Reliance." Uupublished doctoral dissertation, University of Michigan, 1962.

Krebs, A. M. "Two Determinants of Conformity: Age of Independence Training and *n* Achievement," *Journal of Abnormal and Social Psychology*, 56 (1958), 130–131.

L'Abate, L. "Personality Correlates of Manifest Anxiety in Children," *Journal of Consulting Psychology*, 24 (1960), 342–348.

Lahtinen, Pirkko. "The Effect of Failure and Rejection on Dependency." Unpublished doctoral dissertation, University of Michigan, 1964.

Lavin, D. E. *The Prediction of Academic Performance*. New York: Russell Sage Foundation, 1965.

253

Leighton, D. C. "The Distribution of Psychiatric Symptoms in a Small Town," *American Journal of Psychiatry*, 112 (1956), 716–723.

Lewis, M., Meyers, W. J., Kagan, J., and Grossberg, R. "Attention to Visual Patterns in Infants." Paper presented at the meeting of the American Psychological Association, Philadelphia, September, 1963.

Lunneborg, P. W., and Lunneborg, C. E. "The Relationship of Social Desirability to Other Test-Taking Attitudes in Children." Paper presented at the meeting of the American Psychological Association, Philadelphia, September, 1963.

MacCorquodale, K., and Meehl, P. "Preliminary Suggestions as to a Formalization of Expectancy Theory," *Psychological Review*, 60 (1953), 55–63.

Mahone, C. H. "Fear of Failure and Unrealistic Vocational Aspiration," *Journal of Abnormal and Social Psychology*, 60 (1960), 253–261.

Mandler, G., and Watson, D. L. "Anxiety and the Interruption of Behavior." In C. D. Spielberger (ed.), *Anxiety and Behavior*. New York: Academic Press, 1966, 263–290.

Marks, R. W. "The Effect of Probability, Desirability and Privilege on the Stated Expectations of Children," *Journal of Personality*, 19 (1951), 332–351.

Martire, J. G. "Relationships Between the Self Concept and Differences in the Strength and Generality of Achievement Motivation," *Journal of Personality*, 24 (1956), 364–375.

McClelland, D. C. *The Achieving Society*. Princeton: D. Van Nostrand Co., 1961.

———. *Personality*. New York: Dryden Press, 1951.

———. "Risk Taking in Children with High and Low Need for Achievement." In J. W. Atkinson (ed.), *Motives in Fantasy, Action and Society*. Princeton: D. Van Nostrand Co., 1958, Chap. 21.

McClelland, D. C., Atkinson, J. W., Clark, R. A., and Lowell, E. L. *The Achievement Motive*. New York: Appleton-Century-Crofts, 1953.

McClelland, D. C., and Friedman, G. A. "A Cross-Cultural Study of the Relationship Between Child-Training Practices and Achievement Motivation Appearing in Folk Tales." In G. E. Swanson, T. M. Newcomb, and E. L. Hartley (eds.), *Readings in Social Psychology* (rev. ed.). New York: Henry Holt & Co., 1952, 243–249.

McGee, R. K. "Response Style as a Personality Variable: By What Criterion?" *Psychological Bulletin*, 59 (1962), 284–295.

McGhee, P., and Crandall, V. C. "Beliefs in Internal-External Control of Reinforcements and Academic Performance," *Child Development*, 39 (1968), 91–102.

Mischel, W. "Delay of Gratification, Need for Achievement and Acquiescence in Another Culture," *Journal of Abnormal and Social Psychology*, 62 (1961), 1–17.

———. "Preference for Delayed Reinforcement and Social Responsibility," *Journal of Abnormal and Social Psychology*, 62 (1961), 1–7.

Mixson, R. J. "Motivational Determinants of Persistence in and Attrition from an Engineering Program." Unpublished doctoral dissertation, Princeton University, 1966.

Moss, H. A., and Kagan, J. "The Stability of Achievement and Recognition

Seeking Behavior from Childhood to Adulthood," *Journal of Abnormal and Social Psychology*, 62 (1961), 543–552.

Piaget, J. *The Moral Judgment of the Child*. Glencoe, Ill.: Free Press, 1948. (Originally published in 1932.)

————. *The Origins of Intelligence in Children*. New York: International University Press, 1952.

Phillips, B. N. *An Analysis of Causes of Anxiety Among Children in School*. Austin: The University of Texas, 1966. (Final Report to the Office of Education, U.S. Department of Health, Education, and Welfare: Project No. 2616, Contract No. OE–5–10–012.)

Raphelson, A. "The Relationships Among Imaginative, Direct Verbal and Physiological Measures of Anxiety in an Achievement Situation," *Journal of Abnormal and Social Psychology*, 54 (1957), 13–18.

Raynor, J. O., and Smith, C. P. "Achievement-Related Motives and Risk Taking in Games of Skill and Chance," *Journal of Personality*, 34 (1966), 176–198.

Robbins, L. C. "The Accuracy of Parental Recall of Aspects of Child Development and of Child Rearing Practices," *Journal of Abnormal and Social Psychology*, 66 (1963), 261–270.

Rorer, L. G. "The Great Response Style Myth," *Oregon Research Institute Research Monograph*, 3 (1963), No. 6.

Rosen, B. C. "The Achievement Syndrome: A Psychocultural Dimension of Social Stratification," *American Sociological Review*, 21 (1956), 203–211.

————. "Race, Ethnicity and the Achievement Syndrome," *American Sociological Review*, 24 (1959), 47–60.

Rosen, B. and D'Andrade, R. "The Psychosocial Origins of Achievement Motivation," *Sociometry*, 22 (1959), 185–218.

Rosenzweig, S. "An Experimental Study of Repression with Special Reference to Need-Persistive and Ego-Defensive Reactions to Frustration," *Journal of Experimental Psychology*, 32 (1943), 64–74.

Rotter, J. B. *Social Learning and Clinical Psychology*. New York: Prentice-Hall, 1954.

Ruebush, B. K. "Children's Behavior as a Function of Anxiety and Defensiveness." Unpublished doctoral dissertation, Yale University, 1960.

Samelson, F. "Agreement Set and Anticontent Attitudes in the *F* Scale: A Reinterpretation," *Journal of Abnormal and Social Psychology*, 68 (1964), 338–342.

Sarason, S. B. "The Measurement of Anxiety in Children: Some Questions and Problems." In C. D. Spielberger (ed.), *Anxiety and Behavior*. New York: Academic Press, 1966, 63–79.

Sarason, S. B., Davidson, K. S., Lighthall, F. F., Waite, R. R., and Ruebush, B. K. *Anxiety in Elementary School Children*. New York: John Wiley & Sons, 1960.

Sarason, S. B., Hill, K. T., and Zimbardo, P. G. "A Longitudinal Study of the Relation of Test Anxiety to Performance on Intelligence and Achievement Tests," *Monographs of the Society for Research in Child Development*, Serial No. 98, Vol. 29 (1964), No. 7.

Sarnoff, I., Lighthall, F. F., Waite, R. R., Davidson, K., and Sarason, S. B.

"A Cross-Cultural Study of Anxiety Among American and English School Children," *Journal of Educational Psychology*, 49 (1958), 129–136.

Sears, P. S. "Correlates of Need Achievement and Need Affiliation and Classroom Management, Self-Concept and Creativity." Unpublished manuscript, Laboratory of Human Development, Stanford University, 1962.

Silverman, J. "Temperament, Sex, and Cognitive Styles." Unpublished manuscript, National Institute of Mental Health, 1966.

Silverstein, A. B., and Mohan, P. J. "Test Anxiety or Generalized School Anxiety?" *American Journal of Mental Deficiency*, 69 (1964), 438–439.

Singer, J. L. *Daydreaming: An Introduction to the Experimental Study of Inner Experience.* New York: Random House, 1966.

Siss, R. "Expectations of Mothers and Teachers for Independence and Reading and Their Influence upon Reading Achievement and Personality Attributes of Third Grade Boys." Unpublished doctoral dissertation, Rutgers University, 1962.

Skinner, B. F. *Walden Two.* New York: The Macmillan Co., 1948.

Slovic, P. "Value as a Determiner of Subjective Probability." Unpublished doctoral dissertation, University of Michigan, 1964.

Smith, C. P. "Achievement-Related Motives and Goal Setting under Different Conditions," *Journal of Personality*, 31 (1963), 124–140.

———. *Child Development.* Dubuque, Iowa: Wm. C. Brown, 1966.

———. "Relationships Between Achievement-Related Motives and Intelligence, Performance Level, and Persistence," *Journal of Abnormal and Social Psychology*, 68 (1964), 523–532.

Solomon, D., Busse, T. V., and Parelius, R. J. "Parental Behavior and Achievement of Lower-Class Negro Children." Paper read at APA, Washington, September, 1967.

Sontag, L. W., Baker, C. T., and Nelson, V. L. "Mental Growth and Personality Development: A Longitudinal Study," *Monographs of the Society for Research in Child Development*, 23 (1958), Serial 68.

Stolz, L. M. *Influences on Parent Behavior.* Stanford, Calif.: Stanford University Press, 1967.

Strodtbeck, F. L. "Family Interaction, Values and Achievement." In D. C. McClelland *et al.* (ed.), *Talent and Society.* Princeton: D. Van Nostrand Co., 1958, 135–194.

Taylor, J. A. "A Personality Scale of Manifest Anxiety," *Journal of Abnormal and Social Psychology*, 48 (1953), 285–290.

Tolman, E. C. *Purposive Behavior in Animals and Men.* Berkeley: University of California Press, 1949.

Tomkins, S. S. *Affect, Imagery, Consciousness.* Vol. I, *The Positive Affects.* New York: Springer, 1962.

———. *Affect, Imagery, Consciousness.* Vol. II, *The Negative Affects.* New York: Springer, 1963.

Torgoff, I. "Parental Developmental Timetable: Parental Field Effects on Children's Compliance." Paper read at the meeting of the Society for Research in Child Development, Pennsylvania State University, 1961.

Tyler, B. B. "Expectancy for Eventual Success as a Factor in Problem Solving Behavior," *Journal of Educational Psychology*, 49 (1958), 166–172.

Tyler, F. B., Rafferty, J., and Tyler, B. "Relationships Among Motivations of

Parents and Their Children," *Journal of Genetic Psychology,* 101 (1962), 69–81.

U.S. Bureau of the Census. "Methodology and Scores of Socioeconomic Status." Working Paper No. 15. Washington, D.C., 1963.

——. *U.S. Census of population: 1960. General Social and Economic Characteristics, Maryland.* Final report PC (1)–22C. Washington, D.C.: Government Printing Office, 1961.

——. *U.S. Census of population: 1960. General Social and Economic Characteristics, United States Summary.* Final report PC (1)–1C. Washington, D.C.: Government Printing Office, 1961.

Veroff, J. "Assessment of Motive in Children." Progress report submitted to USPHS, 1953.

——. "Assessment of Motives Through Fantasy." Paper given at Midwestern Psychological Association, 1961.

——. "Theoretical Background for Studying the Origins of Human Motivational Dispositions," *Merrill-Palmer Quarterly,* (1965), 3–18.

Veroff, J., Atkinson, J. W., Feld, S., and Gurin, G. "The Use of Thematic Apperception to Assess Motivation in a Nationwide Interview Study," *Psychological Monographs,* 74 (1960), 12, Whole No. 499.

Veroff, J., Feld, Sheila, and Crockett, H. "Explorations into the Effects of Picture Cues on Thematic Apperceptive Expression of Achievement Motivation," *Journal of Personality and Social Psychology,* 3 (1966), 171–181.

Veroff, J., Feld, Sheila, and Gurin, G. "Achievement Motivation and Religious Background," *American Sociological Review,* 27 (1962), 205–217.

Veroff, J., Goldsmith, R., and Taylor, Linda. "Effects of Achievement Motivation and Self-Esteem on Generalization of Children's Preference." USPHS Final Report (MH–10554), 1966.

Veroff, J., and Pearlman, S. "The Initial Effects of Desegregation on the Achievement Motivation of Negro Elementary School Children," *Journal of Social Issues.* In press.

Watson, D. "Relationship Between Locus of Control and Anxiety," *Journal of Personality and Social Psychology,* 6 (1967), 91–92.

Watson, J. B. *Psychological Care of Infant and Child.* New York: W. W. Norton Co., 1928.

Welsh, G. S., and Dahlstrom, W. G. (eds.), *Basic Readings on the MMPI in Psychology and Medicine.* Minneapolis: University of Minnesota Press, 1956.

Weiner, B. "Implications of the Current Theory of Achievement Motivation for Research and Performance in the Classroom," *Psychology in the Schools,* 4 (1967), 164–171.

Wenar, C. "Competence at One," *Merrill-Palmer Quarterly,* 10 (1964), 329–342.

White, R. W. "Competence and the Psychosexual Stages of Development." In M. Jones (ed.), *Nebraska Symposium on Motivation.* Lincoln: University of Nebraska Press, 1960.

——. "Motivation Reconsidered: The Concept of Competence," *Psychological Review,* 66 (1959), 297–333.

Winer, B. J. *Statistical Principles in Experimental Design*. New York: McGraw-Hill Book Co., 1962.

Winterbottom, Marian R. "The Relation of Childhood Training in Independence to Achievement Motivation." Unpublished doctoral dissertation, University of Michigan, 1953.

——. "The Relation of Need for Achievement to Learning Experiences in Independence and Mastery." In J. W. Atkinson (ed.), *Motives in Fantasy, Action and Society*. Princeton: D. Van Nostrand Co., 1958, 453–478.

Witkin, H. A., Dyk, R. B., Faterson, H. F., Goodenough, D. R. and Karp, S. A. *Psychological Differentiation*. New York: John Wiley & Sons, 1962.

Worell, L. "The Effect of Goal Value upon Expectancy." *Journal of Abnormal and Social Psychology*, 53 (1956), 48–53.

Yarrow, L. J. "Research in Dimensions of Early Maternal Care," *Merrill-Palmer Quarterly*, 9 (1963), 101–114.

Yarrow, M. R., Campbell, J. D., and Burton, R. V. "Reliability of Maternal Retrospection: A Preliminary Report," *Family Process*, 3 (1964), 207–218.

Index

Black, A. E., 82
Bradburn, N. M., 190
Brim, O. G., Jr., 238, 239
Burton, R. V., 216

California Psychological Inventory, 35, 36, 42
Callard, E., 68, 74, 80, 82
Campbell, J. D., 216
Caplovitz, D., 190
Caretaking demands, 120, 121, 137, 148
Child, I. L., 82, 106, 137
Childrearing practices, 228–235
    age of demands, 81
    development of achievement-related motives and, 104–109, 136–139
    religion and, 53, 54, 120
    use of playpens and, 53–54
Childrearing questionnaire, 148
Childrearing values, 6, 7, 123–126
    measure of, 149
Children's Social Desirability Scale, 26, 27
Clark, W. H., 30
Coding procedures, 66
Coding reliability, 66, 227
Coleman, J. S., 17
Columbia Mental Maturity Scale, 68
Comparative Poor Self-Evaluation Factor, 172, 177
Competence, 48–49, 54, 215, 216
    self-evaluation of, 48, 229
    self-ratings of, 121
Competition, 5, 8, 9, 47, 50, 55, 57, 118, 126
Competitive and individual achievement, 7, 225, 232
Coopersmith, S., 61
Conditional love, 127–128, 208
Conformity, 56
Conscientious achievement, 125
Content analysis of children's stories, see Coding procedures
Corrective feedback, 216
Crandall, Vaughn J., 2, 21, 25, 47, 58, 61, 62, 111
Crandall, Virginia C., 2–4, 11, 25, 58, 87, 202, 203, 205, 212, 213, 214, 222, 224, 230, 238, 239, 243, 245
Criticism of child, 42, 54, 108, 109
Cronbach, L. J., 155
Crowne, D. P., 58

D'Andrade, R. G., 42, 106, 108, 128
Daydreams, 193
Defensiveness, 7, 44, 71, 83, 111, 115, 133, 141, 152, 192, 211, 223
    definition of, 116
    goal setting and, 134, 142

Defensiveness (*cont.*)
    parental, 109
    self concept and, 129
Defensiveness Scale for Children, 115, 152, 164
Dependence, 6, 54, 109, 123
    teacher ratings of, 121–122
De Pree, S., 82
Desegregation, 69, 83–85, 95, 97
Development, stages of, 52–53
Developmental assertions, 68
Differentiation, 51, 56
Difficulty of tasks, socially defined, 5
Direction of effects, 217
Disposition expectancy, 12
Dreams, 193
Dunn, J. A., 172

Effectiveness, sense of, 51
Egocentrism, 50
Embedded Figures Test, 63–64, 89–90, 226
Epps, E. G., 195
Expanded Test Anxiety Scale for Children, 173–179, 198
Expectancy, 9, 15–18, 22, 82, 202, 213–214, 238–240
    definition of, 12–14, 205
    discrepancy between IQ and, 23–24, 27
    measure of, 14, 19, 21
    motivational interpretation of, 16, 43
    prediction of behavior from, 15–21
    realism of, 28, 29
    of reinforcement, 3, 11, 13, 14, 17
    sex differences in, 3–4, 11, 16, 21–40, 223
    value and, 11, 14, 25, 202
Expectancy estimates, 16, 22, 27, 30, 37, 41, 43
    changes in, 31, 32
    realism of, 31–32, 38, 41
    relation to IQ of, 23
    similarity of reinforcement and, 18, 19, 20
External control, 230
Extrinsic rewards, 44

Failure, effect of, 94–95
    See also Success and failure
Fantasy achievement motivation, 64, 71
    age trends in, 75–77, 222
    See also Achievement motivation
Fantasy measure of integrated achievement motivation, 76, 97
Fear of failure, 57–58, 64, 85, 246
Fear of success, 5, 58, 85, 90–91
Feather, N. T., 2, 16, 25, 43, 60, 192, 230, 239

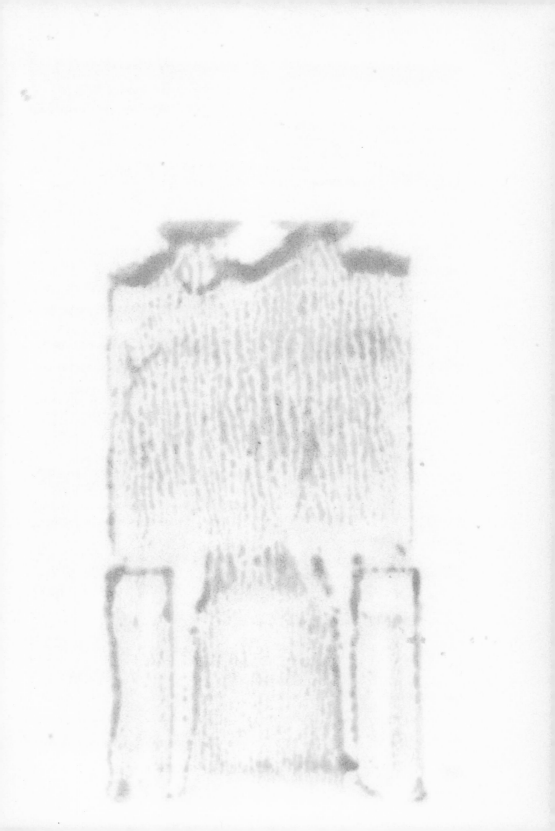

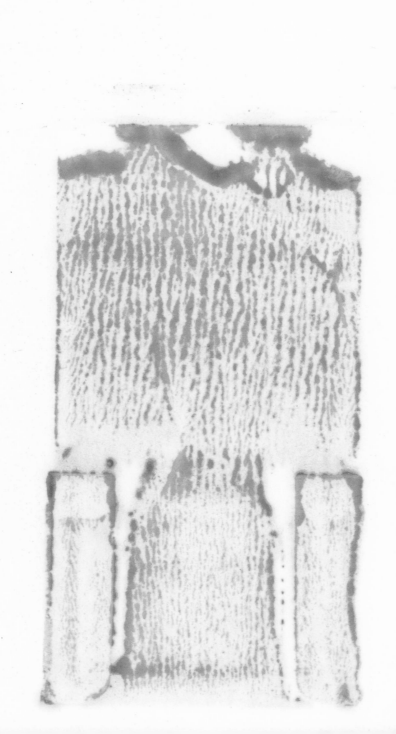